T0326474

BUSINESS ETHICS *AND* CATHOLIC SOCIAL THOUGHT

Selected Titles from the Moral Traditions Series

David Cloutier, Andrea Vicini, SJ, and Darlene Weaver, editors

BUSINESS ETHICS *AND* CATHOLIC SOCIAL THOUGHT

EDITED BY DANIEL K. FINN

GEORGETOWN UNIVERSITY PRESS / WASHINGTON, DC

The publisher is not responsible for third-party websites or their content. URL links were active at time of publication.

Library of Congress Cataloging-in-Publication Data

Names: Finn, Daniel K., 1947– editor.
Title: Business ethics and Catholic social thought / Daniel K. Finn.
Description: Washington : Georgetown University Press, 2021. | Includes
    bibliographical references and index.
Identifiers: LCCN 2020027071 | ISBN 9781647120733 (hardcover) |
    ISBN 9781647120740 (paperback) | ISBN 9781647120757 (ebook)
Subjects: LCSH: Business ethics—Religious aspects—Catholic Church. | Social
    ethics—Religious aspects—Catholic Church.
Classification: LCC HF5387 .B86765 2021 | DDC 261.8/5—dc23
LC record available at https://lccn.loc.gov/2020027071

22 21   9 8 7 6 5 4 3 2 First printing

Cover design by Jeremy John Parker

In memory of
Edward D. Kleinbard
1951–2020

CONTENTS

ACKNOWLEDGMENTS

This volume is the result of the work of the Institute for Advanced Catholic Studies, and my gratitude as editor goes first to Fr. James Heft, SM, the recently retired president emeritus of the institute. His vision for scholarly attention to what the Catholic intellectual tradition can contribute to contemporary life has enlivened this and all the projects of the institute. Also at the institute, Shelia Garrison and Becky Cerling were of great help in making our authors-only conference such a success.

Thanks also go to the authors whose insights illuminate some of the most pressing difficulties in the relation of religion and business today. Their thoughtful contributions and generous listening have enriched each other's chapters in ways that I think will be obvious to the reader.

I am indebted to Al Bertrand, Elizabeth Crowley Webber, Alfred Imhoff, and all the support staff at Georgetown University Press who made this book possible.

I extend deep gratitude to Judy Shank, whose invaluable help with the manuscript made my job so much easier.

Finally, I want to thank Tom and Julie Condon, of San Marino, California, for sharing the hospitality of their home for an evening to make our conference an even richer experience.

Introduction

Daniel K. Finn

Can a religion whose founder taught love of neighbor as the most fundamental moral principle give moral approval to profit-seeking business firms in a global economy? An adequate answer to this question by Christians is more complicated than most answers to the question presume.

Most of the existing literature on the morality of business in a global economy falls into two categories. The first is business ethics, itself a vast array of issues and approaches focusing largely on improving the decisions of managers at all levels within the firm. Much of this work is philosophical and does not draw on religious themes. Scholarship in Christian business ethics—like its philosophical counterpart—tends to focus on the interpersonal moral issues at stake and the values and virtues appropriate to them, such as honesty, integrity, fair treatment, and transparency.

The second category comprises analyses of the morality of economic systems, most typically capitalism and socialism. Here, too, much of the scholarship is philosophical, not theological. Within the Catholic tradition, the theological approaches to these systemic questions have relied heavily on modern Catholic social teaching, articulated by popes and bishops since the late nineteenth century. The literature in this second category either tends to overlook the character of individual business or treats business generically as a positive or negative force, depending on the author's assessment of capitalism.

The Institute for Advanced Catholic Studies, at the University of Southern California in Los Angeles, has for more than a decade sponsored the True Wealth of Nations research project. This is an inquiry into the relation of religion and economic life that periodically brings together a group of scholars from various disciplines to discuss fundamental questions. At the end of each of these authors-only conferences, the group reflects on what additional issues related to faith and economics require deeper scholarly attention. A concern that has arisen in these conversations is the character of a truly Catholic assessment of the morality of business.

Most scholarship on the morality of business of both types identified above addresses important issues but also leaves unaddressed fundamental questions that the present volume aims to investigate. What would a moral assessment of business look like if it asked not only questions identified with interpersonal ethics but also those articulated more broadly in Catholic social thought? To answer this question, this volume presents ten chapters in three parts.

Part I—which comprises chapters 1 and 2—presents preliminary evidence for consideration in the later chapters. Chapter 1, by Regina Wolfe, summarizes interviews with three Catholic CEOs who have spent their careers at firms of different sizes and characters. There is no claim here to a scientific sampling of national CEO opinion. Instead, the interviews provide a series of concrete problems and situations that prove fruitful for the scholarly reflections of the authors of the volume.

Chapter 2, by Jennifer Herdt, identifies the roots in both Christian and secular history of several underlying issues addressed in this volume. The chapter points to five key historical developments: the commercial revolution of the eleventh and twelfth centuries, the rise of the mendicant orders in the thirteenth, the development of a credit economy and the role of Franciscans in debates about property and poverty, the rise of Protestantism (including Max Weber's claims about the roots of capitalism), and "the emancipation of self-interest" from Adam Smith onward. Each of these has been influential in the development of the modern business firm and its claims to moral legitimacy.

Part II—which comprises chapters 3, 4, and 5—examines the internal dynamics of business. Chapter 3, by Andrew Yuengert, arises from the recognition that business firms, especially large ones, depend more and more on management science. This reliance generates a threefold gap in the way businesses managers conceive of their tasks: gaps between theory and practice, between business science and business ethics, and between the moral life of the business leader at work and in the rest of life. Practical wisdom is proposed as the virtue of a business leader capable of bridging the three divides. The chapter ends by addressing how businesses leaders employing practical wisdom might operate differently, and how business schools might incorporate an appreciation of practical wisdom into their curricula.

Chapter 4, by Gregory Beabout, begins with a discussion of the differences in the motivations of college students preparing for careers in business and medicine, the former more likely to speak about making money while the latter aim to help others. The chapter distinguishes two types of business professionals based on their understanding of their own motives: the moneymaker and the business person concerned with promoting a positive social impact. How these two characters understand agency and autonomy differently is clarified by the use of Alasdair MacIntyre's distinction between modern "Morality" and "Neo-Aristotelianism." The "grammar" of Neo-Aristotelianism provides a more helpful self-understanding for the business person concerned with positive social impact.

Chapter 5, by Mary Hirschfeld, begins with the recognition that modern debates about capitalism have most often entailed competing moral narratives: capitalism as exploitation versus capitalism as liberation. Pope Francis has used rhetoric that seems to place him within the exploitation narrative, but a more careful reading indicates that he is not entering into that secular debate. Rather, the pope offers a fundamental critique of tendencies in modern culture on both sides, which he dubs the technocratic paradigm. As he says, "This paradigm exalts the concept of a subject who, using logical and rational procedures, progressively approaches and gains control over an external object." In contrast, Hirschfeld argues, Francis offers a "creation paradigm" that enables business leaders to resist arguments for profit-maximization and requires a conversion to a new way of thinking about the goods we seek and the way we seek them.

Part III—which comprises chapters 6 through 10—addresses the wider responsibilities of business. Chapter 6, by Kenneth Goodpaster and Michael Naughton, begins with the recognition that the purpose of any institution is fundamental; it provides both meaning and legitimacy. This purpose is best understood in terms of an "institutional insight" informed by the common good. The conventional distinctions within business ethics that focus on the shareholder or stakeholder are helpful in critiquing a profit-maximization strategy but are inadequate for describing the purpose of business. Only through a robust and deep sense of purpose will employees be committed to operationalizing the firm's strategy, and the common good is necessary to provide specific content to the institutional role and purpose of business in society. The chapter draws on Catholic social teaching, but the message of the chapter is applicable far beyond Catholic or Christian business leaders.

Chapter 7, by David Cloutier, starts from the recognition that the most fundamental moral legitimation of businesses is that they provide the goods and services that consumers value. But to what extent does this creation of value correspond to what the Catholic tradition means by the responsibility of a business to produce "good goods"? The answer proceeds in four stages. First, there are the general principles regarding good goods in Catholic social thought, including some more explicit norms for judgment about such goods. Second, these norms are put in dialogue with empirical accounts of how consumers actually make choices in advanced economies. Third, presumably acting out of self-interest, firms do attempt to shape consumer agency, often in ways that can contradict Catholic social thought. Fourth, our moral judgments about good goods are enriched by attention to the collective character of consumption, which requires attention to broader structures within which consumers and firms exercise their respective agencies.

Chapter 8, by Martin Schlag, begins with the problem that too many of the moral critiques of capitalism assume that morality must be protected from markets. A more adequate approach asks under what conditions market activity itself is moral. A first-person perspective is essential for business ethics because it presses us to address fundamental questions about the various goods we pursue in business and whether the lower goods we aim at will actually promote the higher goods we hold to be more important. Thus, in Catholic social thought, we should reject what some have called "the Benedict Option" (building a Christian island of sanctity and stability amid the sea of modernity) and instead embrace "the Benedict Project" (the Pope's own proposal for "an encounter and dialogue with other ways of life and with elements that can lead to a new synthesis"). Incorporating the common good in our structuring of institutions (both the market and institutions of society) then becomes an essential part of a responsible life in business.

Chapter 9, by Edward Kleinbard, attends to two fundamental reasons for endorsing Pope John Paul II's conception of a social mortgage on property ownership. The first is the Judeo-Christian understanding of the material world as a gift from God. The second is the fact that so much of the prosperity of the prosperous is due to good luck: our genetic inheritance, the resources of our parents, and many influential events in our lives that are beyond our control. Those of us fortunate enough to be prosperous should respond with gratitude and a willingness to recognize a kind of social mortgage on our prosperity. Because recent economic analysis finds that government investments in the poor and social infrastructure generate "inclusive growth," a social mortgage that generates tax revenue to be spent in these ways is both morally and economically beneficial. Public policy to accomplish these goals can then be understood as a form of insurance, where all contribute to a common pool of resources that is employed to assist those in need of help.

Chapter 10, by Martijn Cremers, investigates the typical economic support for markets. The prevailing argument in economics for the moral superiority of markets is rooted in the two fundamental theorems of welfare economics. This leads many economists to limit the role of government to promoting a competitive market equilibrium and redistributing wealth but not undertaking other expenditures because that would reduce economic efficiency. The advantages of this goal include three important "shared goods" of market competition that benefit even those who are not themselves involved in a particular market transaction: information sharing, risk sharing, and discipline sharing. The fundamental problem with this economic analysis is that a competitive market equilibrium rarely occurs in practice because of the regular failure of three conditions essential to it: that there be at least a rough equality in access to information, power, and control among market participants. Such failures can be harmful not only to individuals but also to businesses.

Taken together, these ten chapters offer the reader a range of insights into how and to what extent Catholic social thought can offer a moral approbation of business firms, their activities, and the lives of those who lead them.

PART I

PRELIMINARY
EVIDENCE

CHAPTER 1

CEO Perspectives on Morality and Business

Regina Wentzel Wolfe

This volume aims to assess the morality of business in the tradition of Catholic social thought. Each of us, the authors of these chapters, is a scholar and teacher. We recognize that our reflections will be shallow if we are not in touch with business as it exists today, and for this reason, a number of us are regularly in contact with business leaders. Still, in order to ground the conversations that have led to this volume, we begin with a summary of interviews with three CEOs.

People of faith whose day-to-day lives are taken up with the daily routine of business may not use the language of philosophy and theology to describe their understanding of the relationship of religion and economic life. Yet it is clear that the three individuals interviewed for this project do not separate the two. In their own way, each shows a strong grounding in the basic principles that undergird Catholic social thought. The three individuals represent a cross section of the US economy: a small, family-owned company; a publicly traded small or medium-sized enterprise; and a *Fortune* Global 500 company. It is important to recognize the interviews are not part of a random sample and no attempt is being made to generalize about CEOs based on the interviews. The purpose of allowing them to tell their stories is to provide examples of people who take seriously a principled life.

David A. Bochnowski chairs the executive board of Peoples Bank SB and its parent company, NorthWest Indiana Bancorp. Before this, he served as CEO and president of both companies. He began at Peoples Bank in 1977 as the bank's legal counsel. The bank, which currently has just under 300 employees, was founded by his grandfather in 1910. A graduate of

Georgetown University's Walsh School of Foreign Service, he holds a juris doctorate degree from Georgetown University Law School and a master's degree in African Studies from Howard University.[1]

Thomas E. Holloran is a Minnesota native who began his career as an attorney specializing in business and securities law. He worked with the founders of Medtronic to incorporate the company and to take it public. Holloran joined Medtronic's Board of Directors at that point and served on the board until the mandatory retirement age of seventy. During his years at Medtronic, which currently employs close to 100,000 people, he served as general counsel, executive vice president, and president. After his time at Medtronic, he was chair and CEO of an investment banking firm.[2]

Joan S. Wrenn is CEO of Hudson Precision Products, where Wrenn and her sons, who will succeed her, represent four generations of leadership in this family-owned and -operated company that has seventy or so employees. Founded as Casey-Hudson Company in 1906, the company was floundering when Wrenn's grandfather bought it in 1932. The company produces precision-machined parts and assemblies used by companies in a variety of industries, including electronics, medical devices, automotive, and aerospace.

THE PURPOSE OF BUSINESS

Without exception, these leaders believe that businesses are meant to meet the real needs of their customers and clients. This is to be done by providing high-quality goods and services. Although all recognize that profit is essential to longevity and the thriving of any business enterprise, all believe that there is more to business than profit. On a day-to-day basis, the respective businesses that these executives have led have been consistent with this broader understanding of the purpose of business.

Holloran, who was involved in drafting Medtronic's mission statement, characterizes this attitude well: "The mission statement has been the model of how that company has operated for all the years since the middle 1950s. It defines the purpose of the company to make products that will alleviate pain, extend life, and restore health. In a nutshell, that's why that company exists." "There's nothing in the mission statement about maximizing shareholder return," he notes. "All of the shareholders have done extraordinarily well over the years," he observes, and adds, "There is one segment of the mission statement on profit, but it is so the company can go forth and recognize success in the rest of the mission."[3]

For her part, Joan Wrenn harkens back to the philosophy that her grandfather brought to Hudson Precision Products in 1932: "You're not in business to make the family wealthy. You're in business to have a product you deliver ethically to the market at a fair price." She is clear that it is the responsibility of the ownership of the company to make certain that happens.

This theme is echoed by David Bochnowski, though there is a bit of a twist. His grandfather, a Polish immigrant who came to northwestern Indiana to work in the foundries, had an entrepreneurial spirit. "Working in the foundry wasn't enough for him," Bochnowski recounts. "He had a dance hall and saloon, which in those early days had the only safe in the neighborhood. People literally brought their money and put it in the safe because they trusted him." As time went on, the people placing their money in the safe recognized that the money could be used to help others in the community. "They decided," Bochnowski continues, "as long as we're going to do this, we ought to do it legally and get a banking charter, which is what they did." "The bank's roots," he adds, "are really more as a cooperative or neighborhood association. It was designed to help others do better. That's part of the long-standing culture of the company."

A STAKEHOLDER RATHER THAN A SHAREHOLDER APPROACH

Given their understanding of the purpose of business, it is not surprising that all three CEOs adopt a stakeholder approach to business rather than a shareholder approach. Holloran was the most direct. "I'm much more a stakeholder person," he admits. "I was a CEO of an investment banking firm and there I felt that I was helping people with their retirement, with the educational needs of their children. With the stakeholder model, I think shareholders come out just fine," he insists. "If you're well run, there will be over time an advancement of the price of the shares of the stock. That's all you can ask for," he concludes.

Bochnowski is clear. "A banking charter is a stakeholder charter," he contends. "You're supposed to take the resources that are entrusted to you and use them for economic gain within the community." Besides, he continues, "If you're not relevant to your community and your customers, you're not going to be in business for that long. That's the challenge of today, as a matter of fact." Here, he points to technological advances as a driver for the way business is done.

Customers are important stakeholders for Wrenn as well. "If we focused only on profit, there would be companies we'd no longer be able to do business with," she asserts. "For example, there's a company we've been doing business with for forty-seven years, and we're still making the same part for them. We know how to make the part well enough not to make mistakes or get into problems," she continues, "and that's big because there is no margin for error in manufacturing our products; the cost of a mistake is huge. If we really know how to do the work and it's easy enough for us to accomplish, then we can afford to make a little less money on it because there isn't as much risk," she explains. "The risk factors are incredible because of the precision needed. We've known three generations of owners at that company." Large corporations have been among Hudson's customers since the company's early days. "In 1934, we did business with Motorola on a handshake," Wrenn remarks. It was a time when relationships were central to business transactions.

Referencing suppliers, whom she also considers to be among Hudson's primary stakeholders, Wrenn says, "Some of them send up trial balloons to see if you're watching. They'll slip in all types of things, like an environmental surcharge on plating. How many invoices does it take to notice and ask what's this about?" "Or," she adds, "they raise prices. They quote a price and then when it comes to getting the invoice, which may be two or three months later, the invoice doesn't reflect the agreed-on price. It happens all the time. It did not used to happen. It is happening all the time. Or somebody will say, 'You don't understand our expenses.' And I have to say, 'You don't understand the word *commitment*.' Most of the time we can find a new vendor but some of the time we can't. We really have to watch everything—no more verbal agreements," she observes, and notes, "there are customers that don't want to get to know you." Still, the personal touch persists: "While we can't give gifts anymore, we do send handwritten religious Christmas cards. We get more people thanking us for that." That said, Wrenn is clear, "Business can become impersonal if you let it. It's just the way it is," she says with a resigned tone in her voice.

Not surprisingly, given the size of their companies, both Wrenn and Bochnowski also focus on employees when considering stakeholders. With only seventy employees, Wrenn is clear: "You take care of your employees as you take care of your family." She provided numerous examples of what that has meant over the years. They range from mentoring and working with employees until they master the task rather than firing them to finding ways to help financially when there is an unexpected illness, death, or other event. Wrenn is clear that this must be done without belittling or being paternalistic but rather respecting each person's human dignity.

She also reflected on a time when a supervisor came to see her about people who were at the top of their pay grade. "He had a list of people who hadn't had raises in six years and was worried about them. I asked him to let me sit with it a while. I wanted to think about how we could respond. Jobs are very different in our business. There're only six jobs that are identical, so we do have gradations," she explains. "We can structure this. While much of the work is task oriented, there's also the soft stuff. One of the fellows, I remember, did a lot for people. We decide we could raise his salary for what he did for people. Yes, there's the structure," she admitted, referring to the pay scale, "and you have to balance the structure. But there are exceptions," she contends, "because there are people who are exceptional. At the end of the day," she insists, "you find a way somehow to compensate them and thank them without distorting the structure, because you can't do that."

At Peoples Bank, which has fewer than 300 employees, "we're pretty big on the profit sharing side of things," Bochnowski states. "Depending on the performance of the company, our profit-sharing match, which is on the retirement match, is generous. It can go as high as 12 percent. The bonus system, which we call our incentive system, is, again, tied to performance—what's our earnings per share, what's our return on assets, what's our return on equity. Those are all shareholder measures; but at the same time, if you want a high-performing bank, all three of those need to align in a very positive way. We're saying to employees, if the bank does well and we perform as we think we should, then you, individually, will do well. All of this is described in the proxy statement for shareholders," Bochnowski observes.

"We want the shareholders to be happy," he says, and explains the management team and board's perspective: "How do we drive their happiness? We drive their happiness with strong performance. Who drives strong performance? All of us who are here every day." From his perspective, it's important for employees to have a stake in the outcome of their work: "We know, for instance, that we have to compete with Chicago salaries. We've known forever that if people want to go to work in Chicago they can make more money there, but they have to commute every day and do all the things that go with that. At the same time, we've got to stay competitive within the local market, otherwise they will go to Chicago," Bochnowski acknowledges.

"While pay is important," he admits, "so are work conditions. We try to create a family environment here and it seems to work. If people truly feel that there's a benefit from their labor individually and, while they're sitting next to one another, collectively, then they stay. We have a very low turnover in this company. I think it's because of the overall work conditions," he contends. "Every year, we participate in the 'best places to work in Indiana' survey, which is conducted by a third party. Based upon those answers—and employees have the right to comment on every aspect of the job, to say whatever they want to say—we've consistently been named one of the best places to work in Indiana in our size category, less than 300 employees."

According to Bochnowski, of the four senior leaders in the company, two are women; one heads information technology and the other is the general counsel. "However," he admits, "in terms of women's participation, we have not made the progress we need to make in the board room. We've had two women on the board for a while, but that needs to change. I do think it's going to resolve itself," he contends. The problem is a result of a variety of circumstances. As he notes, "In a company like ours, you can't just kick someone off the board." For the most part, this has meant waiting for someone to retire. "There are five of us, all men who came on the board quite a number of years ago; we're between the ages of sixty-nine and seventy-two, so we're all going to be retiring from the board at about the same time. This will provide the opportunity to increase the number of women," he contends. In this regard, he notes that, "like everything else in America, 50 percent of the time our product goes to a woman, maybe more often than that. We have to figure out a way to address the issue of greater representation of women on the board and do it in a professional way. The question is whether we can find women entrepreneurs running companies that need between one- and ten-million-dollar loans, which is our company's sweet spot, who are willing to risk taking time from their businesses to come into a board room. It's an interesting question," he reflects.

HUMAN AGENCY AND AUTONOMY

None of the interviewees used the term "agency" specifically, though they did address the issue of employees' sense of purpose as well as the degree to which employees have the autonomy to make decisions and act on them. Given the differences in industries and size of the enterprises, the responses varied. Wrenn is clear that at Hudson they avoid rigid rules and regulations for the most part. "Take an easy issue, for instance," she says. "We have broad regulations about time off or days of absences, where other companies might institute disciplinary procedures after five days of absence. We have an employee who is a soccer player—he's still here, has worked for us for thirty-seven years—a number of years ago, he got to the point in his soccer career where he was missing on Monday mornings. His daughter would call him in sick. This became a habit, and everybody knew about it. He'd be told this isn't going so well, and he'd respond, 'Oh, yes, yes. . . .' Finally, one day I thought, 'This psychologist—and that's what I am—could do an intervention here and it's going to work.' He didn't appear on next Monday. On the Tuesday, I found him. 'You have a minute?' I asked. Then I told him, 'I want you to put in as much effort to getting here on Monday morning as you give to playing soccer.' He looked at me and said, 'Mrs. Wrenn, you're absolutely right.' He never was missing again," she adds.

"If you're going to take the time and energy to manage things in that way, then you don't need all these rules and regulations. But how many people do that?" she asks. "My son tells me it's diminishing in our industry. The biggest of the companies I'm referring to has 150 people, others have 24, or 50, or 70 like we do. You can't blame people for changing their attitude or just following the rules," she admits. It's this change to "letter of the law" responses that she sees as a big difference in the industry.

She shares another story that points to Hudson's business model. "We have an engineer who when we first hired him asked me, 'You own the company and you're here?' He continued, 'the last place I worked I was number 351. I never had a name, I was just number 351.' They kept such a distance from their employees that they didn't even know their names," she says, shaking her head. "There's a radical difference in the way we relate to employees. It takes a lot of energy to operate the business knowing the person and dealing with the person," Wrenn acknowledges. "It will be interesting to see the next five years around here because we have a lot of new people. Can we bring them into our philosophy so that they don't take us for granted and abuse the system?" she wonders.

At NorthWest Indiana Bancorp and People's Bank, personal agency and autonomy are a bit more complicated. "Legally, we have to take any application for a home loan," Bochnowski notes. "But on the commercial banking side we can decide about loans; it may be a request from an industry we don't serve, so we're not going to entertain that loan. We work mostly with entrepreneurs," he indicates. Those are the people and companies with whom relationships are built.

In terms of employees' capacity for making decisions and acting on them, Bochnowski points out that "senior management is concerned about having checks and balances in place so that somebody doesn't go off the rails and no one knows about it. We want our employees to be independent while knowing what their boundaries are," he remarks. "We don't want to run a company that tells employees they should be afraid to make a mistake. If money goes out the door, that's a problem; we get all that." Bochnowski believes it is important for employees to recognize that management knows employees are "doing their best every day within the boundaries of what the institution is trying to accomplish. In addition, employees are expected to use their independent judgment to make decisions. If they're not comfortable with the decision they're making or it's above their pay grade, they need to go ask somebody else," Bochnowski declares.

Related to this is the need to be certain that employees know they can and ought to take action if they believe something is out of place. "We do have a hotline that not only shareholders and customers can use but employees can use as well," Bochnowski explains. "We give employees two choices. Tell us or tell the hotline. The hotline goes to a third party anonymously. They just tell us what was reported, and we act on it. We tell employees that if they contact the hotline we will respond, and we do. But our policy does not require us to tell the employee what the investigation determined, though we will say that we are investigating," he adds. "Nor will we tell the employee if action was taken, because of human resource issues and all the rest. Though if someone has made a hotline report and a person is no longer with the bank or their duties have changed, they can figure it out," he observes. "We had an interesting case where one person then filed a complaint—this is all public record—with the Indiana Civil Rights Commission claiming that they had reported something that we had not followed up on. Our defense was, yes, we did, and it was all in camera, but we had no responsibility to go back to the employee for the obvious reasons. The Civil Rights Commission exonerated us, but it's interesting how these things can unfold in someone's mind. The person who filed that complaint and claimed we didn't do anything ultimately left the company of their own accord. We apparently didn't fix it as quickly or as publicly as this person's standards said we should have. But it did get resolved," Bochnowski confirms. "What was interesting for me was how people think you should or shouldn't act. In fact, I thought we acted appropriately, and I thought, under the circumstances, swiftly. When someone makes an accusation, the worst thing you can do is accuse someone of something they didn't do," he insists. "You have to find out and be sure of the facts, and that takes a while."

In considering employees' sense of purpose, Holloran points to the need to "phrase what you're doing in human terms. The more that's done, the more people enjoy work and feel that they're accomplishing something that helps other people," he contends. Such an approach or attitude "is unique to some companies. I can only speak to the companies I've been involved with, but all of them have had some involvement with human need. In general," he continues, "you have to give employees some reason for having pride in their work. Their compensation can be somewhat based on the financial well-being of the company, too, but I think they need more than that. People today have choices. I think the more they feel they are doing something worthwhile with their life and their job, the better the company runs."

When it comes to top executives, Holloran is emphatic: "I think that executive compensation is out of whack. I think it's unduly rewarding at the top end now. At least for the top executives, it's up to the board to craft what the expectations are and even weave them into the compensation plan. The board has a significant role to play in what people work for and what they value. The board is influential. It does the hiring and over the years we hired managers at Medtronic that we thought were congruent with the mission of the company. We rewarded them on the elements we wanted them to develop," he notes.

"Who is on your board is important," Holloran insists, "and what their concept of the company is. When there are vacancies, they should be filled by people who will be very helpful to what the aims of the company are. Almost invariably, they're reelected by the shareholders." Noting the importance of board orientation and formation, he points out the need to "give your board the opportunity of seeing not just top management but at least the next layer or maybe even the layer below that." One strategy to do this, he posits, "is the all-day seminar that gives the board access to the next layers of management. It's a very useful tool; it helps board members see what people are doing and also how the company is developing talent."

VIRTUES

All three interviewees were adamant. Honesty and integrity are essential! "Certainly, one paramount virtue is honesty," Holloran states. "Not just in the sense of not taking things that aren't yours, but honesty in evaluating what's happening in the organization. I suppose it's honesty and candor." Bochnowski reiterates this: "Honesty, integrity, and a reputation for fair dealing are necessary." They make an impact on the company's "reputation within the community," and having a good reputation is crucial to the bank's long-term viability. This is true not only for the organization as a whole but also for individual employees.

"We just had our corporate retreat last week." Bochnowski recounts. "Part of the discussion—this was really, really interesting—was 'What's our culture?' What's our culture as a board? What's our culture as management? How do we fit all this together? What are the boundaries? What is it that we do or don't do? It just knocked me over. I asked the CEO about it, and he said, 'I remember we did a retreat like this; it was just a management retreat and it was right around the time that Volkswagen's actions were coming to light.' He went on, 'When we were done, you said you wanted to take a minute and just talk to our group about how we all thought that happened, and how would we prevent something like that from happening here? We had a 45-minute or hour discussion on that.' Even though I've passed on the leadership of the company," Bochnowski continued, "it's very clear that that conversation left an impression on him and on the management group." The relationship of having an unblemished reputation and institutional culture are clear for Bochnowski, who insists, "Institutional culture is important, and the tone is set at the top."

Wrenn echoes this sentiment. "In talking about all this, I'm finding out how totally ingrained I am in our philosophy. It's grounded in family values and faith values," she notes. Referring to her earlier comment about once having done business with Motorola on a handshake, Wrenn acknowledges, "the challenges are basically ethical." Here, she's not only thinking about the company's business philosophy but also about the products it produces.

MORAL QUALITIES OF GOODS AND SERVICES

"We make parts for other people's products," Wrenn states. "The general public doesn't even know about our industry, precision machining. We have bomb fuses, we have prosthetic knees, we have tools, we have collets for power tools, we have medical devices, we have all kinds of things," she explains. "One of the priests I know asked me one day, 'Well how do you feel about making parts for bombs?' I said, 'Well, I'll give you a very concrete example. We make parts for bombs that blew up Desert Storm, and we made parts for gas valves that regenerated the area directly, part to part. So how do I feel about it? Somebody is going to do it, so we're doing it. If you tell me that morally I shouldn't make parts for bombs, I want to know why not? They protect us as well.' It's a double edge," she admits. "That's probably the only thing in this entire business that I would say has some real moral tie to it. None of the other products have that. We'd be agreeing on all the other products we make."

Wrenn has another ethical concern that clearly disturbs her: "As a company in the product design supply chain, I've seen companies that focus on maximizing returns with no interest for the longevity of a product." "What I really cannot tolerate," she declares, "is when you get the message from a customer that a product you're working with has a lifespan that's unnecessarily short. That's not what we make. The parts we make are metal and are substantial. They're not plastic that will melt under heat. We're not involved in that kind of thing. Still, it's incredibly annoying to get the message from someone that a $700 dollar item is going to last about ten years. No, no, no," she says emphatically. For her this is an ethical issue, but she admits it's counter-productive to approach it as such. Instead, "we find ourselves in a position to talk about the lifespan of the item, and sometimes we can get a little edge of influence and they come back with, 'Maybe you're right; maybe we've got the wrong idea of how long it's going to last.' That's come up twice in particular cases I remember."

Holloran is also clear, "There is a moral dimension when considering the quality of goods and services. It's not just in the medical device industry. It's much beyond that," he contends, "in the food products, for example. Well, we've seen some terrible falsehoods in the automobile industry. It's easy to see in the medical products, but it goes way beyond that. Personally," he remarks, "I've never been on the board of a company that I didn't think was making a useful and important product. I don't think I want to serve on a board of a company that isn't doing something useful for the economy or the consumer. If I'm not motivated, how can I, if I'm the CEO, motivate the employees, if I don't believe in what we're doing?" he asks.

Bochnowski, too, is concerned about the quality of services provided and ensuring that those services are provided in an ethical manner. As noted above, in community banking a reputation for fair dealing is crucial to customer satisfaction and company growth. But these things are also affected by external factors beyond the control of the bank's management and governance structures.

One such external factor is technology. "Currently, in this industry technology is moving the business, inconveniently quickly," he points out. "I don't know what your kids do for banking," he continues, "but I bet they do it on their smartphones. My kids can't understand why I still balance my checkbook. They keep telling me all I need to do is check online for my balance. Instead of the business being the early adopter, it's the customers that are driving it to try new technologies. The extent to which people want speed now, particularly with lending decisions, raise many very good questions, such as how you know your boundaries and how you know what you can or can't do." The bank has established processes to address customers' desire for timely responses but at the same time ensure that boundaries are maintained and solid business decisions are made.

Another external factor focuses on customer perception of the industry in general: "We have customers who say they like doing business with us, but they don't do all their business with us. They believe that if there's ever a problem with banking, the government isn't going to let the big guy fail. It's a mind-set. Regardless of what the capital rules are and that we're examined once a year, that we're audited every year, that we have internal auditors in the bank and that we have all those checks and balances the perception is that if there's a real problem the big guys are going to survive and we will not," he states. "Customers don't care that we've been in business all these years and have a great capital position." He points to the trend line: "Back in the 1980s we had 15,000 to 16,000 bank charters in the United States, and we're now down to about 5,000 to 6,000, with the thought that it's going to go to 3,000," he reports. "Some of that is because some retirement plans are to exit the business; then there are the many burdens we have to put up with to run a bank—that's another reason some exit the business." "As an example—this is a mind blower," he suggests, "we had a day when we had over a million attempts to hack into our system." While maintaining high ethical standards and providing quality services is critical from Bochnowski's perspective and go a long way to explain the bank's success, they are not always sufficient to overcome some of these external factors.

SELF-INTEREST AND THE COMMON GOOD

Of all the interviewees, Wrenn is the one who sees shifts toward a more self-interested approach in doing business. Hudson is a long-standing member of the Precision Machine Products Association; her son was president of the association. "He tells me," she reports, "that some companies are putting in defense mechanisms with customers and employees to solidify things and putting in more rules and regulations to protect themselves from being taken or being abused. He's hearing people say, 'You can't be good to people anymore because they'll take advantage and use you.' I think it's a creeping disease." "The creeping disease," she explains, "is that people who feel that they can still run their company like we do are being told, 'you're a fool. You're leaving yourself open to transgressions.' Of course, we could respond that way, too, and put in guidelines and rules to keep things from happening. But when those things are tight . . ." she pauses and references the story of the soccer player mentioned earlier and the time and energy it takes to lead in a way that has high expectations for employee attitudes and behavior and yet is not ridged and rule bound.

"Our community involvement is in the educational sphere," Wrenn says. "We work with a local school that has a manufacturing technology program." At base, however, for Wrenn, contribution to the common good centers on employees. "I think our responsibility is to our employees," she maintains. "If you can contribute financially to the community at large, fine, but not to the detriment of the company because then you are not meeting your responsibility to your employees."

She recounts a conversation she overheard between her sons. "One of our sons tells the other one, 'This is a social service, you realize. If you took the assets of this business and sold the whole thing, we'd all come out better, but we've got seventy people we're employing, and for this six-month period that's been the goal, to keep these people employed.' Once," she reports, "it was a three-year period where the goal was to keep people employed. From that aspect, I think we're very different."

"There is no place for narrow self-interest in our company," she declares. "If we focused only on profit, we would do things very differently. We would not do work with certain customers; we would not make products for them. We would say we need 'x' number of profit margin at the end of the job, regardless. If we had to scale back to make that profit, we'd be making more money, but we wouldn't be employing seventy people," she observes.

Echoing his grandfather's philosophy in founding the bank, Bochnowski asserts, "You're supposed to take the resources that are entrusted to you and use them for economic gain within the community. You have to worry about your shareholders, and you have to worry about the community. In banking, in particular," he explains, "there's something called the Community Reinvestment Act, which has teeth. If you don't reinvest in the community, if you don't do what your charter says you're supposed to do, the people who grant you the charter get upset. They can take it away or they can make it very difficult for you to grow or to do things you want to do until you correct what they perceive as the issue. It's a carrot-and-stick approach," he states.

"We tend to go with housing, education of children, and environmental concerns," he notes. "Living in the Chicagoland area, with steel mills, oil refineries, and so forth—we may be the rust belt but we still make a lot of stuff and environmental concerns are significant, particularly for our children and grandchildren. It's a big deal with them," he contends. "If a local little league team wants a sponsorship for $150, we do that. But any real dollars typically are focused on specific issues. We try to stay away from cultural issues. We tend not to help causes because you have to help both sides or you appear to be choosing sides."

Noting that people can choose to work almost anywhere, he acknowledges that most employees have their roots in the Midwest and choose to work there. "They are people who have chosen to stay in this community and make their mark here. What we talk about is that if we do well, the community does well. We have to support the community. At the bank, we have something called the Community First Committee; there're no management people on it. The employees do fundraising throughout the year and the bank matches dollar-for-dollar each year. The committee decides who gets the money. For example, they made a $25,000 five-year commitment to a Boys and Girls Club in Gary, Indiana. At the same time, the bank made a separate $25,000 contribution, so a total of $50,000, to something that really helps a particular segment of the community. Employee engagement in the community is a big deal," he observes.

"I want to go back to the question of narrowly self-interested business," he says. "When I read that, I thought of my Georgetown Jesuit education. Yes, we want that business to succeed because the country succeeds when the economy succeeds; we want people to be fairly rewarded; we want everybody to be happy," he admits. "But the whole Georgetown experience says you can't save yourself by yourself. You can only save yourself by helping others. At least for me, all those interests—I'm not sure I know how to define Catholic interests anymore—but I know what the faith interest was that was taught to all of us and it was more an example. I don't know that Georgetown taught any of us to memorize the *Catechism* or any of the things that have caused people to be turned off by the Church; it was more 'this is how life should work if you follow the example of Christ and the Apostles.' There's just something about this whole big picture of we're not in this alone. We're in this together. That seems to permeate how we treat our employees here, it permeates how we deal with the community, and it permeates how we try to deal with our shareholders."

There's no doubt about Holloran's position. "I tend to say 'no' to narrow self-interest. I think people want to lead their business lives in a way that gives them gratification and feelings that they're helping society as a whole. I think businesses should give part of their profits away, and I think they should encourage their employees to do the same, which is what Medtronic is doing now with their employee matching program," he points out.

Unlike the other two interviewees, Holloran supports business advocacy. "I think businesses do have an obligation to influence social, political, or economic environments in the societies where they operate," he argues. "For a long time the Food, Drug, and Cosmetic Act didn't cover medical devices. I was a part of a medical products trade group, and I was a witness in both the House and the Senate on the hearings when the Food, Drug, and Cosmetic Act was amended to include devices. I actually wrote a segment of what I thought should be included in the bill, which," he admits, "was totally ignored. Devices are now qualified much in the same way that drugs are. The US is very slow in this. The result is that the new product developments are happening in Europe. So yes," he concludes, "I think it's important, and it goes beyond self-interest. It goes to public interest." Finally, he remarks that if academics and researchers really look, "they will find as many strongly moral people in business as they will find on their own faculty. The idea of most business people being dishonest or excessively greedy is misplaced," he declares.

CONCLUSION

Although the interviewees only rarely used terminology familiar to those studying and doing research in Catholic social thought, there are a number of things we can learn from their stories. First, each of them leads a company that is profitable, but none of them seek profit for profit's sake or solely for the benefit of owners and/or shareholders. Rather, profits also function as a means to stay in business, pay adequate wages, and provide worthwhile goods and services to customers. For each, the company mission is front and center, the touchstone in serving stakeholders, including the communities in which they operate.

In addition, though they seldom mention religion, all three are implicitly spiritual in their approach to business and to their stakeholders. It is clear that all have a deep respect for the dignity of human persons in general and their own employees in particular. They see in business a way of providing purpose and meaning to people's lives while at the same time contributing to the common good of the communities—local or global—in which the business operates. This attitude underscores their approach to profits noted above; it is an approach that is consistent with Catholic social thought.

Not surprisingly, the term "agency" is not used by any of these leaders. Notice, however, that each takes responsibility—personal responsibility—for the company and its direction and actions. In doing so, they clearly exhibit personal agency. This sort of personal responsibility is simply part of who they are as human persons and how they manage their organizations.

NOTES

1. For more information, see "Peoples Bank: Officers & Directors," http://investorrelations .ibankpeoples.com/OD.
2. For a fuller biography, see University of Saint Thomas, "The Thomas Holloran Legacy," www.stthomas.edu/hollorancenter/about/legacy/.
3. The statement to which Holloran refers is the fourth of six points in Medtronic's Mission Statement: "To make a fair profit on current operations to meet our obligations, sustain our growth, and reach our goals." The entire Mission Statement can be found at www .medtronic.com/us-en/about/mission.html.

CHAPTER 2

Commerce and Communion in the History of Christian Thought

Jennifer A. Herdt

This volume investigates the conditions for the moral legitimacy of business in Catholic social thought. Many of the characteristics of businesses and markets today are new. Yet business as we know it arose from earlier forms of trade and commerce that have fundamentally shaped today's firms. And our thinking about business, whether religiously or scientifically, has developed out of earlier conceptions of economic life. As a result, this opening chapter addresses some of those historical precedents that are most consequential for any assessment of the morality of business in the twenty-first century.

It is hardly surprising that cultural understandings of trade and business have shifted dramatically over the past two millennia, because the social world itself has changed so much in that time. Yet Christian reflection on economic life has been a constant—an ongoing effort in each era to assess contemporary practices and to guide and transform them toward a greater love of God and neighbor. Any chapter-length treatment of this topic can offer no more than a few broad strokes, so I focus on three key figures and moments in this history: the Franciscan poverty debates, John Calvin's economic thought, and Adam Smith's founding of political economy. Some surprising things emerge.

First, in a radical reaction to the dislocations introduced by a new money economy, the Franciscans' rejected any sort of ownership of property. And yet they were at the same time pioneers in developing theories of relative price, defending the social value of merchants, and creating the predecessors of today's banks. Second, although John Calvin broke new ground in his teachings on usury, and like the other Protestant reformers insisted that full devotion to God could be lived out in ordinary occupations of the laity in the world, most of his economic teachings stood in continuity with the main channels of prior Christian reflection. He condemned luxury, taught that property ownership is stewardship, and rejected the idea that wealth is a sign of God's favor. Third, although Adam Smith is famous for his reference to an "invisible hand" that leads to beneficial market outcomes different from the intentions of market actors, he did not advocate the unfettered pursuit of self-interest. Rather, he insisted that reason and humanity required that the market be regulated with a view to its impact on the poor and disadvantaged.

From the beginning of the Christian tradition, certain fundamental themes animated reflection on trade, profit, and wealth. It is challenging to discern just how to live out these insights in our own constantly changing social and economic environment. But it was similarly challenging for the mendicant orders to address the new realities of urban life and a money economy, for Scholastics to assess new forms of lending that might or might not be usurious, and for Christian thinkers to discern how best to serve genuine human flourishing amid the decline of feudalism and the rise of capitalism. The point of attending to these historical sources is that there is wisdom for today in the Franciscan insistence on making need the measure of value, in Calvin's insistence on the stewardship of wealth, and in Smith's recognition that the unfettered pursuit of self-interest does not automatically redound to the common good. There is much to gain from understanding the ways in which Christian economic reflection has unfolded within changing contexts in the past.

CHRISTIANITY IN THE ANCIENT WORLD

Trade and manufacturing prospered in the ancient Mediterranean world and were the key to the strength of the Roman Empire. This did not mean, however, that the life of business was respected. Leisure was prized as freedom; work was denigrated as enslavement. The life of a philosopher was leisure; that of a merchant, work. Plato saw the need for "producers" in his ideal republic but ranked them below the auxiliaries and the guardians. These values were taken over into early Christianity's elevation of contemplation, but there the traditional Hellenistic disdain for the merchant life as work rather than leisure was joined with quite different concerns inherited from the Hebrew tradition—notably, an insistence on God's concern for the poor.

Jesus proclaimed the poor blessed; he said that it was more difficult for the rich to enter the kingdom of heaven than for a camel to pass through the eye of a needle (Luke 6:20; Matthew 19:24). His advice to the rich young man was to give away all that he had in order to follow Jesus (Matthew 19:21). Even though this was understood as a counsel of perfection rather than as an obligation binding all Christians, it decisively shaped Christian attitudes toward wealth.[1] As Clement of Alexandria remarked in the second century, "If no one had anything, what room would be left among men for giving? . . . He who holds possessions, and gold, and silver, and houses, as the gifts of God . . . and knows that he possesses them more for the sake of the brethren than his own . . . is he who is blessed by the Lord."[2]

Although radical Christian voices urged all believers into a life of voluntary poverty, insisting that wealth taints and corrupts, more moderate voices regarded wealth itself as neutral or good, in that it enables sustained giving and provides sustenance to the poor. These concerns are taken up later in this volume in a number of ways. In chapter 7 David Cloutier asks what a Christian view of material possessions means for businesses wanting to produce good goods; in chapter 6 Kenneth Goodpaster and Michael Naughton apply these convictions to the notion of "institutional insight" within the firm; and in chapter 9 Edward Kleinbard addresses the implications of the "social mortgage" implicit in property ownership.

Poverty was a central feature of monastic life as it took shape in the fourth and fifth centuries. The sixth-century Rule of Saint Benedict rejected private ownership by monks, seeking explicitly to recreate the form of Christian community described in the Book of Acts: "The whole group of those who believed were of one heart and soul, and no one claimed private ownership of any possessions, but everything they owned was held in common" (Acts 4:32).[3]

THE COMMERCIAL REVOLUTION

From the sack of Rome in 410 CE up to the eleventh century, Western Europe remained largely a subsistence agrarian economy. This began to change with the cessation of invasions from the north, as trade routes became safer and cities grew.[4] Over the course of the "Commercial Revolution" of the eleventh and twelfth centuries, the economy became money based; coins were minted, an interconnected economy developed, and investment grew.[5] Money was seen as having "a mysterious power to represent the value of ordinary useful things."[6] It made it possible to tally up not simply stocks of various commodities but also wealth as such. The monasteries became major sites for the increase of wealth, and monks took pride in tracking that increase.

But tensions existed between different understandings of wealth. All agreed that wealth should be devoted to the service of God and neighbor, not private indulgence. But was monastic wealth best invested in jeweled chalices and elaborate architecture, as at Cluny? Or was it better to reinvest profits in the purchase of land, accumulating wealth? Bernard of Clairvaux championed this latter, Cistercian model as the proper stewardship of talents, leading to their multiplication. In turn, Cluny was increasingly seen as hoarding wealth and tying it up unproductively, no longer as suitably glorifying God.[7] In chapter 6 Goodpaster and Naughton apply an analogous understanding of productivity to the modern business firm.

With the emergence of a money economy and a preoccupation with increasing wealth, usury became a major preoccupation. The prohibition against moneylending had deep roots, reaching back into the Deuteronomic prohibition on lending at interest to fellow Hebrews (Deut. 13:19–20). Gratian's *Decretum* defined usury as "expecting to receive back more than you have given" in a loan, focusing on the sinful intention embedded in this expectation.[8] As the discussion evolved, moneylending was condemned; yet the sale of land rents was not, nor was the activity of merchants. The latter forms of activity were regarded not as hoarding wealth but as using or investing it for the sake of the common good. The private gain was considered incidental. In fact, in the twelfth century, merchants were directly compared with ascetic monks who impoverished themselves for the sake of something of higher value: "The merchant left his house to go to the market, the cleric left his domains to learn Wisdom: the former sold everything he possessed, the latter gave up everything, even himself."[9] Hence, merchants and monastics could be viewed as cooperating in the pursuit of the common good, over against the greed of money lenders.

The rise of the merchant class went hand in hand with the growth of the cities. Within feudalism, peasants exchanged agricultural products and military service for the use of land and for protection from manorial lords. In growing cities, serfs could escape bondage, but they were also subjected to new forms of insecurity, while merchants and craftspeople could become prosperous without owning land. Initially, merchants were merely servants of manorial lords: "They would trade, exchange and lend, as much for their own profit as because they were authorized to do so by their lords."[10] They enriched their lords, to be sure, but also themselves, and they gradually acquired independent power, moving freely about in conducting business: "wealth and its secrets were being mastered more by people who were not masters in the highest meaning of the term."[11]

THE MENDICANT ORDERS

These far-reaching social and economic changes associated with the rise of cities and merchants, and the dislocations associated with them, stimulated intensive reflection not just on wealth and profit but also on the meaning of ownership, need, and poverty. Indeed, the first school of moral theology grew up in the late twelfth century around Peter the Chanter as a site for wrestling with conflicts arising in a world that needed credit but prohibited usury.[12] None were more fully involved in this reflection than the members of the mendicant orders, the Dominicans and Franciscans.[13] The mendicant orders were an urban phenomenon. The older monastic orders had been rooted in place and tied to the land; monks farmed, made wine and beer, and engaged in prayer and contemplation. The mendicants were on the move. Their emergence and identity were thus bound up intimately with major economic shifts associated with the growth of the cities.

The Dominican order was founded in 1216 to oppose heresy and preach the Gospel. Dominic perceived a need for men of God who were free to travel to areas where informed preaching was needed—especially the cities.[14] Dominic and his associates regarded it as quite proper that they, like the Apostle Paul, be sustained by gifts from the communities they served. The Dominicans quickly became rooted in the university (a new urban phenomenon), and devoted themselves not just to doctrinal theology but also to reflecting on property, money, price, and profit.

Albert the Great and his student, Thomas Aquinas, drew on Aristotle to develop new defenses of private property, over against a patristic consensus that property was nothing more than a concession to sin, needed in order to maintain public order. Private property, they argued, encouraged good stewardship of material resources and effective coordination of human activity; it was beneficial to individuals, families, and communities.[15] Economic activity could be a site for the cultivation of virtuous human agency that contributed to genuine human flourishing. A monetary investment in another man's business (a financial partnership) was legitimate; it was a form of ownership, sharing in the risk of the enterprise. It was not a loan, because a borrower still owes the principal even after bankruptcy.[16]

Francis represented a more radical challenge to the rising money economy. For Francis, mendicancy did not simply enable a new kind of mission to the people; it *embodied* that mission, expressing a new valorization of poverty as the life lived by Christ and an approximation to life before the fall of Adam and Eve. Whereas the Dominicans regarded voluntary poverty as compatible with accepting endowments in support of the order, the Franciscans did not. Francis regarded physical separation from money and ownership as essential: to be poor was to wear rags, to wander, to beg, to touch animals and outcasts, those outside civil human existence.[17] Having stepped outside the ordinary structures of human life, Francis questioned the capacity of money to measure value. Only poverty, he argued, allowed one to grasp the true value of things and to see that needs can be satisfied only through relational connections.[18] This question of the true value of things is echoed later in this volume by the concern of David Cloutier with good goods, of Kenneth Goodpaster and Michael Naughton with participative goods, and of Mary Hirschfeld with the technocratic paradigm.

THE FRANCISCAN POVERTY DEBATES

For Franciscans, money was a form of hoarding, impeding the direct circulation of goods. Poverty freed one for loving relationships with others. The Franciscan Rule of 1223 therefore specified: "Let the Friars appropriate nothing for themselves, not a house, nor a place, nor anything else."[19] This was understood as a rejection of both individual and common property. Franciscans rejected any *proprietas* and accepted only *usus*; they were not to own but only use those things needed to support life.[20] This radical stance elicited intense debate over more than a century. Pope Gregory IX, in a 1230 bull, *Quo elongati*, insisted against early critics that the Franciscans were indeed living without any rights but only had the use (*usus*) of things. Pope Innocent IV added that this was possible because what the Franciscans used were things properly owned by the Roman Church.[21]

Critics such as William of Saint-Amour argued that Christian perfection does not require giving up all property; the early Christians owned property in common, and hence Franciscan poverty did not represent an improvement on the usual practice of monastic life.[22] Without property, he pressed, how could the Franciscans perform acts of charity to the poor? Gerard of Abbeville went further, arguing that the Franciscans could not possibly avoid owning property: insofar as a share of the common possessions of the Church rightfully belong to the poor, a share rightfully belongs to the Franciscans.[23] Further, it was not legally possible to "use" food and other consumables without owning them, because *dominium* without use applied only to objects the substance of which was not diminished through use.[24] Whenever the Franciscans were given gifts, ownership was thereby transferred to them.[25]

For Bonaventure, this represented a misconception of "use." "Simplex usus," he argued, was legally indifferent, not a mode of *dominium*; it was simply "permission to use for the substance of life," not a transfer of ownership.[26] The created state of humankind in the Garden was not one of common property but of simple communion of goods, *communio*. The Franciscans, like Christ and the apostles, were approximating this prelapsarian state. Pope Nicholas III, endorsing Bonaventure's views, added the notion of factual use, "*usus facti*": the use of those things necessary for sustenance, quite apart from having or acquiring any rights to these things.

But the attacks continued through the 1270s and 1280s, led by the secular theologians at Paris, Henry of Ghent and Godfrey of Fontaines, culminating in a 1322 papal declaration that the Franciscan order was heretical. Pope John XXII insisted that it was not possible to distinguish between *dominium* and *usus facti* when it came to consumables. To deny that the Franciscans had the *right* to use those things (a right of ownership) that they consumed was to say that they were committing an injustice in using them. The Franciscans could not claim to be exemplary without admitting that they did in fact have property rights.[27] Although the Franciscans continued to defend themselves, it was this position that finally prevailed against them.

Alongside their theoretical refusals of property ownership, the Franciscans were also forced to create new forms of practical relationship. They needed to rely on others who did not aspire to Christlike poverty, and who were willing to handle money on their behalf, receiving donations intended for their support and buying the goods that met their daily needs.[28] The Franciscans harbored no illusions that all Christians would embrace voluntary poverty. Indeed, some defended their way of life in part because it left more resources for the rest of the populace.[29]

Franciscans also depicted themselves as experts on use and value who could thereby be of service to others in analyzing market society from a disinterested point of view. For example, Bonaventure argued that even ostentatious clothing might not be useless for some, but rather an appropriate sign of authority.[30] By the end of the thirteenth century, the Franciscans had developed quite a sophisticated understanding that need, and therefore value, were not absolute but rather context dependent. This led to an understanding of how prices are determined in markets: "The value of things and professions, of goods, and people, is formed by considering, case by case, the generally recognized usefulness, the variable abundance, and also the subjective degree of appreciation these realities receive from people."[31]

THE FRANCISCAN ROLE IN THE RISE
OF A CREDIT ECONOMY

This understanding of relative price paved the way for a surprising develop-ment: the Franciscans could view merchants as similar to themselves, as experts in evaluating value. Hence, merchants were to be regarded as socially useful and as rightfully earning compensation for their expertise, in the form of profit. In 1212, Peter Olivi wrote:

> As the artisan's ability and activity legitimately procure him profit, so the merchant's activity, evident in his careful examination of the value and price of things, and his ability to determine a fair price by paying attention to the smallest details rightfully enable him to earn a profit, since, staying in a variable range of fair prices, he is useful to others just because, in this way, they will learn to calculate more accurately the prices and values of things.[32]

Hence, somewhat paradoxically, the Franciscans contributed to a new valorization of the merchant way of life. And while the Franciscans them-selves could, of course, not become merchants, laypeople who joined the lay confraternities linked to the Franciscan order were often merchants. In fourteenth-century French and Italian cities, members of the Third Order of Saint Francis were often given sensitive public responsibilities because they were seen both as civic-minded and disinterested and as having a refined grasp of the art of understanding price and value.[33]

The Franciscan Alexander Lombard, writing at the end of the thirteenth century, wrote a tractate on usury that identified twelve sorts of cases when it was legitimate to receive more in return from an original amount loaned.[34] Over the course of the thirteenth and fourteenth centuries, further excep-tions were carved out. If a loan caused real damage to a lender, for instance, he could claim compensation in the form of *damnum emergens*.[35] If a lender lost out on an opportunity to buy something and sell it at a profit by virtue of hav-ing made a loan, he could require of his debtor an equivalent, *lucrum cessans*.[36] And if a loan involved risk of loss, the lender could demand a compensatory *periculum sortis*.[37]

Even as theological argument created theoretical space for a credit-based economy, merchants, who circulate wealth in service to the common good, were sharply distinguished from usurers, who immobilize capital by lending money simply in order to gain more. This distinction was bound up with a self-serving and hypocritical Christian anti-Judaism. Jews were invited to settle in European cities because they were not bound by Christian prohibitions against usury. They therefore served a critically important urban role as bankers for societies increasingly dependent on the availability of capital. However, their activities, unlike those of merchants, were not viewed as forms of service to the common good. How could they serve the common good when they were not properly members of the community at all, and rarely full citizens? Traditional Christian anxieties about the presence of Jews in their communities were in the fourteenth and fifteenth centuries increasingly focused on regarding Jewish usury as the foil over against which Christian merchant activity could be exonerated from critique and valorized as socially beneficial.[38]

One final development is worth mentioning in connection with the Franciscans. In late-fifteenth-century Italy, they created the Monte di Pietà, a new kind of financial institution that formed the basis of modern banking. As originally conceived, merchants donated money to the Monte to be lent at very low interest to the poor. In this context, moneylending was a form of charitable activity and service to the poor; the interest charged served only to cover the costs of the enterprise. This sort of moneylending, unlike that of the Jews, was framed as public service, which helped to eliminate poverty by enabling the poor to establish small businesses.[39]

Controversy raged nonetheless, with Dominicans (against the Franciscans) insisting that the expenses of the institutions should be borne by the lenders, not the borrowers. The legitimacy of charging interest to borrowers was affirmed by the Fifth Lateran Council in 1516. Once the payment of interest was allowed, the Montes had a way to sustain themselves apart from ongoing charitable gifts and gradually became institutions that lent to businesspeople as well as to the poor. Thus the road was paved for the acceptance of noncharitable lending institutions and for the charging of interest that is used to sustain a business.[40]

Despite their embrace of radical poverty, then, the Franciscans played a key role in legitimating the activities of merchants and the rise of a credit-based economy. The criterion was always service to the common good: "poverty and wealth could appear contiguous and complementary in building the common good, if they gave substance to the choice of acting, every day, in sight of a definition of common welfare."[41] These late-medieval Franciscan ideas remain fundamental in today's deliberations about the morality of business in Catholic social thought. This is evident throughout this volume, including the concerns for the common good within business, as articulated by Goodpaster and Naughton, and with the responsibilities of business for the broader social context within which it operates, as Martin Schlag argues.

THE PROTESTANT ETHIC AND
THE SPIRIT OF CAPITALISM

Long before the upheavals of the Protestant Reformation, the fourteenth century witnessed significant economic change. Manorialism in Western Europe declined; serfs were freed in efforts to increase the yield of land, resulting in migration to the cities and a large urban proletariat, often unemployed.[42] The Hundred Years' War (1337–1453) spurred on the centralization of the French and English states, accompanied by increased rates of taxation that burdened populations decimated by the Black Death (1347–51). Social unrest mounted. In commercial cities, tensions developed between powerful merchants and craft guilds, and between these and the urban poor. The guilds tended to enact restrictions on the trade of merchants; monarchs, who relied on credit from wealthy merchants, supported their efforts to reduce these restrictions. Hence commerce grew and the gap between rich and poor expanded. The influx of precious metals from the New World fed the development of banking and caused inflation that further burdened the poor during the sixteenth century; wages did not keep up with the cost of living. It was hardly surprising that movements for religious renewal were often bound up together with social and political movements, even as the former can in no way be reduced to the latter.

The powerful influence of Max Weber's *Protestant Ethic and the Spirit of Capitalism* has made it difficult to bring into proper focus the changes introduced into economic thinking and practice in the Reformation era.[43] According to Weber, Protestantism (particularly the Reformed traditions) drove the development of capitalism by way of its notion of vocation or calling.[44] No longer were "vocations" limited to those who accepted the counsels of perfection and turned their backs on the world, embracing lives of poverty, chastity, and obedience. Each Christian received a divine calling, and that vocation might well be to a life of business. Further, Weber argued, Calvinists regarded economic prosperity as a sign of divine election, and their affirmation of double predestination drove a restless pursuit of assurance of election. Protestants were "inner-worldly ascetics," who labored in a highly organized and disciplined fashion, while condemning luxury and self-indulgence.[45] Because profits could not be consumed, they were reinvested, driving economic growth.

Perhaps the first thing to be noted in taking stock of Weber's thesis is simply how much continuity there was between Protestant and Catholic (i.e., between early modern and late medieval) economic thought. Critiques of luxury continued unabated, as David Cloutier makes clear in chapter 7 below.

Catholics and Protestants alike affirmed the right for a merchant to receive a profit adequate to compensate for cost, time, labor, and risk, while insisting that merchants were not justified in exploiting the plight of others and selling their goods at prices as high as possible.[46] Luther, echoing earlier Franciscan reflection on the just determination of prices, argued that this sort of exploitation could be avoided if goods were "valued at the price for which they are bought and sold in the common market, or in the land generally."[47]

Much has been made of Calvin's departure from tradition in refusing to condemn usury as such.[48] However, Calvin's innovation was less dramatic than often depicted. The process of defining usury in ever-narrower terms had been under way for centuries, carving out space for the growth of credit-based economies. Calvin simply pointed out that the argument had become merely semantic. Usury was rightly condemned wholesale if understood as lending practices that exploited the poor or extracted interest in cases in which the borrower acquired nothing more from the loan than the actual value of the money.[49] If usury so defined is condemned, however, this leaves room for approving forms of lending at interest that put money to productive use. Alternatively, one might say that usury itself is not always bad, but only when exploitative. Calvin endorsed the latter approach, arguing that Scripture did not intend to rule out all lending at interest. In doing so, he contextualized and historicized biblical texts condemning usury and rejected Scholastic arguments concerning the unproductive character of money. This built on groundwork developed gradually within the context of the medieval Commercial Revolution.

The rejection of monastic life, and the concomitant affirmation of ordinary lay occupations, constituted the most significant cultural shift in Protestant territories. Calvin rejected both luxury and asceticism: "If we ponder to what end God created food, we shall find that he meant not only to provide for necessity but also for delight and good cheer."[50] Similarly for grasses, trees, fruits, wine, and flower—they are intended to delight as well as sustain life, and to lead human beings to God: "All things were created for us that we might recognize the Author and give thanks for his kindness toward us."[51] This does not mean that wealth is to be equated with spiritual blessing. Calvin unequivocally rejects the notion that wealth is a sign of God's favor or poverty a sign of divine rejection:

> As, on the one hand, the most of men, judging of the favor of God from an uncertain and transitory state of prosperity, applaud the rich, and those upon whom, as they say, fortune smiles; so, on the other hand, they act contemptuously towards the wretched and miserable,

and foolishly imagine that God hates them, because he does not exercise so much forbearance towards them as he does towards the reprobate. The error of which we speak, namely, that of judging wrongfully and wickedly, is one which has prevailed in all ages of the world.[52]

Wealth tempts us to rely on ourselves and our own power rather than on God; poverty can teach us to trust in God.[53] Mary Hirschfeld addresses a twenty-first-century version of many of these issues in chapter 5 of this volume.

Possession is rightly understood as stewardship. All the things that we have are "as it were, entrusted to us, and we must one day render account of them."[54] Wealth is to be consecrated to God, and this consecration is shown in generosity to those in need. The rich are God's deputies; by virtue of the fact that they have been given more than they need, they are charged with the responsibility of acting in God's own person, to distribute good as God does. It is theft to defraud poor neighbors of good things one has been given in trust in order to benefit them. God distributes wealth unequally in order to provide opportunities for the circulation of wealth, for reciprocal exchanges of God's good gifts, such that human society will be built up by its imaging of God's own generous giving and taught how to accept God's good gifts: "while they communicate to each other mutually according to the measure of gifts and of necessity, this mutual contribution produces a befitting symmetry, though some have more, and some less, and gifts are distributed unequally."[55]

The institution of private property fosters virtuous agency—in particular, responsibility and diligence—and it is appropriate that property be used first to take care of the needs of one's household; but beyond this, it is legitimized only by its circulation, not its accumulation.[56] Here there was substantial continuity with medieval economic thought, with its refusal to regard property rights as absolute; private property is legitimate because and insofar as it serves the common good. The magisterial Reformation in this respect maintained a traditional position over against humanists who appealed to Roman law to justify largely unfettered rights to private property and against movements of the Radical Reformation that regarded private property as itself sinful and sought to establish new forms of common ownership, in effect extending to laypeople some of the ideals embodied in medieval monasticism.[57] As the other chapters in this volume demonstrate, this "middle" position is characteristic of today's Catholic social thought as well.

It was in this context that Calvin emphasized vocation: "Each individual has his own kind of living assigned to him by the Lord as a sort of sentry post so that he may not heedlessly wander about through life."[58] By embracing this vocation and its associated duties, the Christian can be confident that he or she is acting as a good steward. Further, even the lowliest occupations are elevated when lived as callings: "No task will be so sordid and base, provided you obey your calling in it, that it will not shine and be reckoned very precious in God's sight."[59] There is no special value in voluntary poverty or asceticism; God's good gifts are to be used productively, neither hoarded, nor squandered, nor exploited unsustainably.[60] Contemplation is not essentially better than work, for in working in ways that serve the common good, human beings serve and glorify God and share in God's own productive activity.[61] We can see this sort of connection between business productivity and Christian faith in many places in the interviews of CEOs by Gina Wolfe in chapter 1.

This is not the place to attempt a thorough assessment of Weber's causal claims concerning the Protestant ethic and the development of capitalism. Suffice it to say that Weber's thesis has been roundly criticized from a number of directions. R. H. Tawney, one of Weber's early critics, noted that Weber's analysis was focused primarily on later Calvinism, which had been transformed by intervening economic developments that could not be attributed to Calvinism.[62] Calvin's emphasis on work as participating in God's providential care for the common good is quite alien to the mind-set that captivated Weber, one in which the pursuit of profit is taken as an end in itself. Historians have argued convincingly that the divergence between the economic fortunes of East and West did not occur until the Industrial Revolution, and indeed that parts of China and India were more prosperous and productive than Western Europe before that time.[63] And Renaissance Italy has been defended as the real birthplace of European capitalism.[64] Indeed, some have argued that capitalism developed in a more unregulated fashion in Catholic territories that continued to pay lip service to the prohibition of usury.[65]

Some scholars still find aspects of Weber's thesis compelling. For it was the cities where Reformed Protestantism was strong that became economically dominant in the sixteenth century—successively, Antwerp, Amsterdam, and London.[66] This may not have been due directly to greater industriousness on the part of Protestants, but it does seem to have resulted in part from a decreased number of religious holidays, a lengthening of the workday, and the economic impact of the dissolution of monasteries and sale of monastic lands.[67] These social changes were indeed related to the Protestant sanctification of worldly existence, extending even to business activity. Weber wrongly attributed the economic vitality of Reformed cities, and Reformed industriousness, to anxiety over election, but there was a kernel of truth to his analysis, and his provocative thesis continues to spur scholarly inquiry to the present day.[68]

POLITICAL ECONOMY AND THE RISE
OF CAPITALISM: ADAM SMITH

Adam Smith is recognized today as the founding father of "political economy," predecessor to the modern-day discipline of economics. Although not the first to use the term "division of labor" to refer to specialization, he articulated with persuasive clarity how the division of labor enhanced national wealth and prosperity.[69] He wrote in the context of the Scottish Enlightenment, which represents the high-water mark of enthusiasm for the positive social effects of commerce. Commerce was valued as a civilizing force, which by bringing distant peoples into contact with one another and fostering sympathetic understanding would ensure not just prosperity but also virtue.[70] Today we recognize the dark side of this discourse, which served to legitimate colonial empires.[71] In the eighteenth century, many Scots, regarding Scotland essentially as a British colony, saw in commerce not only a path to economic independence and flourishing but also to the healing of religious and political factions.[72]

Smith is best known, however, not for his account of the division of labor but for his notion of the "invisible hand"—even though he used the term only three times, and only once in *The Wealth of Nations*. This passage has made him the darling of free market economists, for it is frequently misinterpreted to support the notion that public good is promoted most effectively when individuals pursue their private self-interest unencumbered by regulation:[73]

> As every individual, therefore, endeavours as much as he can both to employ his capital in the support of domestic industry, and so to direct that industry that its produce may be of the greatest value; every individual necessarily labours to render the annual revenue of the society as great as he can. He generally, indeed, neither intends to promote the public interest, nor knows how much he is promoting it. By preferring the support of domestic to that of foreign industry, he intends only his own security; and by directing that industry in such a manner as its produce may be of the greatest value, he intends only his own gain, and he is in this, as in many other cases, led by an invisible hand to promote an end which was no part of his intention. Nor is it always the worse for the society that it was no part of it. By pursuing his own interest he frequently promotes that of the society more effectually than when he really intends to promote it. I have never known much good done by those who affected to trade for the public good. It is an affectation, indeed, not very common among merchants, and very few words need be employed in dissuading them from it.[74]

Despite scattered texts implying that the pursuit of self-interest may be providentially turned to common benefit, Smith makes clear that ordinarily it is up to human beings to scrutinize policies to avoid distortion by special interests. Commercial society, in Smith's account, has two primary benefits: it maximizes wealth, raising the welfare of both rich and poor; and it fosters freedom, by transforming patterns of dependency. Where the vast majority were once directly dependent on the powerful few, in a commercial society, all are indirectly dependent on many, as markets develop and interlock in complex ways.[75]

Smith did not, however, believe that commercial society, or any "invisible hand" operating within it, could guarantee equality or social justice. Further, he argued that such a society generates a host of vices: vanity, pride, duplicity, indifference.[76] The nation must combat these vices by cultivating countervailing virtues, notably the virtue of beneficence.[77] Although Smith does not identify the technological paradigm cited by Pope Francis and explored by Mary Hirschfeld in chapter 5 of this volume, he did recognize that otherwise beneficial social arrangements often generate moral problems that individuals in society need to address. Society must intervene in markets in order to redress the suffering that arises even within the most flourishing commercial society. Smith insisted, for instance, that "no society can surely be flourishing and happy, of which the far greater part of the members are poor and miserable. It is but equity, besides, that they who feed, cloath and lodge the whole body of the people, should have such a share of the produce of their own labour as to be themselves tolerably well fed, cloathed and lodged."[78]

A living wage, he argued, is the lowest wage "consistent with common humanity."[79] He worried that workers paid by the piece would overwork themselves, and he contended that employers should "listen to the dictates of reason and humanity" in allowing adequate time for rest.[80]

Smith was struck by the unintended effects of human actions, and how the pursuit of profit in the market can be publicly beneficial. But he certainly did not conclude that no one need be directly concerned with promoting the public good. The self-interest of merchants leads them to seek to form monopolies, for instance, and Smith regarded these as clearly detrimental to the public and in need of regulation.[81]

BEYOND SMITH: EMANCIPATING SELF-INTEREST

If Smith is not to blame for giving his blessing to unrestrained capitalism, who was? The answer can only be summarized here, attending briefly to the demotion of divine Providence (and with it, the problem of theodicy it caused) and to the rough equivalent that eventually evolved, which included a dependence on self-interest and a redefinition of the discipline of political economy as value neutral.

Smith was hardly alone in linking the analysis of the workings of political economy with reflection on divine providence. Indeed, this is a striking characteristic of European economic thought during the seventeenth and eighteenth centuries. The modern natural law tradition from Grotius onward had reasoned from observed features of human social behavior to conclusions concerning God's intentions and design for humankind. For instance, the fact that human beings were needy and vulnerable, lacking in thick fur or sharp claws, was taken as an indication that God intended them to band together for mutual security, building societies. The discourse of political economy grew out of a context shaped by this sort of providentialist natural law reflection.[82]

Yet a belief that economic life was part of the providential design of a God who is both good and omnipotent inevitably led to theodicy problems in the face of undeniable suffering and inequity to which the economy gave rise.[83] Malthus's pessimistic focus on scarcity and diminishing returns played an influential role here.[84] One tack to explain so much suffering was to try to show that benefits outweighed harms—for example, following Malthus in arguing that the misery and death that limited the number of the poor were unfortunately necessary for the long-term well-being of society. But another solution won out, rooted in a new way to interpret self-interest that facilitated a value-neutral conception of the discipline of political economy.

As Mary Hirschfeld also argues in chapter 5, an important dimension of this development has been explored by Albert Hirschman in his classic text *The Passions and the Interests: Political Arguments for Capitalism Before Its Triumph*.[85] Seventeenth-century thinkers became intrigued with the possibility of using one set of passions to control another and, in particular, for using the "calm" passion of profit to control or displace warlike passions. These useful passions came to be described as "interests" and were regarded not as fallen and sinful vices but as part of humankind's created endowment and as fundamentally beneficial, if properly balanced.

Weber's analysis might lead us to expect that it was Protestant thinkers who led the way in this elevation and transformation of the passions. But this was an ecumenical movement. Thomas Wright (1561–1624), the English Catholic author of *The Passions of the Minde in Generall* (1601; 1604), is a striking case in point. Wright argued that the concupiscible and irascible passions had been given to humankind by God in order to allow them "to provide for themselves all those things that are profitable, and to avoid all those things which are damnifiable."[86] Wright regarded self-interest and virtue as going naturally hand in hand: "What can more deterre men from wickednesse then their own private losse, or move them more to vertue then their owne present gaine?"[87] We tend to think of Mandeville, and his catchphrase "private vices, public benefits," as the origin of the even more striking notion that vicious behavior itself serves the common good.[88] However, other thinkers several decades earlier were exploring similar notions; John Houghton, for instance, wrote in 1681 that "those who are guilty of Prodigality, Pride, Vanity, and Luxury, do cause more wealth to the Kingdom, than loss to their own estates."[89]

With this conception of interests as beneficially generating a larger good, one might have expected that the elimination of Providence would release reformist energies because the economic system would need human direction if it were no longer viewed as divinely designed to benefit the common good automatically. And this was in fact the case, to some extent. In England, the 1850s witnessed the Christian socialism of F. D. Maurice, Charles Kingsley, and others.[90] Leo XIII initiated the tradition of Catholic social teaching with his 1891 encyclical *Rerum novarum*. During the same period, Abraham Kuyper sought to develop a thoroughly Christian form of economic thought from within a Dutch Calvinist perspective.[91] This moral conviction that our participation in economic life should contribute to the common good is reflected in many of the chapters in this volume, including in Gregory Beabout's stress on communal flourishing and Martin Schlag's argument that businesses are responsible for the broader context in which they operate.

Yet during this period, mainstream economic thinking came to be wholly detached from theological reflection. Indeed, nineteenth-century British theologians, some of whom were also economists, fed the development of political economy as an autonomous science by arguing that it should be a realm of value-neutral fact, to be used as a means to the pursuit of ends identified by theology.[92] They failed to anticipate how aggressively the logic of the market would take over, defining human flourishing in purely material terms and abandoning any further reflection on the ends of economic life. The door was opened for the glorification of the pursuit of profit and of free market capitalism, and the arguments from economic science that perfectly competitive markets improve human welfare, as Martijn Cremers investigates in his chapter in this volume.[93] A critique of these realities is a central part of the defense of practical wisdom by Andrew Yuengert and the diagnosis of "teleopathy" by Goodpaster and Naughton in later chapters.

CONCLUDING REFLECTIONS

Where, then, does this narrative leave us? On one hand, the economy today has changed dramatically. Where households could once upon a time aspire to relative self-sufficiency, and "economy" referred to the management of the household, now systems for the production and consumption of goods and services entail interdependencies that extend around the globe. Yet human beings remain much the same—creatures that can be harmed by want and violated by injustice, whom Christians understand as cherished and summoned by God to participate as agents in the self-gifting communion of the divine life. The creative activities of making, buying, and selling goods and services are rightly understood as part and parcel of human response to this divine summons.

Work is not slavery. Neither wealth nor ownership nor profit is intrinsically evil. These things can be humanly fulfilling and good when they are not exploitative, when they take their place in a mutually beneficial circulation of goods and services that builds up community and serves the common good—a common good we must now grasp as extending to the earth and its creatures.

Work should leave room for contemplation and fellowship. Wealth should be held in trust. Ownership is not an unlimited right. There is no invisible hand to prevent human selfishness from doing harm or to guarantee that efficient markets will be just markets. The challenges of holding corporations responsible are immense and extraordinarily complex. The first, critical step is taken in acknowledging that we may not evade this shared responsibility, that we have been placed in the garden to till and keep it, to live in harmony with one another and with our fellow creatures, circulating for common nourishment what Earth has given and human hands have made. The rest of the chapters in this book explore just what all this means for business in the twenty-first century.

NOTES

1. See Peter Brown's rich discussion in *Through the Eye of a Needle.*
2. Clement of Alexandria, "Who Is the Rich Man?" XIII; XVI, 594–95. On Augustine's variation on this theme, see Brown, *Through the Eye of a Needle,* 378. I have discussed Augustine's views of wealth and almsgiving in Herdt, "Eudaimonism and Dispossession," 97–112.
3. Rule of Saint Benedict, 123.
4. Bloch, *Feudal Society,* 3–56; Little, *Religious Poverty,* 7.

5. Little, *Religious Poverty*, 15–18; Benson and Constable, *Renaissance and Renewal*, xvii–xxx; Bloch, *Feudal Society*, 421–37. For an overview of developments in Italy, see Schlag, "Economic and Business Ethics," 180–81.

6. Todeschini, *Franciscan Wealth*, 13.

7. Todeschini, 19, 47.

8. *Decretum*, C.14.q.3, c.I: col. 735; see Wood, *Medieval Economic Thought*, 159.

9. Zachary of Besançon, "Unum ex quattuor, sive de concordia evangelistarum," *Patrologia Latina* 186: 77, quoted by Todeschini, *Franciscan Wealth*, 21.

10. Todeschini, 14.

11. Todeschini, 15.

12. Little, *Religious Poverty*, 175.

13. Little, 156–58.

14. Todeschini, 31.

15. Little, *Religious Poverty*, 176–77; Hirschfeld, *Aquinas*, 161–90; *ST*, II–II, q. 66, a. 2.

16. Little, 178–79.

17. Todeschini, *Franciscan Wealth*, 61–64.

18. Todeschini, 69.

19. Francis of Assisi, *Regula Bullata*, c. 6, in *Die Opuscula des Hl. Franziskus von Assisi*, ed. K. Esser (Spicilegium Bonaventurianum XIII), Frottaferrata (Rome) 1989, cited by Mäkinen, *Property Rights*, 11.

20. Mäkinen, *Property Rights*, 193.

21. Innocent IV, Ordinem Vestrum, in *Bullarium Franciscanum*; Mäkinen, *Property Rights*, 193–94.

22. William of Saint-Amour, *De quantitate eleemosynae*, 328–29; Langholm, *Economics*, 146.

23. Langholm, 278.

24. Mäkinen, *Property Rights*, 196.

25. Mäkinen, 197.

26. Mäkinen, 198; Bonaventura, *Apologia pauperum*, 1269.

27. Mäkinen, 203; Langholm, *Economics*, 147–48.

28. Little, *Religious Poverty*, 165.

29. Todeschini, *Franciscan Wealth*, 83.

30. Todeschini, 85.

31. Todeschini, 115.

32. Peter John Olivi, *De contractibus, de emptionibus et venditionibus*, quoted by Todeschini, *Franciscan Wealth*, 118.

33. Todeschini, *Franciscan Wealth*, 130; Little, *Religious Poverty*, 207. On Olivi's contributions, see Schlag, "Economic and Business Ethics," 184–90.

34. Lombard, *Tractatus de usuris*, 1307, discussed by Little, *Religious Poverty*, 182.

35. Noonan, *Scholastic Analysis*, 115–16.

36. Noonan, 116.

37. Noonan, 129.

38. Todeschini, *Franciscan Wealth*, 151–56.

39. Todeschini, 174–78.

40. Noonan, *Scholastic Analysis*, 294–310.

41. Todeschini, *Franciscan Wealth*, 194.

42. Biéler, *Calvin's Social and Economic Thought*, 4.

43. Ernst Troeltsch advanced a similar argument in 1911, emphasizing the significance of the blessing Calvin gave to lending at interest and hence to capitalism, in his *Social Teachings of the Christian Churches*. Max Stackhouse offers a brief overview of some of the most influential responses to Weber's thesis; Stackhouse, "Weber," 310–14.

44. Weber, *Protestant Ethic*, 155–64, 170–72, 180.

45. Weber, "Asceticism, Mysticism and Salvation," 542.

46. Luther, "Trade and Usury," 248.

47. Luther, 250.

48. See, e.g., Tawney, *Religion*; and Visser 't Hooft, *Background*. For a balanced discussion, see Noonan, *Scholastic Analysis*, 365–67.

49. See Bieler, *Calvin's Economic and Social Thought*, 403–16; and Valeri, "Religion," 123–42.

50. Calvin, *Institutes*, III.X, 720.

51. Calvin, X, 721.

52. Calvin, *Commentary on a Harmony of the Evangelists*, on Matthew 6:24.

53. Calvin, on Matthew 6:27.

54. Calvin, *Institutes*, III.X, 723.

55. Calvin, *Commentary on the Epistle of Paul to the Corinthians*, 2 Corinthians 8:14.

56. Calvin, *Commentary on the Acts of the Apostles*, Acts 2:45.

57. However, the view that Roman law defended absolute property rights is largely a construction of the nineteenth century, Jakab, "Property Rights," 106–31.

58. Calvin, *Institutes*, III.X, 724.

59. Calvin, III.X, 725.

60. Calvin, *Commentary on Genesis*, 2:15.

61. Calvin, *Harmony of the Law*, on Exodus 20:8.

62. Tawney, *Religion*, xi, xiii.

63. Pomeranz, *Great Divergence*.

64. Cohen, "Rational Capitalism."

65. Sayous, "Calvinisme," 227; cited by Bieler, *Calvin's Social and Economic Thought*, 447.

66. Gorski, "Little Divergence," 167.

67. Gorski, 168; Jan De Vries, "Industrious Revolution," 249–70.

68. Among recent works, in addition to those already noted, see Lehmann and Roth, *Weber's Protestant Ethic*; Ghosh, *Max Weber*; and Barbalet, *Weber, Passion, and Profits*.

69. Campbell and Skinner suggest that the first exposition of the term "division of labor" was Sir William Petty, writing in 1690; *Wealth of Nations*, I, 13.

70. Hont and Ignatieff, *Wealth and Virtue*; Phillipson, "Culture and Society," 407–48.

71. See, e.g., Chakrabarty, *Provincializing Europe*.

72. Herdt, "Religion," 12–13.

73. See, e.g., Friedman, *Capitalism*; and Stigler, *Economist as Preacher*. Stigler, 136, remarked of Smith's *Wealth of Nations* that it "is a stupendous palace erected upon the granite of self-interest." For a powerful critique of this narrative, see Kleinbard, *We Are Better*, 31–37; and see Kleinbard's reflections in chapter 9 of this volume.

74. Smith, *Wealth of Nations*, IV.ii, 456.

75. On these two benefits identified by Smith, see Hanley, *Smith*, 15–22.

76. Hanley, 102–3.

77. Hanley, 175–208.

78. Smith, *Wealth of Nations*, 96.

79. Smith, 86.

80. Smith, 100.

81. Smith, 267.

82. On the *Wealth of Nations* precisely as natural theology, see Waterman, *Political Economy*, 88–106; also see Haakonssen, *Natural Law*.

83. Oslington, *Political Economy*, 112–13.

84. Waterman, *Political Economy*, 114–18; Waterman, *Revolution*, 58–112.

85. Hirschman, *Passions*.

86. Wright, *Passions*, 1604: 21, quoted by Barbalet, *Weber*, 95.

87. Wright, *Passions*, 326; quoted by Barbalet, *Weber*, 96.

88. Mandeville, *Fable*.

89. Quoted by Appleby, *Economic Thought*, 171.

90. For an overview, see Preston, "Christian Socialism."

91. Kuyper, *Lectures on Calvinism*.

92. Waterman, *Political Economy*, 107–26; Waterman, *Revolution*, 113–70.

93. On the rise of neoliberal economics proper, see Jones, *Masters*, esp. 113–15. For a nuanced theological assessment, see Hirschfeld, *Aquinas*.

PART II

THE INTERNAL DYNAMICS OF BUSINESS

CHAPTER 3

Practical Wisdom and Management Science

Andrew M. Yuengert

The inquiry into the morality of business undertaken in this volume requires attention to a fundamental shift in business practice, particularly in large firms: a reliance on "management science" in making business decisions. The change has simultaneously generated resistance. Critiques of management science (and of business education that teaches it) often point to recent financial crises and scandals as evidence of the flaws in current practice.[1]

These critiques highlight a threefold gap in the way management science and business managers conceive of their tasks: gaps between theory and practice, between business science and business ethics, and between the personal moral life of the business executive and the norms and roles of commerce and finance. They also assert that the resources of management science as it is currently practiced are insufficient to bridge the gaps. Management science must look outside itself for the resources. This chapter argues that "practical wisdom" is what is needed.

Alasdair MacIntyre provides one way to understand this dissatisfaction with management science. He notes that every tradition of inquiry contains a set of questions and difficulties that are "insoluble antinomies," known to those in the tradition as intractable questions or oversights. If these problems become pressing enough, some will begin to "ask whether the alternative and rival tradition may not be able to provide resources to characterize and to explain the failings and defects of their own tradition more adequately than they, using the resources of that tradition, have been able to do."[2] A growing body of research explores the resources of virtue ethics, especially the virtue of practical wisdom, as an alternative, or at least a supplement, to management science. All three of the CEOs interviewed in chapter 1 stressed the central role of virtues. Yet, because practical wisdom and the other virtues are from "an alternative and rival tradition," it is difficult to graft them on to the existing intellectual framework of management science. Practical wisdom works inside the three blind spots of management science: in the gaps between theory and practice, between ethics and science, between the roles and norms of commerce and the moral life of the person. Its location in the blind spots gives the virtue tradition something to offer management science, but it creates a problem of translation: how can management science see what virtue ethics has to offer, especially because it does not notice that it has any blind spots?

Two common responses to the challenge of virtue ethics reduce the prospect of intellectual exchange considerably. First, management science might domesticate the virtues so they will behave themselves in the scientific household, defining them to fit into quantifiable categories to avoid any need to deal with the challenge they actually present. Virtues get translated into observable personality traits driving behavior, or nothing more than instrumentally useful habits that promote profitability. Second, management science might leave the virtues to run wild outside the scientific household, but still maintain the strict separation between "values" (the domain of virtues) and the scientific analysis of "fact" (the domain of management science). From this second response, we get virtue ethics as a separate course module in a business ethics curriculum that is already kept strictly separate from management science. Yet as David Bochnowski reports in his chapter 1 interview, a more holistic commitment to virtue, which he credits to his "Georgetown Jesuit education," is fundamental to responsible business leadership.

Neither of these responses is likely to understand fully or harness effectively what the virtue tradition can offer. Practical wisdom's integration of facts and value, of theory and practice, and of the demands of business and the demands of the good life cannot be fully appreciated by those who insist on a strict separation of ethics and management science. To take practical wisdom seriously as an alternative approach to business management, it must be employed on its own terms, as fully part of the virtue tradition.

This chapter is a targeted review of the business literature on practical wisdom, emphasizing its implications for businesses and business schools. The first section outlines the three intellectual divisions that are natural consequences of the technocratic mind-set of management science. The second section introduces practical wisdom as the virtue of a business leader, emphasizing its ability to bridge the three divides. The third section suggests what it would mean to take practical wisdom seriously: how businesses might operate differently, and how business schools might incorporate practical wisdom into their curricula.

THREE DIVIDES IN BUSINESS

Management science is a systematic investigation of the rationalized, efficient control of business operations toward the goal of profitability.[3] To achieve this end, it has adopted the methods of applied science and engineering: careful theoretical specification and analysis of the internal and external business environments—of inputs, output, human resources, finance, operations, markets, and regulation. This theoretical work is followed by the operationalization of these concepts by appropriate measures and proxies, and careful research into the causal structure of the theoretical model and what it is designed to illuminate. The goal of research is a greater understanding of the levers by which businesses can maximize profits through institutional design, efficient resource use, and appropriate incentive structures.

The engineering approach of management science is not unique to business schools; it is merely one expression of the technocratic worldview, the subject of chapter 5 in this volume, by Mary Hirschfeld. Technocratic approaches are decidedly "third person." Their goal in business is to convert any concrete challenge facing particular persons into a "decision problem," formulated so that someone who is not making the actual decision, but who is expert in the abstractions, can make it. People, locations, machinery, and money are rendered comparable by being translated into measurable resources. Raw uncertainty is tamed by converting it into probability distributions. The inner states and intentions of everyone involved—owners, managers, workers, and customers—are unmeasurable, and thus are ignored in favor of observable actions.

The spectacular success of modern technocratic methods in raising material living standards (combined with a collapse in our ability to disagree about ends reasonably[4]) explains the appeal of technocratic approaches like management science. Indeed, it would be foolish for any manager or owner to eschew these crucial tools. Nevertheless, there are losses in understanding that accompany the gains from technocratic methods. Various critiques argue that the dominance of technocratic methods in business and in business schools gives rise to the same problem: the separation of business as it is conceived and practiced from the moral life as it is conceived and lived out.[5] This separation is observable on the three levels already mentioned.

First, there is an unbridged gulf between the analysis provided by management science and its daily application in business. However finely tuned its abstract categories, management science can never be sufficient for running a business. There will always be something left out of the analysis—something that is an imperfect fit for the circumstances. The scientific method is analytical, operating at a distance on abstractions (models, assumptions, quantities, functional relations). Business decisions are by contrast synthetic, combining technical knowledge with knowledge of particular circumstances to bring deliberation to the point of action. Because management science purposefully overlooks synthetic skills and knowledge, it leaves the impression that the analytical expertise of business research is sufficient to fully inform business practice.

Sumantra Ghoshal calls this mistake "the pretense of knowledge"—the exclusion of important phenomena and behavior from the academic knowledge base. These are excluded because they are difficult to quantify, leading to "absurdities in theory" (e.g., understanding justice as efficiency) and "dehumanization in practice" (employing deterministic economic theories to justify morally questionable workplace practices).[6] Warren Bennis and James O'Toole similarly argue that the narrowness of the scientific method leads to equating business practice with technocratic method. They counter that business is not another academic discipline; it is a "profession," whose task is to "call upon the work of many academic disciplines."[7] The "profession" of business must bridge the divide between research and practice: "The problem is not that business schools have embraced scientific rigor but that they have forsaken other forms of knowledge."[8]

A second divide within business is the gap between business ethics and the other business disciplines. These disciplines operate with methods that exclude ethical considerations from their subject matter. Ghoshal notes that the scientific aspirations of academic business disciplines preclude human intentionality (the arena of ethics) as a causal force.[9] Consequently, business ethics becomes a course that is tacked on in the business curriculum, unable to ground practices of management, finance, or marketing. In the face of such a stark divide between business research and ethics, it is not surprising that when business research attempts to draw on ethics, it tends to put ethics at the service of profits.[10] To students formed in an environment where business can put ethics at its service but is itself isolated from the demands of ethics, ethics is a set of moral exhortations that one can either take or leave. Ethics can only *hope* it will be heard, speaking (or shouting) across the gulf that divides it from management science.

Even some ethical theories leave unchallenged the strict separation between management science and ethics. Utilitarianism, because it does not call into question the ends that arise from individual preferences, can make use of the insights of this deterministic analysis because it also refuses to question the content of preferences.[11] Deontological approaches, which are themselves analytical, likewise pose little threat to the methods of management science. Miguel Alzola emphasizes the close fit of deontological ethics (which evaluates action only as it conforms to duty) and positive analytical method (which evaluates action without regard to psychological state and intention).[12] The analytically derived imperatives of deontology do impose external constraints on the options available to management science, but once certain actions are forbidden, the structure and content of the analysis itself goes on.[13] The gap is not quite as wide as before, but ethics still does not inform business decisions.

The third divide is more personal than the first two: the gap between the roles and norms at work and those that prevail elsewhere in life. Technocratic conceptions of business leave the impression that ethical considerations are an irrelevant distraction. There is some truth to this because technical practice governs much of accounting, financial analysis, and operations. The morals of the accountant are only indirectly relevant to the creation of an income statement.

Nevertheless, Bennis and O'Toole insist that many of the most critical business decisions are not technical and must be approached through a broader exercise of reason that includes ethical reflection: "How does a culture of celebrity affect leadership? How should a CEO be compensated? How does one design global operations so they are at once effective and equitable? What is the purpose of a corporation beyond the creation of shareholder value?"[14] More concretely, CEO Joan Wren reports in chapter 1 on the importance of being able to make exceptions to standard policies, clearly an exercise of practical wisdom. It is a mistake to shoehorn these questions into the narrow space of profit-maximization. This denies a place for the moral life in the worklife of the business executive.

In *After Virtue*, MacIntyre notes that the division between the role one plays in business and the role one plays elsewhere is part of a more significant moral confusion; business is only one of many social spheres, and "modernity partitions each human life into a variety of segments, each with its own norms and modes of behavior."[15] Many people have unfortunately given up on the possibility of a unified narrative of life, which would make action morally intelligible. The struggle to live a unified life fosters growth in wisdom and human flourishing. A unified narrative also makes it less likely that one might justify actions in business that would shock one's moral sensibilities in any other sphere.

The three gaps outlined above generate questions that modern technocratic theory cannot answer. The disciplines of management science are not oblivious to these divides, but they make little effort to grapple with them directly. Nonetheless, some appeal to institutional and structural forces outside business to bring the two sides of the divide into uneasy alignment. There are two theoretical descriptions of how this alignment might be achieved; each relies on a combination of discernible systemic order and public policy action.

First, "liberal" theories argue that competitive markets, though they do not operate on moral principles, offer systemic incentives that curb the worst moral excesses in business and reward innovation and service. Competitive pressures do not make businesses moral, but, as David Cloutier investigates in chapter 7, they will constrain them to serve consumers. Second, more interventionist theories expect competition to result in monopoly, exploitation, and the manipulation of consumer desires. Because competition will not compel businesses to serve customer interests, the state must draw on economic research to regulate market activity and curb business excesses.[16]

Neither of these structural solutions expects much from business, or from business ethics. Neither integrates the ethical and technocratic sides of business, but each attempts to reconcile them at a broader, systemic level, thus reducing some of the tensions and contradictions of the technocratic approach. Any critique of technocratic approaches must acknowledge these attempts to address the internal tensions, while at the same time offering an alternative that addresses the tensions directly, so that inadequate systemic solutions need not carry the entire burden of reconciliation.

PRACTICAL WISDOM AS AN ORGANIZING CONCEPT FOR MANAGEMENT

If we understand management as an exercise in practical wisdom, we can bridge the divides in management science. To take up this offer of integration, however, we must accept practical wisdom on its own terms, as a moral and intellectual virtue, and not as a purely technical exercise.

Management science relies on the analytical, third-person distance afforded by abstraction. In contrast, practical wisdom is excellence in first-person decision-making, emphasizing the first-person account given by Martin Schlag in chapter 8 of this volume. The starting point in the virtues tradition is human action, described not in abstract quantitative categories but as human beings confront it. When they make choices, human beings do not have the luxury of separating fact from value, of taking their goals and purposes as fixed and preexisting, or of assuming well-defined probability distributions covering every possible outcome. They must grapple with decisions in circumstances that unfold piecemeal and unpredictably. They experience the consequences of action or inaction personally. More importantly, they confront the particularities of concrete choice without abandoning reasoned reflection on their actions.

The species of reason that grapples with first-person choice is not rigorous third-person analysis—but it is reason nonetheless. When practical wisdom gives an account of itself, it offers rough outlines and general descriptions, not well-specified objective functions, constraints, and optimizing algorithms. According to Aristotle, the vagueness of its reflections is not, however, a sign of unreason or intellectual sloppiness; it is a consequence of the imprecision of the problem of choice itself: "Our discussion will be adequate if it has as much clearness as the subject admits, for precision is not to be sought for alike in all things. . . . It is the mark of an educated man to look for precision in each class of things just so far as the nature of the subject admits."[17]

A Brief Aside on Catholic Social Teaching, Virtue, and Practical Wisdom

Modern Catholic social teaching (the modern tradition of papal encyclicals) has deep roots in the virtue tradition. The popes speak the language of the virtues and draw on resources from the virtue ethics tradition. They routinely invoke the importance of practical wisdom in the political order for the common good.[18] They point out the contributions of the virtues (including practical wisdom) in business.[19] The design of effective institutions and solutions to social problems likewise requires this virtue.[20] Even the formation of lay leaders for effective Christian social action requires practical wisdom.[21]

Yet the history of Catholic social teaching—and the history of the Catholic moral theology that informs it—is not a straightforward history of virtue ethics. Servais Pinckaers identifies two competing theories within the history of Catholic moral theology.[22] First, "moralities of happiness"—which draw on Aristotle, Augustine, and Aquinas—are more closely aligned with the tradition of virtue ethics. Second, "moralities of obligation" begin with precepts of the moral law and their claims on human action; apart from binding moral obligation, human action is entirely free from ethical evaluation or constraint.

Practical wisdom plays a much-attenuated role in moralities of obligation; its job is not to discern the obligations of morality, and it need not accept their binding authority. When action is unimpeded by obligation, practical wisdom pursues its ends in messy, chaotic circumstance; when action is constrained by moral obligation accepted by the will, practical wisdom pursues its ends within the constraint. In moralities of obligation, virtues become inner dispositions that dispose us to *accept* moral obligations (a goodwill). In moralities of obligation, practical wisdom merely puts already-accepted precepts into practice and will be unable to fully integrate business and ethics.

Catholic social teaching has been influenced by and draws on both theories of obligation and theories of happiness. Moralities of happiness are not dominant within academic reflections on this tradition. Many significant academic reference works on Catholic social teaching rarely mention the virtues or practical wisdom.[23] Consequently, although practical wisdom appears in the documents of Catholic social teaching, those whose chief concerns are principles and the obligations they impose can overlook it. Even many treatments that draw explicitly on the virtues tradition admit that the virtues are only implicit in the encyclicals; their importance must be argued and cannot be taken for granted.[24] Domenec Mele states as much in his outline of the place of virtue in Catholic social teaching: "For a long period, Catholic Social Teaching placed great emphasis on principles, but virtues were always there although they often remained implicit."[25]

Catholic social teaching is a crucial resource for reflection on business management, but to the extent that it draws on moralities of obligation, it will not remedy the divisions within management science. Business needs practical wisdom, rooted in the Neo-Aristotelian tradition, and the related "moralities of happiness" in Catholic theology. The full promise of practical wisdom for how we conceive of business and the academic business disciplines is most apparent when it is placed more completely within the Neo-Aristotelian tradition.

Virtue Is Practical

Practical wisdom is a virtue; it is excellence in making decisions that are humanly good—not just good management decisions or good technical decisions, but good decisions for a human being *as* human being. Its general nature, as a *virtue*, is crucial to understanding what practical wisdom offers in management science. Aristotle defines virtue as "a state of character concerned with choice, lying in a mean, i.e., the mean relative to us, this being determined by a rational principle, and by that principle by which a person of practical wisdom would determine it."[26]

Every part of this definition is essential. To leave any part of it out—to cut virtue down to size to fit it to the scientific method—is to risk overlooking what virtue offers.

First, virtue is "a state of character concerned with choice." It is not just habitual orientation toward a moral principle, a strong desire to be good. All the virtues are *practical*—they help us make good decisions—because the moral life is inescapably practical.

Second, the practical choices to which virtues incline us lie in a mean "relative to us." Humans must deliberate and act in highly contingent circumstances; "what to do" depends on those singular circumstances that face the person making the decision. Choice is more than a complex analytical problem; contingencies both within the agent's character and external to him multiply the ways a decision can go wrong. The difficulty in defining what is at stake in a decision, and in finding the right balance between goods and circumstance, makes virtue necessary.

Third, the choices made possible by virtue are "determined by a rational principle." Virtue is not mere habit; it is a combination of intelligence and disposition. Julia Annas, in *Intelligent Virtue*, draws carefully on the analogy between virtue in human action and virtuosity in skilled activity.[27] In the virtuoso violinist, we recognize a combination of method, habit, and intelligence. The experience of playing is not itself self-conscious; while playing, the violinist does not think about how to play. Yet if asked, she can give an account of what she is doing and how she might improve. Practical reason employs a similarly intuitive discernment about what is possible in the circumstances. Scientific accounts of human behavior overlook this embodied reasonableness of virtue.

The fourth characteristic of virtue in Aristotle's definition is equally intriguing: the rational principle by which choices are made, and to which virtue inclines us, is "that principle by which a person of practical wisdom would determine it." The mean in virtue is found not in a text but in the life and judgment of the practically wise person, just as the best judge of excellent play of the violin is an excellent violin player. The ability to discern the good and to deliberate about what to do is embedded in character. The virtuous can perceive the good "in each class of things," whereas one who lacks the virtues will overlook it.[28]

This fourth characteristic of virtue (its embeddedness in character) also brings to light its social nature. You cannot learn virtue from a book because a formal account cannot do full justice to the perceptiveness and judgment made possible by virtue. You learn virtue in the company and under the guidance of those who have it. Just as you learn music or human skills under the tutelage of those who have them, you become virtuous and practically wise in the community of the practically wise.[29]

The Virtue of Practical Wisdom

The virtue of practical wisdom is already deeply implicated in the definition of virtue in general: all the virtues are concerned with choice, and practical wisdom is the nexus of practical action. Aristotle defines practical wisdom as "a reasoned and true state of capacity to act with regard to human goods."[30] In the *Summa*, Aquinas gives a pithier definition, "right reason applied to action."[31]

The term "action" is liable to be an abstract formulation in the modern analytical mind, as a formalized specification of means, ends, and an algorithm that connects them. Under such abstract formalization, decisions about what to do can be separated from the context in which people act—theory separated from practice, ethics from technique, the life of business from human life "as such," reducing practical wisdom to complex calculation. Practical wisdom, however, makes actual, concrete decisions, and real decisions cannot be made by a third person in a computer lab. Action in the Neo-Aristotelian tradition is profoundly first person, in which the one who acts is fully invested, for better or for worse. Practical wisdom is excellence in this sort of action.

Practical wisdom is defined as excellence in human choice—not choice abstracted from any particularity, but the choice of a person fully engaged in his or her lived circumstances. As a result, practical wisdom must bridge the three divides in business research and education identified above. Those who practice business successfully in the first person must integrate the insights of research and the exigencies of business context; they seek out a conversation between morals and business success; they are troubled by pressure to be different people at work than they are in the rest of their lives. Practical wisdom integrates categories that appear necessarily divided in modern business science.

INTEGRATIVE PRACTICAL WISDOM

Business owners, managers, and workers do not have the luxury of abstract analysis: each must combine theory and practice. At a minimum, if they had to choose between them, they would have to choose practice. Practical wisdom is a description of the experience and practice of acting in the world. As such, it must also give an integrated account of theory and practice, of moral theory and business science, of life inside and outside the commercial social context.

Practical Wisdom and Other Exercises of Reason

Practical wisdom is a virtue, not a passive, unreflective habit. It is an application of reason to all the elements that go into right action, not merely those elements that can be modeled. Aristotle introduces practical wisdom in his treatment of the intellectual virtues. The intellectual virtues are divided into those that apprehend unchanging truths (theory, intuition, and wisdom), and those that apprehend truths that might be otherwise (technique and practical wisdom).

To apply this distinction today, we need to recognize a shortcoming of typical English usage. Although economists and management scientists strongly identify their discipline with *theory* (the truths of mathematics), I argue in *The Boundaries of Technique* that economics and management science are more accurately categorized as *techniques*. Although they draw heavily on mathematics, they make use of statistical and theoretical methods to address those truths of business and the economy that are subject to change and manipulation.[32]

Because both technique and practical wisdom apprehend things that could be otherwise, and because modern management science and economics are techniques, the differences between technique and practical wisdom (and their relationship with each other) are crucial for understanding the proper place of practical wisdom in business and business education. Technique and practical wisdom are distinguished by their ends in two ways.

First, the end of technique is given and fixed, whereas practical wisdom must grapple with both ends and means. Technique develops with the repeated pursuit of similar tasks, geared to a well-defined external output— for example, producing an accounting income statement. Canons of practice channel the activity of the technical expert along well-trodden paths. In contrast, *contingency*—the complex of particularities that, although abstracted away in technical analysis, must be taken into account in actual decisions— puts in question ends as well as means. In chapter 1, CEO David Bochnowski provides an excellent example of practical wisdom at work when he describes the need to decide on the level of "secrecy" appropriate when his firm investigates one employee's complaint against another. Both transparency of process and confidentiality to protect the innocent are goals of a good organization and the business leader must decide how to respect them both simultaneously. Because practical wisdom must grapple with contingency, it deliberates about both ends and means.

A second difference between the ends of technique and the ends of practical wisdom is their respective locations. Technique produces artifacts that are external to the technician, whose goodness can be judged apart from the character of the technician; we need not know who made a clock or wrote a business plan to judge it by technical standards. The outcome of practical wisdom, however, is internal to the one who decides.[33] The struggle to discern what ends are possible and to carry out a plan of action leaves a mark on the character of the person: we become better, or fail to improve, by dint of our actions to realize human goods in our lives and the lives of others. The location of the ends of practical wisdom highlights its intensely personal nature. It is happiness realized, not abstractly measured.

Because practical wisdom does not lend itself to technical description, and because modern reason is defined by formal description and measurement of ends and means, practical wisdom *appears* to be nonrational, inaccessible to the narrow reason of business science. Nevertheless, Aristotle classifies it as an intellectual virtue, an exercise of the intellect. Its end (action in pursuit of human goods) and its operations (counsel, judgment, command) are admittedly imprecise—"precision is not to be sought for alike in all things"—but we can reason about the outline, and discern whether an outline is good or bad.[34]

The outline of practical wisdom in the Neo-Aristotelian tradition is no mere sketch, however. In the *Summa*, Aquinas offers a thorough discussion of the nature of human action and explores the nature of practical wisdom: as a virtue, its operation, its constituent virtues, and failures of practical wisdom.[35] I will not attempt a full treatment here but will only emphasize how practical wisdom acts to bridge the three divides in management science.

Theory and Practice

All concrete decisions share a common challenge: contingency. Contingency is the primal uncertainty that challenges our counsels and judgments. Despite all our efforts to control and systematize our environment, we all have experience of actions for which formulas and rules of thumb are insufficient guides. Estimated probability distributions are only as good as the data. Our reasoning can fail us. The unpredictability of our own character can derail our plans.

Management science abstracts away from contingency, modeling it as probability and attempting to reduce it through measurement and systems of control. By definition, however, contingency is not subject to quantitative methods. We can describe the virtues by which it is discerned and factored into decisions, but we cannot develop formulas to conquer it. Virtue is needed because uncertainty opens up a space where untutored emotions can affect our practical reason. Aquinas discusses a range of virtues that are closely associated with practical wisdom and that grapple directly with contingency.[36] The need for virtues like situational understanding, the ability to call on memory under pressure, shrewd adjustment to surprises, circumspection, and due caution testify to the entrepreneurial character of practical wisdom, which does not merely accept contingency stoically but adjusts to it dynamically. The virtues that manage contingency make little sense in the clean analytical world of management science, which assumes contingency away. Because actual decisions must confront contingency, the virtues associated with practical wisdom are necessary.

Ethics and Management Science

Because of its own decision to avoid value judgments, management science cannot integrate itself into the larger moral and practical considerations of practical wisdom; it is purposefully blind to the resources for such an integration. In contrast, practical wisdom is by its nature integrative; it draws on all reasoned activities (theory, intuition, technique) and combines their insights with its judgment about particulars to make a good decision. Practical wisdom is neither technical nor theoretical, but it *is* reasoned, and reasoned explorations of its nature and operation force us to bridge the gap between theory and practice, between ethics and management science.

In *The Boundaries of Technique*, I outline the relationship between practical wisdom and technique.[37] Technique, because it seeks a limited end, and defines its method with regard to that end, enjoys a real but limited autonomy from the ethics-laden reflections of practical wisdom. One might question the need for a particular technical output (a door from a carpenter, a model from an economist) but, once the need is accepted, the technician proceeds as if the ethical questions do not matter. Yet, the insulation of technique from practical wisdom is not total; we do not absolve technicians of all responsibility for the uses to which their products are put.

Technical analysis begins by standardizing and quantifying the ends of the technique, thus putting them beyond deliberation. It is left to practical wisdom to evaluate whether the end is worth pursuing in current circumstances, and whether the ends of the technique complement or undermine other important ends affected by the decision. In chapter 6, Kenneth Goodpaster and Michael Naughton put a similar stress on viewing immediate decisions in light of broader aims.

It is possible to be better or worse at this sort of integration; practical wisdom consists in being good at it. Bennis and O'Toole claim that management should be considered a profession that draws on many techniques, and they argue that business schools should prepare students for this sort of integration. This is evidence of the need for and possibility of practical wisdom.[38] Discussions of how one becomes good at this sort of integration, and how one carries it out, will not be scientifically rigorous but are not by that fact rendered fruitless.

Business and the Moral Life

As we said earlier, Julia Annas makes extensive use of the analogy between skilled performance and the virtues.[39] By describing the intelligence embodied in, for example, musical or athletic skill—the drive to excel, the interplay between imitation and creative virtuosity, and the good derived from attempts to improve at every level of skill—Annas outlines the nature of virtue, of excellence in living life.

This imaginative leap from excellence in a particular task to excellence in living life in its totality might seem impossible in a culture dominated by the modern analytic style. We are too often resigned to a divided moral existence, accepting one set of norms in the segregated sphere of business and other collections of contradictory norms in other isolated spheres. What is good for business practice need not be good absolutely.

There is no *technical* method for integrating the whole of one's life: analysis examines the parts in detail but provides no rules for putting them together. There is no agreed-upon analytical standard (no single-valued scale) that can compare the goods pursued in various spheres of life. As a result, the choice between conflicting goods appears arbitrary and non-rational. Yet the ordering of lower goods to higher goods is critical for a responsible and fulfilling life, as David Cloutier, Martin Schlag, Kenneth Goodpaster, and Michael Naughton argue elsewhere in this volume. The virtues that enable such an integration must therefore be somewhat invisible to technocratic methods.

Conversely, the virtue tradition takes for granted that it is possible to live a unified life, and that the attempt to be multiple conflicting persons in different spheres undermines human happiness. The unified human flourishing that is the end of practical wisdom is by no means easy or widely achieved, however. The attempt to balance goods realized in different areas of life will force us to compare goods that appear to be incomparable. Difficult business decisions about expanding and downsizing, treating customers and suppliers honestly and fairly, ensuring the survival of a business or shutting it down, involve human trade-offs that are not reducible to profitability, even though profits are crucial for firm growth and sustainability.

A "scale" that can reconcile the conflicting goods and norms of business and other parts of life is by nature difficult to specify exactly. It will express itself differently in different communities and in different lives within those communities, as an account of what it means to live well. The wide variety of integrated accounts of a life well lived does not testify to the impossibility of an integrated view, however. If practical wisdom is a human virtue, then members of one community will recognize, even in the practices and norms of radically different civilizations, echoes of their own desire to live a complete and unified life.

The context for this integration is inescapably personal; it is the life one is trying to lead.[40] It is an achievement, built piecemeal from one's experiences, mentors, failures, and successes. Elijah Millgram notes that the need to choose between seemingly incommensurable goods and to balance the trade-offs among them is itself crucial to understanding what makes for a good life.[41] Kleio Akrivou and Jose Victor Oron echo this insight in their discussion of "the interprocessual self," their general description of the self in virtue ethics.[42] Growth in the interprocessual self occurs in the very struggle to integrate the conflicting goods in one's life. Anyone who avoids these conflicts will fail to grow in practical wisdom.

PRACTICAL IMPLICATIONS

It would be self-defeating to argue that business needs practical wisdom without reflecting on its practical implementation. The technical approaches to business that currently dominate academe are not sufficient to run an actual business. But because practical wisdom bridges the gaps between the science of business, practice, and the moral life, it is incumbent on us to review the efforts to take practical wisdom seriously in business education and business management.

By this point, it should be no surprise that the virtue tradition does not prescribe rigorous, analytical solutions. Just as practical wisdom can only be described in outline and roughly, the guidance for companies seeking to take it seriously is imprecise; nevertheless, having a good outline is better than having a bad one.

An approach to business that takes the first-person perspective of practical wisdom will take seriously those aspects of business practice that are revealed in the first person. Workers, managers, and customers are more than assumed preferences to be manipulated in the service of profits; they are persons whose goals and virtues matter greatly to the operation of the business, and to its evaluation leaders within or observers outside. The perspective of practical wisdom allows us to frame business institutions in a way that places virtues and personal development in their proper places, as part of the common good of business. Also, it generates practical advice for how institutional structure and workplace culture can foster and sustain practical wisdom.

Perspectives on Business Institutions

Profits are a crucial instrumental good, but they are instrumental nonetheless. From the standpoint of practical wisdom, we can begin to discuss what ends profits are supposed to serve and modify our accounts of the institutional challenge of business accordingly.

The common good of a business is its purpose "as a community of persons."[43] Of course, each person in a business community has a different set of goals, but a healthy business allows each to pursue his or her own flourishing in a coordinated way.[44] Brian McCall draws on Aristotle's *Politics* to define business as an "imperfect community," whose members pursue some common ends, but which is not self-sufficient for any member's flourishing.[45] The incomplete common goods of businesses do not detract from their importance. Defined in the *Vocation of a Business Leader* as goods that are truly good, good work, and good wealth, these common goods are humanly important.[46] The common good of the "more perfect" community (the political community) respects and fosters the common goods of imperfect communities while not absorbing or obliterating them.[47]

The challenge of managing a business organization, defined as an imperfect community with its own common good, requires more than technical skill; it requires practical wisdom, analogous to the practical wisdom needed to govern a polity. Because the goal of business is broader than profit-maximization, the management task is correspondingly more complex, bringing to the foreground conflicts between individual interests and community, between the private corporation and the public good, between ethics and science. The interviews with CEOs in chapter 1 describe the practical challenge of making business serve more than profits. Similar arguments are made in chapter 6 by Goodpaster and Naughton, on the contrasts between shareholder/stakeholder and common good conceptions of the firm, and by Martin Schlag in chapter 8, discussing the responsibilities of business for society's moral ecology. It is the task of the manager to put profit in its proper place, as a crucial instrumental good at the service of the more primary goods of the firm: good goods, good work, and good wealth.

An equally important branch of the Neo-Aristotelian business ethics literature frames the institutional challenge differently, drawing not on the *Politics* directly but on the distinction between practice and institution in MacIntyre's *After Virtue*. A "practice" is a socially established cooperative activity that produces "internal goods," which are the growth in virtue (or "excellences") related to the practice.[48] By defining the virtues in this way, MacIntyre embeds them in communities of practice and opens up the possibility of discussing the place of virtue in business. Growth in practical wisdom requires a community of practice. How can this come about, and what might prevent it from happening?

Although practices rely on and foster the virtues, they need external goods: order and structure, and material resources. If the pursuit of the common good of a business is a practice, it will only be sustainable if the business is well run and profitable. MacIntyre emphasized the threat posed by institutions to practices—that the pursuit of the external goods undermines the pursuit of the virtues internal to practices. MacIntyre's assertion has generated disagreement and qualification: some argue that institutions do not necessarily corrode practices, but can support them;[49] others offer examples where practices undermine the institutions that maintain them;[50] others assert that the management of institutions can itself be a practice.[51] This literature provides an important perspective on the arduous task of practical wisdom in organizations: keeping the institution at the service of the common goods contained in practices.

Practical but Imprecise Guidance

A better account of the purpose of the firm (the common good of a business community, the balance between practices and institutions) requires the exercise of practical wisdom. How is this expanded vision of the firm made operational, and how is the practical wisdom necessary to its implementation fostered in business? The literature on practical wisdom and virtue in business offers general guidance.

If a business institution is to be more than a profit-maximizing enterprise, it must keep its broader purpose in mind. A more complex mission must be put in place and sustained. Employing a MacIntyrean framework, Ron Beadle lists the ways managers can lose sight of communal practices: by treating the firm as an ahistorical abstraction, by neglecting their shared life, and by granting no space for practices in corporate missions, focusing entirely on external goods.[52] Geoff Moore and Ron Beadle offer similar advice: corporations should be designed so that they foster an awareness that they exist for the sake of practices, and corporate leadership should remind workers and management of the need for excellent practice.[53] An appreciation that a business has a common good richer than profit-maximization must similarly be fostered through participation and an awareness of a firm's history. Moore argues that trust and active participation—embodied in job design, limits on monitoring, curbs on executive pay, and transparency in leadership—are crucial to creating communities of practice.[54]

Much of the advice from researchers in this field emphasizes that virtuous institutions (which protect practices and foster the virtues that protect practices) and practical wisdom in governance require that businesses hire virtuous people and form employees in the virtues and vision of the organization.[55] The commitment to hiring and training for purposes broader than profit-maximization signals a commitment to placing business in a larger context, as Goodpaster and Naughton argue in chapter 6.

Practical wisdom is transmitted personally, through imitation, mentorship, and examples in many different settings. If practical wisdom is to become an organizing virtue in business, we will need a rich literature of case studies. Helen Alford and Michael Naughton outline a Catholic framework for management in which virtue plays an organizing role, and they review several corporate examples.[56] Michael Naughton and David Specht offer three case studies of attempts to live out the virtues under difficult market conditions.[57] Barry Schwartz and Kenneth Sharpe discuss the ways institutions can suppress the exercise of practical wisdom through excessive compartmentalization, and how practical wisdom might instead be fostered.[58] Brinkman and O'Brien's health care case study describes the intentional organization of a business around the exercise of practical wisdom.[59] T. Dean Maines and Michael Naughton offer a program for professional development, the "Self-Assessment and Improvement Process," as a means of fostering "middle level thinking, . . . the habit or practice of linking moral principles with business realities."[60]

CONCLUSION

Management science adopts a technocratic approach to business, quantifying the various aspects of business and employing mathematical models and statistics to generate a compelling perspective on business practice. For all its efficiencies and insights, however, management science is unable to bridge the three gaps between theory and practice, scientific method and ethics, and business behavior and the moral life of the business executive. These gaps are barriers to placing the analysis of business at the service of the human goods of the persons affected by business. The work of bridging these gaps, of putting this partial analysis into conversation with human flourishing, is accomplished by the virtues. The principal virtue in business is practical wisdom, and its primary task is to integrate knowledge of current circumstance with the insights of management science.

The first step in engaging the practical wisdom tradition is to acknowledge that it exists—that practical wisdom performs a concrete, integrative function in business, that some people are more practically wise than others, and that we can reason about and improve its exercise. When we accept the possibility of reasoning about something that cannot be quantified, we create a space to reflect on practical wisdom and to foster its operations in business. To be sure, the results will not be as satisfyingly exact as constrained optima and statistical point estimates, and the improvements made possible by the practical wisdom approach will not be as quantifiable as those of profit-maximization. Still, they will better reflect the purposes of those engaged in and affected by business. The growing literature on practical wisdom and on the virtues in business shows that this reflection can be fruitful.

Practical wisdom is not a replacement for management science; part of the exercise of this virtue is to put management science more fully at the service of all the goods of business. We need to put management science in conversation with practice, ethics, and the moral life. Practical wisdom makes management science *more* relevant, not less, by more clearly specifying what it has to offer business and what we must add to it. Management science needs the exercise of practical wisdom to avoid the waste of resources that management science becomes when its usefulness is unexamined or taken for granted and to prevent the damage management science can do when it is unguided toward real human ends.

NOTES

1. See Ghoshal, "Bad Management"; and Bennis and O'Toole, "How Business Schools."
2. MacIntyre, *Whose Justice?* 167–68.
3. Management science was once defined more narrowly, as the applied mathematics discipline of operations research. Contemporary definitions, like that in the online *Cambridge English Dictionary*, are broader: "the use of scientific methods and ideas to understand

business and management problems and decisions, or the formal study of management."
See https://dictionary.cambridge.org/us/dictionary/english/management-science.

4. See MacIntyre, *After Virtue.*
5. Ghoshal, "Bad Management"; Bennis and O'Toole, "How Business Schools."
6. Ghoshal, "Bad Management," 79–80.
7. Bennis and O'Toole, "How Business Schools," 97.
8. Bennis and O'Toole, 104.
9. Ghoshal, "Bad Management," 78–79. Economists might respond to this critique that they in fact do take human intentions seriously, through the constrained maximization model; nevertheless, since the ends of human action (preferences) are fixed in this model, its technical, maximizing logic shades into determinism, not human agency. See Davis, *Theory.*
10. Pearce, "Aristotle," 38–39.
11. This is true both of the economic versions of utilitarianism, which emphasizes efficiency, and those versions of utilitarianism that argue explicitly for the maximization of utility as a policy goal.
12. Alzola, "Virtuous Persons."
13. In chapter 20, Beabout compares the different implications of "grammars of virtue' (Neo-Aristotelianism) and "grammars of morality" for how we think about autonomy and agency.
14. Bennis and O'Toole, "How Business Schools," 99.
15. MacIntyre, *After Virtue,* 204.
16. More recently, both approaches have drawn on theories of biological and cultural evolution. See Smith, *Rationality*; and Bowles, *Moral Economy.*
17. Aristotle, *Ethics,* 1.3.
18. Leo XIII, *Rerum novarum,* para. 36; John Paul II, *Laborem exercens,* para. 20; Francis, *Laudato si',* para. 135.
19. Paul VI, *Populorum progressio,* para. 25; John Paul II, *Centesimus annus,* para. 32.
20. Leo XIII, *Rerum novarum,* paras. 55, 56; Pius XI, *Quadragesimo anno,* para. 140; Benedict XVI, *Caritas in veritate,* paras. 47, 65; Francis, *Laudato si',* paras. 63, 124.
21. Leo XIII, *Rerum novarum,* paras. 60; Pius XI, *Quadragesimo anno,* para. 142.
22. Pinckaers, *Sources.*
23. See Himes, *Modern Catholic Social Teaching*; and Curran, *Catholic Social Teaching.*
24. E.g., Alford, "Influence"; Benestad, *Church*; and Mele, "Virtues."
25. Mele, "Virtues," 160; Benestad, *Church.*
26. Aristotle, *Ethics,* 2.6.
27. Annas, *Intelligent Virtue.*
28. Aristotle, *Ethics,* 3.4. Aquinas, *Summa Theologica,* II-II, 45.2, describes a certain connaturality between the good and the perceptions of the virtuous.
29. See Annas, *Intelligent Virtue,* chap. 3.
30. Aristotle, *Ethics,* 6.5.
31. Aquinas, *Summa Theologica,* II-II, 47.2.
32. Yuengert, *Boundaries.*
33. The conflict between internal development and the achievement of external goods is only apparent: practical wisdom is excellence in achieving the human good for oneself and others. A practically wise person who achieves internal goods while wreaking external havoc is a contradiction.
34. Aristotle, *Ethics,* 1.3.

35. Aquinas, *Summa*, I-II, 1-21; II-II, 47–56.
36. Aquinas, II-II, 48–52.
37. Yuengert, *Boundaries*.
38. Bennis and O'Toole, "How Business Schools."
39. Annas, *Intelligent Virtue*.
40. Taylor, "Leading a Life."
41. Millgram, "Incommensurability," 161.
42. Akrivou and Oron, "Two Kinds."
43. John Paul II, *Centesimus annus*, para. 35.
44. See Sison and Fontrodona, "Common Good."
45. Aristotle "Politics"; McCall, "Corporations."
46. Pontifical Council for Justice and Peace, *Vocation*, 17.
47. McCall, "Corporations," 189.
48. Macintyre, *After Virtue*, 187.
49. Moore, "Virtue"; Moore, "On the Implications."
50. Dobson, "Against MacIntyre."
51. Beabout, *Character*.
52. Beadle, "MacIntyre's Influence."
53. Moore and Beadle, "In Search of Organizational Virtue."
54. Moore, "Virtue."
55. Moore and Beadle, "In Search of Organizational Virtue"; Brinkman and O'Brien, "Transforming Healthcare."
56. Alford and Naughton, *Managing as If Faith Mattered*.
57. Naughton and Specht, *Leading Wisely*.
58. Schwartz and Sharpe, *Practical Wisdom*.
59. Brinkman and O'Brien, "Transforming Healthcare."
60. Maines and Naughton, "Middle Level Thinking," 672.

CHAPTER 4

What Are Agency and Autonomy, and What Difference Do They Make for Business?

Gregory R. Beabout

This volume aims to improve the reader's moral judgments about business, judgments that often center on whether seeking a profit leads business to act immorally. When it comes to a moral assessment of those who lead businesses, people usually assume that the motivation driving business managers is their own income. And they surely do care about this. But "money" is only part of the explanation, and at times the lesser part. Just as important are two other often-ignored motivations: agency and autonomy.

In common parlance, "an agent" frequently means someone who acts in the interest of someone else; sports stars have agents who negotiate their contracts. But when we speak of agency as a motivation, we mean the capacity to act, to exert power, to make things happen. Agency in this sense can generate a sense of accomplishment, a sense of "being successful." Even when that success is measured in money, it is the success that is more fundamental.

Closely related to agency is autonomy, which is defined in the *Oxford English Dictionary* as "liberty to follow one's will; control over one's own affairs; freedom from external influence, personal independence." Although business managers do have superiors—even the CEO answers to the board of directors—the sense of accomplishment generated by successful agency is typically tied to a recognition that the manager has made things happen, has made decisions about what others will do and not simply recommendations to a superior.

Together, agency and autonomy are powerful motivating factors in the lives of successful business leaders. For example, Donald Trump, long before his entry into politics, explained that "money was never a big motivation for me, except as a way to keep score. The real excitement is playing the game!"[1]

So what difference do agency and autonomy make for a business and for our moral evaluation of business? The first thing to recognize is that even the definitions given above of these two realities are contestable. It is helpful to recall an insight expressed in one of the key documents of the Second Vatican Council: an essential feature of the modern world is that "the very words by which key concepts are expressed take on quite different meanings in diverse ideological systems."[2] So, puzzling through these questions requires that we are aware that such terms are subject to quite different meanings.

The argument of this chapter unfolds as follows. After noting that students preparing for careers in medicine describe their motivations differently from students preparing for careers in business, I examine the way entrepreneurs describe their motivations in terms of a sense of agency and autonomy. Next, I distinguish between two "types" of business professionals with regard to the self-understanding of motives: the moneymaker and the business person concerned with promoting a positive social impact. I contrast the way these two characters understand agency and autonomy by pointing to Alasdair MacIntyre's distinction between two moral philosophies: a modern, secular ethic that MacIntyre calls "Morality"; and an ethic that retrieves insights from the ancient Greeks, especially Aristotle. Then I show how agency and autonomy are understood within each of these. With this distinction in hand, I suggest that a Neo-Aristotelian moral philosophy is to be preferred for those in or preparing for careers in business because it helps cultivate a disposition and a personal identity as one concerned with promoting a positive social impact. With these distinctions in hand, I revisit the question of motivation to show that the grammar of Neo-Aristotelianism is helpful for the business person concerned with positive social impact. Finally, I reply briefly to objections.

MOTIVATIONS FOR BUSINESS AND MEDICINE

Consider the contrast in the way students pursuing careers in medicine typically describe their motivations as compared with students pursuing careers in business.[3] Students preparing for careers in medicine generally rely on a "grammar of service" to articulate their desires; they voice a desire to "help others." In contrast, students preparing for careers in business typically employ a more utilitarian grammar, even sometimes relying on the vocabulary of egoism: "I want to make money."

Of course, this individualistic or egoistic way of understanding the actions of the business person may involve seeing a public benefit or service to others as a side effect. As Adam Smith is taken to have suggested, an "invisible hand" somehow harmonizes the self-interested actions of individuals to bring forth unintended social benefits.[4] This attitude of self-interest as the underlying motive for business activities is deeply embedded in contemporary culture: business as "profit-maximization" has become the default assumption.[5]

The Complex Motivations for Business

Contrary to what might be expected, when entrepreneurs who have started their own businesses are asked to identify their motivations, their descriptions are complex, going beyond a mere desire for financial success. Consider this advice from an entrepreneur to those considering whether to take the plunge to start a business:

> You will understand how fulfilled it feels to actually follow your dreams and your heart. The reward is not necessarily the money. The reward is in being your own boss and in the art of creating something that you truly own and love. You will learn what it's like to sacrifice external things that make you happy (like drinking and eating out) for things that make you happy internally (like making your business succeed). Of course, a profitable business is what proves your capability in business. However, what truly drives you is not the money; it's the passion and fulfillment you get from following your dreams.[6]

In a similar way, recall the practitioner's perspective described by Regina Wolfe in chapter 1, or consider these statements, in which entrepreneurs articulate their reasons for starting a business:

> "I had a passion about a new idea, and I believed I could make a difference."
> "I wanted to make my own decisions."
> "I wanted to secure the future on my own terms."
> "I wanted to be able to set my own hours."
> "I wanted to do work I believed in and get paid based off what I accomplished."
> "I wanted to follow the beat of my own drum."
> "I wanted my work to be more than a job."[7]

Within these statements we hear a complex set of motivations, including the desire to exercise agency and the desire for autonomous self-determination and self-governance. Starting and running a successful business requires patience, good planning, good judgment, and good execution. Perhaps most of all, it requires determination and self-determination; entrepreneurs need to be able to assess market demand and determine pricing, a budget, a marketing strategy, and a process for taking a project to a point of completion that is sustainable. To carry this out, entrepreneurs need to work cooperatively with others toward a common goal, embracing ever-widening circles: customers, suppliers, employers, investors, and many others.

It may be a coincidence of my own circumstances, but I seem to be seeing an increasing number of business students with richer motivations, especially over the last several years. Some of this may be part of a general cultural shift, as more people are becoming attuned to the social and environmental effects of business activities; another factor is that I am increasingly in social settings where I encounter business students who have social concerns—for example, as part of my participation with a "learning community" (LC) at our university designed for first-year students called the "Ethical Leaders in Business LC."

Because the students who apply to be part of this LC self-select, it is not surprising that they come predisposed to think that their career aspirations in business can be aligned with "ethical leadership."[8] Most of the students in this LC become involved in our university's "Service Leadership" program, which is sponsored by our business school.[9] This program for undergraduate students in the business school involves curricular and co-curricular activities spanning the undergraduate years in which students complete many hours of community service, leadership workshops, and related coursework. In addition, I increasingly encounter students with an interest in "social entrepreneurship," that is, the use of start-up companies to develop, fund, and implement solutions to social and cultural issues. Such students sense that it is possible to start or run a business in a way that brings about sustainable positive social change.

Also, over the last several years, I, a philosopher, have been team-teaching a course with my colleague, Bonnie Wilson, an economist, titled "Markets and Catholic Social Thought." This course draws students from our university's rapidly growing Catholic Studies Centre. To capture the dispositions of the new sorts of students I have in mind, consider this recent newspaper story:

> Austin Smith and Byron Abrigg have a passion for economics and entrepreneurship. The friends, who majored in those subjects at St. Louis University, spent time at the Catholic Studies Centre exploring the link between entrepreneurship and Catholic social teaching.

Now SLU alums and out in the workforce, the two carved time out on a recent afternoon to attend a First Friday Mass in the new chapel at SLU's Boileau Hall. Afterward, they stayed for a talk by Bonnie Wilson, an economics professor who focused on the intersection of economics and theology.

"Entrepreneurship opportunities are one way to help build communities in poverty," Smith said. "One of the strongest things you can do for social justice is to support people from diverse backgrounds who have businesses so they can grow their wealth and economic standing," he said, "which in turn helps them flourish as humans."

It's what the two have dubbed "The Pursuit."[10]

It is not difficult to sense the energy and passion in Austin and Byron as reported in this news story. The quotations give evidence of their enthusiasm for business as a way to serve others, and this energy is even more evident when talking with them. They want to have an impact and make a difference in a way that is good for themselves and for the community.

TWO CHARACTERS: THE MONEYMAKER AND THE PROMOTER OF POSITIVE SOCIAL IMPACT

The answers to our question—"What difference do agency and autonomy make for business?"—will vary greatly, depending on one's perspective. Is the central goal to secure a financially stable professional position, or does one see life as a quest, a journey pursuing a life of authentic fulfillment, self-actualization, and integrated human development in community with others? Let us give names to these two characters: we will call the first *the businessperson as moneymaker*. We will call the second the *businessperson concerned with promoting a positive social impact*.

The point here is not to contrast an evil money-grubber with an idealized altruist, though there may be such people in the world. The *moneymaker* I have in mind is a person dedicated to being honest and acting within the law. Such a person is aware that profits come from well-organized business institutions that provide goods and services for which there is consumer demand. Analogously, the *businessperson concerned with promoting a positive social impact* acknowledges the legitimate role of profit as an indication that productive factors have been used in a manner that corresponds with human needs. Both aim to proceed in a manner that is honest and legal, and both are oriented toward work in the world of business.

Nonetheless, there is a difference in the way these two characters understand the purpose and motivation of their own activities. Further, while each of these perspectives is concerned with matters of ethics, the two operate with different notions of agency and autonomy and with differing moral grammars, a moral grammar being a set of often unconsciously accepted rules for how to live one's life.

Although the term "grammar" is usually associated with the rules embedded in language, some theologians, philosophers, and social theorists have stretched the meaning of grammar to refer to the order inherent in human actions and a way of life. For example, Saint John Henry Cardinal Newman describes the "Grammar of Assent," using the word "grammar" to mean the order implicit in various ways of affirming belief, especially religious belief. The philosopher Ludwig Wittgenstein also stretched the notion of a grammar" to mean a network of rules that determine what does and does not make sense in a particular form of life. The philosopher Alasdair MacIntyre has spent his career criticizing the grammar of modern individualism and trying to retrieve the grammar of virtue. The sociologist Robert Bellah has argued that Americans tend to speak using the grammar of individualism while engaging in forms of life that unwittingly draw from the older moral grammars of civic virtue and biblical faith.[11]

To develop a better understanding of these two characters, it is helpful to attend to a distinction made by Alasdair MacIntyre in *Ethics in the Conflicts of Modernity*. MacIntyre advocates a "Neo-Aristotelian" perspective, similar to the Aristotelian critique of management science provided in Andrew Yuengert's chapter in this volume. He contrasts it with an outlook he calls "Morality" (with a capital M). By using this name, *Morality*, MacIntyre is bringing into focus the presuppositions hidden within most contemporary moral discourse, especially as understood by inhabitants of the modern world who participate in the social practices of advanced capitalism and the contemporary culture of expertise. MacIntyre describes Morality as "a set of impersonal rules, entitled to the assent of any rational agent whatsoever, enjoining obedience to such maxims as those that prohibit the taking of innocent life and theft and those that require at least some large degree of truthfulness and at least some significant measure of altruistic benevolence."[12] Morality finds its natural home in a particular time and place, namely, in contemporary life, especially in settings where people are enjoined to treat humans as autonomous agents, and in secular settings where it is presumed that this way of life is obviously the best and most rational way to live. In this context, actions are frequently treated from the "nonperspectival perspective" of the modern, impartial observer; when one faces a decision, the fundamental values to be considered are freedom, equality, efficiency, and effectiveness. Actions, when treated from the perspective of the impartial spectator, are disconnected from personal particularities such as one's gender, ethnicity, personal traits, social class, religious practices, and beliefs. Without reference to any such consideration, the adherents of Morality propose to offer one or more principles to guide particular actions.

MacIntyre identifies six salient characteristics of Morality. First, its adherents present it as a secular doctrine based on impartial reason. Second, it is held to be universally binding on all human agents, no matter what culture or social order to which one belongs, with precepts that are translatable into every language or culture. Third, its precepts function to set limits on the way one acts, requiring one to act in specific ways toward others, even if it is contrary to one's interests or desires. Fourth, its precepts are framed in highly abstract, general terms, including duty, utility, and rights. Fifth, it is presumed by its adherents, whether liberal or conservative, to be superior to all other moralities. Sixth, its adherents find themselves facing various stock dilemmas to which Morality offers no generally accepted solutions.[13]

It is not difficult to imagine contexts in work and business where it is crucial for professionals to abide by the requirements of Morality—for example, in aviation, health care, engineering, and accounting. In such contexts, work is rightly expected to be conducted according to the standards of Morality.

Given this account of the *businessperson as moneymaker* as one who takes it as given that legal and moral obligations should constrain actions in pursuit of profit, it is sensible that such a person is at home in the world of Morality.

In contrast, the *businessperson concerned with promoting a positive social impact* will tend to understand action in terms of a more robust ethical grammar—that is, a grammar of human goods and the pursuit of higher goods, including the goods of a flourishing life and flourishing communities. Several other chapters in this volume draw from a similarly robust moral and theological grammar to engage issues regarding the practice of business, including those by Jennifer A. Herdt (chapter 2), Kenneth Goodpaster and Michael Naughton (6), Andrew Yuengert (3), David Cloutier (7), Martin Schlag (8), and Mary Hirschfeld (5). To work toward a more fine-grained understanding of this difference, let us examine two accounts of agency.

AGENCY FROM THE PERSPECTIVE OF "MORALITY"

From the perspective of the *businessperson as moneymaker*—that is, from the view of one who operates within the constraints that MacIntyre has called Morality—the meaning of agency may seem initially straightforward: an agent is one who acts, who makes things happen. Agency, so considered, is the ability to act in pursuit of a given end.

To bring this into focus, let us consider a typical "agency dilemma" case where one person, the agent, has agreed to act in the interest of another, the principal. Agency dilemmas arise when the agent has interests and/or knowledge not possessed by the principal. In corporate governance cases, agency dilemmas crop up when the interests of upper management—the agent—do not fully align with the interests of the shareholders.

Agency theory aims to devise ways to diminish such conflicts by better aligning the interests of the principal and the agent. For example, in real estate transactions, efforts to ensure collaboration in a win-win transaction—not only between the buyer and seller but also between the realtor as agent and the buyer or seller as principal—generally involve increased transparency and full disclosure of the various interests of the parties involved. Agency dilemmas can be mitigated by acknowledging the importance of long-term relationships, along with a full explanation of the fundamentals of a particular transaction, all in a context that encourages clarity and accountability.

However, this account of agency includes several serious shortcomings. In corporate governance cases, cooperative alignment of the interests of shareholders (as principals) and upper management (as agents) frequently involves remunerating the agents with stock options to promote an alignment of motives. Critics have raised a series of objections to the practice of remunerating upper management with stock, especially pointing to instances of misconduct by agents during the financial crisis, along with other socially harmful phenomena.[14] Concerning motive, especially in agency-dilemma cases where the agent's self-interest conflicts with the requirements of Morality, it is not clear why an agent would be motivated to act in accord with duty. Further, this account of agency has little to offer with regard to the rather common conflicts that arise between a person's various roles. This account of agency seems to promote living a "divided life," where individuals compartmentalize their lives, living as decent people who function quite normally outside the corporation by drawing a very sharp distinction between work and home, between "the contradictory moral demands of their corporate and noncorporate lives."[15]

When the *businessperson as moneymaker* acts in the role of a corporate agent, one is left without any way to determine or even consider how a given end—typically to increase profits—should be balanced with the pursuit of other legitimate given ends that are part of personal and communal flourishing. Similar themes are echoed elsewhere in this volume by Mary Hirschfeld's analysis of the technocratic paradigm in chapter 5 and Andrew Yuengert's critique of management science in chapter 3.

This point is made, perhaps in an overstated manner, in Joel Bakan's popular book, *The Corporation*.[16] The tone of Bakan's work is signaled in his subtitle, *The Pathological Pursuit of Profit and Power*. Bakan focuses on the corporation as a legal person designed by law to be concerned only with increasing shareholder value. Such corporations compel executives "to prioritize the interests of their companies and shareholders above all others and forbids them from being socially responsible."[17] Corporations, according to Bakan, are pathological and psychopathic in their persistent pursuit of profits. Because the corporation has no conscience, it is a legal person that relates to other persons in a manner that is superficial, manipulative, grandiose, asocial, lacking in empathy and accountability, and unable to feel remorse.[18]

In a certain sense, Bakan's rhetoric is overstated; it seems too strong to state that the corporation "has no conscience," because most corporations pursue their given ends within the constraints of the precepts of Morality and the requirements of legality. Nonetheless, Bakan is onto something important; the grammar of Morality leaves us without any rational way to engage in reflective examination of the way a particular goal fits within larger purposes. Thus, we are left without any robust way of deliberating with others about the worth of a given end, or the place of that given end amid other ends, some less and some more important.

AGENCY FROM A NEO-ARISTOTELIAN PERSPECTIVE

There is a second way to understand what it means to be an honest agent by considering the viewpoint of the *businessperson concerned with promoting a positive social impact*. From this point of view, a different moral grammar is used to articulate a richer understanding of human action and agency, one that gives voice to concerns for a robust evaluation of goods and the good life, and for the flourishing of persons and communities. This difference resonates with the difference between the technocratic and creation paradigms examined by Mary Hirschfeld in chapter 5, and with the call for a deeper understanding of the agency of consumers in chapter 7, by David Cloutier. Consider the range of issues opened up by the philosopher Charles Taylor in his essay "What Is Human Agency?"[19] Taylor begins by pointing to the distinction made by Harry Frankfurt between first-order and second-order desires.

A first-order desire is "simply a desire to do or not do one thing or another."[20] Like all animals, humans have a range of desires that arise on various occasions: to flee or to fight, to eat, to reproduce, and the like. However, human animals seem able to have a complex relationship with their animal desires; humans are capable of being aware of their desires, of wanting to resist particular desires, and sometimes of desiring different desires. This human "capacity for reflective self-evaluation" gives rise to what Frankfurt has called second-order desires.[21]

A second-order desire is a desire for or against a specific first-order desire. For example, a fashion model may have the first-order desire to eat, as well as the second-order desire not to act on that desire to eat so she can maintain a shapely figure. Alternatively, an experimental psychologist may have a first-order desire to eat, along with a second-order desire not to act on that desire to eat in order to complete a research project whose goal is to experience something like the hunger felt by those who are homeless.[22]

But even second-order desires can and should be evaluated because they are only the first of two broad kinds of evaluation of desire that Taylor distinguishes.[23] The second sort of evaluation of desire looks to the kind of life you would be making for yourself—to the kind of person you would be tending to become if you were to act on a given desire. Suppose you have the second-order desire not to act on your first-order desire for food because of spite or envy. For example, you are hungry, but you decline the invitation to dinner in order to refuse to acknowledge the hospitality of someone; or consider a hungry person gripped by envy and the desire to have a physique even more shapely than that of an acquaintance. In these examples, an awareness of both the first-order desire (for food) and one's second-order desire (not to act on one's desire for food) give rise to broader questions about what kind of person one wants to become. Do you want to become a spiteful or envious person?

Raising this sort of question involves recognizing that acting on your desires, including both first- and second-order desires, also contributes to confirming or consolidating yourself as a certain kind of agent, perhaps as one who is spiteful or envious or on the contrary as one who rejects spite and envy. Taylor describes a "strong evaluator" as the sort of person who can reflect on the full range of the disparate and jumbled desires, and then take up the quest to govern those desires in an ordered manner directed to becoming a particular sort of person.[24]

As I begin to make strong evaluations about my second-order desires, my capacity for reflective self-evaluation moves beyond simple judgments about whether I should act on this or that urge; as a strong evaluator, I begin to reflect on my agency by considering the narrative of my human existence and asking what it would mean to live a complete life. Extending the previous examples, one might ask, "Should I really desire to be a fashion model? an experimental psychologist?" Thus, one might reflectively recognize that doing this action will confirm a certain path in my life and strengthen my dispositions toward becoming a certain kind of agent. A significant part of what it means to act with human agency, as Taylor notes, includes this sort of reflective capacity in which one acts as a strong evaluator who sees "desires in an additional dimension."[25] Agency involves deliberating and deciding about "different possible modes of being for the agent."[26] A strong evaluator goes deeper than seeing a choice between two first-order or even second-order desires, such as standing firm or fleeing, or between acting on one's urge to flee or withstanding such an urge. The strong evaluator sees in such a circumstance a choice between acting like a coward (and tending to become one) and doing what is worthier, nobler, or more integrated.

On Taylor's account, the strong evaluator eschews the cowardly act in order to become a courageous and honorable human being. A strong evaluator understands agency in terms of acting or restraining one's actions with an eye toward contributing to, confirming, and consolidating one's character as a certain kind of agent: virtuous or vicious, profound or superficial, noble or base, more or less fulfilled, more or less refined.[27] As Taylor puts it, the strong evaluator judges actions as belonging to qualitatively different modes of life: "fragmented or integrated, alienated or free, saintly or merely human, courageous or pusillanimous."[28] The strong evaluator assesses the worth and depth of desires: "To characterize one desire or inclination as worthier, or nobler, or more integrated, etc. than others is to speak of it in terms of the kind of quality of life which it expresses and sustains."[29]

Understood in these terms, real agency then involves conceiving of one's life as a narrative while reflecting on what kind of life one desires, or what "kind of subject that these desires properly belong to."[30] This understanding of human agency, described by Taylor, is endorsed by MacIntyre, who characterizes this account of agency as Neo-Aristotelian. Agency, according to this philosophy, involves cultivating habits of reflective awareness in which one asks "what kind of agent must I become if I am to achieve or contribute to the achievement" of worthwhile goals?[31] Agency, understood this way, involves actualization, and it involves more than focusing on this or that action; human agency points toward questions of deep purpose in which an agent journeys toward increasing awareness of the depth and worth of one's purposes and the relation of higher and lower goods one strives for. A similar argument is made by Kenneth Goodpaster and Michael Naughton in their treatment of the virtues and the moral-cultural sector.

I am suggesting that from the perspective of the *businessperson concerned with promoting a positive social impact*, one will find oneself on a quest that involves a moral grammar that is more robust than what is on offer from the duties of Morality. This retrieval of the ancient grammar of the quest, made contemporary in terms of a quest for an integrated life of personal and communal flourishing, involves a sense of agency that goes beyond acting in accord with a set of precepts or duties. As Taylor puts it, human agency from this perspective involves acting as a strong evaluator. It entails seeing one's life as a narrative while cultivating reflective awareness that allows one to deliberate and act with others to achieve worthwhile goals. Andrew Yuengert makes a similar argument in his critique of management science in chapter 3.

AUTONOMY FROM THE PERSPECTIVE OF MORALITY

Consider now the notion of autonomy, first as it is understood in the grammar of modern, secular Morality and then from a grammar of Neo-Aristotelianism. It is helpful to begin with the duty ethics of Immanuel Kant, as he is widely recognized as contributing more than any other thinker to the modern understanding of autonomy. His duty ethics emphasizes the obligation to respect every rational agent as an end in itself, and the theme of autonomy plays a central role in his thought.

Kant begins his famous essay "What Is Enlightenment?" by pointing to humanity's emergence from self-inflicted immaturity. His attitude is modern and progressive; he presupposes that, in previous (darker) eras, humans were trapped in laziness and cowardice, afraid to reason for themselves, and thus willing to submit to the authority of others. He chides his reader: "It is so convenient to be immature!" In Kant's view, to become enlightened is to become mature or grown up, and thus to be able to act on one's own reasons, without having to seek permission from an authority or from tradition. Personal autonomy, understood this way, is the capacity to make decisions for oneself and to pursue a course of action in one's life.

In the *Grounding for the Metaphysics of Morals*, Kant claims that the "principle of autonomy is the sole principle of morals."[32] In his view, my rational will is autonomous insofar as I govern my practical affairs in obedience to reason, and not as a response to any sort of external, nonrational pressure. Accordingly, he draws a sharp distinction between actions that are autonomous and those that are "heteronomous" (i.e., are influenced by a force such as emotion, desire, or particular circumstances). For Kant, an action is autonomous insofar as it is self-determined and self-legislated; so understood, autonomy involves the ability to free myself from my emotions and desires in order to view my situation in an impartial manner, reflectively discovering on my own what duty requires.

Among Kantians and Neo-Kantians, there is a vast literature with extensive debates, distinctions, and clarifications. It is impossible to do justice to every aspect or interpretation advanced by Kantians with regard to autonomy, but it is helpful to point to an important distinction by asking, "What does it mean to treat someone with respect as an autonomous agent?"[33] Asking about the meaning of respect brings to light a deep but subtle difference between two ways of understanding autonomy. These can be called "radical autonomy" and "ordered autonomy."[34]

"Radical autonomy" entails the freedom both to make one's own choices and to define for oneself one's own conception of the good. From this radically individualistic outlook, I can choose for myself anything I want, so long as it does not violate the autonomy of others. In contrast, "ordered autonomy" means that I am free to make self-determining choices but subject to the moral law. This way recognizes that there is an objective moral order discoverable (at least in part) by every person. Hence, ordered autonomy is the freedom to use my power of self-determination responsibly in accord with the objective moral order.

These two ways of interpreting personal autonomy have given rise to several strands of post-Kantian interpretations of autonomy. First, perhaps the most dominant of these is the strand of modern liberal individualism, with its emphasis on personal autonomy, along with tolerance, the liberty of non-interference, and a sense of equality. Second, some strands of individualism advocate a radical notion of autonomy in which the only limit to one's desires is the autonomy of others; advocates of value-neutral procedural and methodological individualism thus tend to view each agent as free to do whatever one wants so long as it does not violate the autonomy of others. Third, another post-Kantian strand is more postmodern and expressivist; autonomy thus understood stipulates that each individual is free to pursue what one wants and to express oneself as one wants. This form of radical autonomy is summarized in the words of US Supreme Court Justice Anthony Kennedy: "At the heart of liberty is the right to define one's own concept of existence, of meaning, of the universe, and of the mystery of human life."[35]

Some scholars interpret Kant's account of autonomy as pointing to the need to engage questions of deep purpose and substantive issues about flourishing and a good life. This move—to interpret Kant's account of morality as a form of ordered autonomy (in which one has a duty to constrain one's actions by using one's power of self-determination in accord with the moral law)—occurs because there are at least three features of radical autonomy that seem to require more fundamental or substantive matters.[36] First, the power of self-determination is not merely a negative liberty (i.e., not simply a freedom from external coercion); it is also a positive liberty (i.e., freedom to choose). But the individualism of radical autonomy—this purely formal value-neutral procedural methodology—offers no answer to the question of what autonomy is *for*. Second, the positive liberty of self-determination (the freedom to choose) gives rise to the question of what standard will be used to guide choice. Third, treating oneself and others as radically autonomous agents falsifies the self's relations to others because it falsely presumes that every self is always an independent adult with no need to ever rely on another in a spirit of friendship and humility. For these sorts of reasons, there have been many efforts to integrate Kant's emphasis on autonomy with the Aristotelian emphasis on flourishing.[37]

AUTONOMY FROM A
NEO-ARISTOTELIAN PERSPECTIVE

If we reach back before the modern era, we find a grammar in which the concept of autonomy has a much older and richer history. By some accounts—such as Jerome Schneewind's *The Invention of Autonomy*—Kant was responsible for the "invention" of autonomy. But this ignores other, older ways of understanding autonomy. While appropriating key features of the ancient notion of autonomy, I am following MacIntyre in calling this "Neo-Aristotelian," though I am extending MacIntyre's work here, as he does not provide a detailed account of autonomy.

There are several problems with the word "autonomy." First, autonomy is not a central notion in Aristotle's thought. Further, while there are scholars who have gone to lengths to set out an Aristotelian account of autonomy by carefully attending to Aristotle's texts, that is not my purpose here.[38] Instead, my aim here is to provide a broad overview of a range of meanings and issues that come into focus when we attend to the ways the notion of autonomy was employed in the grammar of the ancient Greeks, along with some of the ways this was modified later in the tradition of the Greeks, the Romans, and the medieval Latins. I call this account of autonomy Neo-Aristotelian primarily to distinguish it from the modern notion as found, for example, in Kant.

As the etymology of the term suggests, autonomy (αὐτ ὁ νομος) is an ancient Greek term. Attending to the various ways in which the term was before to Kant helps bring into focus some of the richness of the concept. The idea of autonomy emerged during the transitional period from the Homeric epics to the Golden Age of Greece and the period of the great philosophers of Athens. As John Cooper put it, "The term 'autonomy' itself derives from classical Greek, where it was applied primarily or even exclusively in a political context, to civic communities possessing independent legislative and self-governing authority."[39] This political sense of the term, with reference to "autonomous communities," reappears in later historical periods and in various contemporary contexts. Monasteries are sometimes considered autonomous communities, as are microstates, such as Lichtenstein and Monaco, and political regions, such as Catalonia in Spain. In the United States, the citizens of certain states, such as Texas and Vermont, are sometimes inclined to think of their own states as autonomous in this sense. Similarly, companies and organizations that are self-governing and which have a distinctive culture may be thought of as autonomous communities in this sense.

It is generally agreed that one of the first times that the word "autonomy" appears in writing with reference to an individual (rather than to a community) is in *Antigone*, the great play by Sophocles. The central character, Antigone, refuses to obey the unjust decree of King Creon that forbids her from providing a decent burial for her dead brother. King Creon, surprised by her audacity, sentences her to death. As she takes her place to be punished, the chorus speaks of her as being sentenced "of her own law" (αὐτόνομος).

The Greek, αὐτ ό (*auto*) reflexively refers to oneself, (or in the plural case, themselves), while νομος (*nomos*) generally refers to law, customs, or social norms, though *nomos* can also connote singing or vocalizing or naming. In a sense, Antigone's autonomy is literally her self-legislating or self-naming. Scholars have noted that, in ancient Greek, autonomy can suggest the connotation of being strange or uncanny or weird.[40] Certainly it was strange for a woman in antiquity to stand against the authority of the ruler, but she does so by appealing to a personal insight into the law of Zeus, which Antigone claims is eternal. So, one deep feature of the notion of autonomy is a sort of uncanny strangeness in which an individual is willing to take a stand against an authority or against a society's manner of proceeding; the autonomous individual discerns that a ruler's decree is not binding. Antigone is willing to suffer her punishment, but her sense of self requires her, she thinks, to take a stand and to act against Creon's decree.

The story of Antigone has strong parallels with the story of the trial and death of Socrates. In Plato's dialogues, Socrates is presented as one who governs himself by taking up the shared quest to understand and embody the virtues more adequately. In contrast with some of his interlocutors, who are swayed at times by emotions and desires, Plato repeatedly depicts Socrates as one who exercises self-mastery and self-determination.

These same qualities are held up by Aristotle as features integral to the life of human flourishing. Aristotle addresses himself to a person experienced in life, a listener poised to take a leadership role in the life of a community. He explicitly states that his lectures are "not suited for a young man." As such, he assumes that his listener has reached a level of maturity such that one can practice the virtue of *sophrosyne* (moderation) without being mastered by stray desires. In chapter 2 Jennifer Herdt provides a helpful account of the tradition of the virtues in the Christian tradition.

Though Aristotle does not provide a detailed treatment of autonomy, he considers a series of related puzzles that have implications for understanding it. He notes that our actions are up to us, at least some of the time, and to some extent. Although each of us is given specific tendencies as part of our biology and upbringing, our character development depends in part on our voluntary actions and deliberate decisions. We tend to praise and blame people for their voluntary actions, while feeling sympathy and pity for countervoluntary ones, which may result from force or a lack of knowledge. Force can be either physical or psychological; a lack of knowledge can involve either ignorance of relevant particularities or of relevant principles. Negligence of particularities or principles is excusable only when it is not voluntary, and it is culpable when it comes from a lack of due care. Aristotle considers the unusual circumstance in which sailors decide to jettison cargo during a storm to save their ship. He reasons that the act is voluntary in a sense; though in another sense, it was the stormy conditions that made it seem most reasonable to throw the goods overboard. In general, Aristotle confirms what most take as common sense: we are each responsible for our actions and (with some qualifications) for our character states.

Although Aristotle provides little direct focus on the notion of autonomy, he treats more frequently the related notion of "autarky" (αὐτάρκεια) or self-sufficiency. There is a widely recognized tension in Aristotle's account of self-sufficiency. Throughout most of the *Nicomachean Ethics*, Aristotle treats self-sufficiency in political terms; he states that the common good of a political community is greater than the good of a single citizen, suggesting that political expertise, which aims at the self-sufficiency of a political community, is the highest and most architectonic practice. As Aristotle writes, "Even if the good is the same for a single person and for a city, the good of the city is a greater and more complete thing both to achieve and to preserve."[41]

However, near the end of the *Nicomachean Ethics*, Aristotle seems to shift his focus to the contemplative activity of an individual human. He praises the activity of reflectively contemplating truths that are always, everywhere, and eternally the case—or at least cultivating the desire for such wisdom (*philosophia*) because such activity is what is most complete. He notes that the pleasures of philosophy are "amazing in purity and stability,"[42] and that the activity of philosophy, pursued in leisure for its own sake, is almost divine, opening up a life almost "higher than the human plane."[43] Thus, contemplative activity is praised by Aristotle as the most self-sufficient of all activities.

Later Stoic thinkers widely praised these same qualities.[44] Within the Christian tradition, during both the patristic and medieval periods, self-mastery and self-governance were likewise praised as qualities conducive to a flourishing life.[45] The Rule of Saint Benedict emphasized autonomous, self-governing communities, whose members practice the virtues and have a share in a common life.

It is worth noting that some contemporary thinkers might bristle at referring to these ancient and medieval examples as instances of autonomy. After all, monks who live according to Saint Benedict's rule are encouraged to practice obedience: "The first degree of humility is obedience without delay. This is the virtue of those who hold nothing dearer to them than Christ."[46] This Benedictine sense, in which autonomy is a feature of a self-governing social unit in which the members of the group order themselves according to standards that arise out of their community of practice, is a feature of medieval villages, shires, guilds, and other self-ordered groups whose internal order is gradually deciphered, put to use, and regulated by the members themselves. It is this sense of autonomy that seems to be used in the Vatican Council II document *Gaudium et spes* concerning the autonomy of the arts and scientific disciplines.[47]

More could be added to this survey, but suffice it to say that, contrary to Schneewind's claim that Kant "invented" autonomy, there is a long tradition that stretches back many centuries before Kant in which discourse on autonomy developed, forming a deep moral grammar with concerns beyond Kant's.

In its primary sense, one might say that Neo-Aristotelian autonomy is a feature of particular communities. Each social group or community of practice (a polis, a monastery, a village, a guild, and an academic discipline, along with civic groups and cultures) may be autonomous to the degree that the members of the group regulate themselves according to an internal order deciphered through local experience and embodied in their local conditions.

Autonomy also applies to the actions of individual persons as agents. So long as the agent acts voluntarily and with sufficient awareness, then both the act and the agent may be said to be self-governed. It is important to recognize that, on this account, personal autonomy is a project, an accomplishment, and a gift. With each self-determined act, one becomes more deeply confirmed in one's ability to act in a self-determined manner; self-governance is deepened with each self-governed act, and self-mastery is more fully accomplished with each act of self-determination.

At the same time, the project and accomplishment of self-governance do not arise in a vacuum; one finds oneself in the middle of the journey toward self-mastery only after many years of having been supported and encouraged by others to develop self-determination. The urge to act on one's own is given as a gift, not self-created out of nothingness; so, too, the social conditions in which one can grow and make progress in the project of accomplishing self-mastery are a gift rather than a self-creation.

A Neo-Aristotelian understanding of autonomy is implied in the perspective of the *businessperson concerned with promoting a positive social impact.* To act in a self-governed manner in the course of one's personal narrative, and in the unfolding of communities of practice of which one is a member, is a task, an accomplishment, and a gift.

RECONSIDERING MOTIVATIONS FOR BUSINESS

Recall the case of Austin and Byron, the recent graduates who expressed their desire "to help build communities in poverty" and to support people from diverse backgrounds "so they can grow their wealth and economic standing, which in turn helps them flourish as humans." In describing their lives as a "pursuit," we can sense a richer notion of human agency and autonomy at play in their grammar.

To get at this difference, allow me to recount another story. While Byron and Austin were seniors at our university, they served on the executive board of our university's entrepreneurship club. In that role, they hosted a speaker, Michael Strong, who delivered a presentation on the topic, "How Entrepreneurs and Conscious Capitalists Can Eliminate Global Poverty." Michael Strong is the cofounder (with John Mackey, CEO and cofounder of Whole Foods) of Freedom Lights Our World, a nonprofit dedicated to "liberating the entrepreneurial spirit for good," that has spawned programs such as Peace Through Commerce, Accelerating Women Entrepreneurs, and Conscious Capitalism. When Strong spoke at our business school, he challenged our students to consider, "What if all those who engaged in business were committed to a deeper purpose, and all those committed to doing good were entrepreneurial and enterprising?"

After the talk, I had the opportunity to share a meal with Strong, Byron, Austin, and several other students, all of whom shared an interest in philosophy, economics, entrepreneurship, and Catholic social thought. At a certain point during the meal, Strong commented that he found these students to be quite remarkable. He noted that it is unusual to encounter people who can speak in the language of markets and entrepreneurship yet are also able to speak in an informed manner about integral human development that promotes human flourishing and the common good.

Most of us who work at mission-driven universities where we hope to provide this sort of education can point to instances when our educational goals seem to have taken hold. Part of what is crucial for this sort of integrated education is the opportunity for interdisciplinary efforts, where faculty and students from a range of disciplines are able to bring multiple perspectives together.

REPLIES TO OBJECTIONS

Several criticisms might be raised concerning a Neo-Aristotelian grammar of agency and autonomy. First, does it not promote hubris or false pride if we encourage business professionals to think of themselves as concerned with promoting a positive social impact? In other words, does the Neo-Aristotelian grammar of virtue, flourishing, and the common good actually end up promoting a self-congratulatory sense of oneself as morally superior? The answer is "no." Important here is a crucial feature of the Neo-Aristotelian understanding of agency: the importance of reflective awareness when engaging in practical deliberation with others. Cultivating authentic agency and self-determination requires the exercise of humility and reflective self-awareness, including a willingness to listen to those able to help us see our blind spots.

Second, someone might object that there is no single economic or entrepreneurial model that accords with Neo-Aristotleianism. What precisely is being proposed in encouraging business professionals to think of themselves as promoting a positive social impact? Is the proposal to work as a social entrepreneur, or to focus on small-scale local ventures, or to focus on global equality, or on social cooperatives, or on adopting the "triple bottom line" accounting framework with its emphasis on people, profits, and planet, or on adopting the framework of "total societal impact" or "effective altruism"? Does this Neo-Aristotelian moral grammar, coupled with the concern to promote a positive social impact, point to activities such as socially responsible investing or microfinance or open-book management or the initiatives of the "Economy of Communion" project? The answer here must be that there have been a wide range of efforts to propose alternative models for engaging in business, and many of these models seem compatible with the grammar of Neo-Aristotelianism.

CONCLUSION

By examining various senses in which people speak of human agency and autonomy, I have distinguished between two moral grammars: Morality and Neo-Aristotelianism. In setting forth these grammars, I hope to have suggested that, while each can be transforming, the grammar of Neo-Aristotelianism is more robust, and thus has something more important to offer. For business practitioners and for university students preparing for careers as business professionals, I hope to have shown that the grammar of Neo-Aristotelianism is better suited toward embodying a self-identity as a *businessperson concerned with promoting a positive social impact.*

NOTES

1. See President Trump's Twitter page, https://twitter.com/realdonaldtrump/status/51093 5518360895488?lang=en.
2. Second Vatican Council, *Gaudium et spes*, 4.
3. This is developed more fully at the beginning of my book *Character of the Manager*, 10–16.
4. The classic formulation of this view is typically traced to Adam Smith: "He intends only his own gain, and he is in this, as in many other cases, led by an invisible hand to promote an end which was no part of his intention." See Smith, *Wealth of Nations*, chap. 2, para. 9. For a detailed discussion, see Meeropol, "Another Distortion."
5. For well-known examples from popular and academic writers, see Friedman, "Social Responsibility," 122; and Jensen and Meckling, "Theory," 305–60.
6. Seetubtim, "10 Reasons."
7. The popular literature on entrepreneurship includes many articles in which entrepreneurs reflect on their motivations for going into business. E.g., see Harkless, "20+ Entrepreneurs"; Morgaine, "8 Reasons"; and Brandon, "Why I Started a Business."
8. Saint Louis University, "Ethical Leaders in Business Learning Community," www.slu.edu /housing/living/learn/ethical-leaders.php.
9. Saint Louis University, Service Leadership Program at Richard A. Chaifetz School of Business, www.slu.edu/business/degrees-programs/service-leadership-program.php.
10. Brinker, "SLU Catholic Studies Centre."
11. Bellah et al., *Habits of the Heart*.
12. MacIntyre, *Ethics*, 65.
13. MacIntyre, 115–16.
14. E.g., see J. Boatright, "From Hired Hands," 471–96; Moore, "Virtue," 293–318; and Rodgers and Gago, "Model," 189.
15. Bakan, *Corporation*, 56.
16. Bakan, 2.
17. Bakan, 35.
18. Bakan, 57.
19. Taylor, "Agency," 15–44.

20. Frankfurt, "Freedom," 7.

21. Frankfurt, 7.

22. These examples are from MacIntyre, *Ethics*, 3.

23. Taylor, "Agency," 16.

24. Taylor, 24ff.

25. Taylor, 25.

26. Taylor.

27. Taylor, 16.

28. Taylor, 16.

29. Taylor, 25.

30. Taylor.

31. MacIntyre, *Ethics*, 87.

32. Kant, *Grounding*, 45.

33. E.g., see Sensen, *Kant*; Kühler and Jelinek, *Autonomy*; and O'Neill, *Autonomy*.

34. See Beabout, "What Counts as Respect?" 28–42.

35. *Planned Parenthood of Southeastern Pa. v. Casey*, 505 US 833, at 851.

36. See Beabout, "What Counts as Respect?" 35–41.

37. The literature seeking to put Kant and Aristotle in closer conversation with one another is vast. E.g., see Korsgaard, "Aristotle and Kant"; Aufderheide and Bader, *Highest Good*; Hill, "Happiness"; and Stohr, "Virtue Ethics."

38. E.g., see Allmark, "Aristotelian Account," 41–53.

39. Cooper, "Stoic Autonomy," 1–29.

40. E.g., see Withy, "Authenticity," 239–53.

41. Aristotle, *Nichomachean Ethics*, 1094b8–11

42. Aristotle, 1177a26.

43. Aristotle, 1177b27.

44. Cooper, "Stoic Autonomy," 1–29.

45. E.g., see Carey, *Augustine's Invention*; Taylor, *Sources*; and Austin, *Aquinas*.

46. *Rule of St. Benedict*, chap. 5.

47. Second Vatican Council, *Gaudium et spes*, 36, 41, 55–56, 59, 71, 75.

CHAPTER 5

What Is the Technocratic Paradigm, and Must Business Be Structured by It?

Mary Hirschfeld

This volume investigates the moral legitimacy of business in Catholic social thought. To do that, we need to confront the secular argument that seeks to secure this moral legitimacy in the conviction that firms pursuing maximum profits will act in a way that produces widespread prosperity.[1] It is an ethic that evaluates the moral quality of acts by evaluating the outcomes that are thereby generated, regardless of the intention of the individual. By contrast, the Catholic tradition emphasizes the question of whether given actions are intrinsically good. For Christians, a morally good act must be rooted in morally good intentions; and morally good intentions should reflect love of neighbor. This chapter explores Pope Francis's notion of "the technocratic paradigm" as a fundamental challenge to the belief that maximizing profits should be the aim of business.

Pursuing wealth as an end in itself is disordered (i.e., sinful), especially if it is pursued without regard for our neighbors.[2] Yet the modern embrace of markets rests on the faith that the best way to achieve socially good outcomes is for individuals to pursue their narrow self-interests without regard for the welfare of their neighbor. As Adam Smith suggests, my appeal to my butcher's self-interest is far more likely to get me dinner than is an appeal to his neighborly love for me.[3]

On this view, traditional Christian morality would paradoxically leave our neighbors worse off than they would be if we simply pursued our own private gain. To use biblical language, the modern view suggests that if we want good fruit, we need bad trees. There is thus a tension between one moral frame-work that focuses on one's acts and intentions and another that focuses on the outcomes produced by one's acts.

One way to minimize this tension is to move to a more modern ethic that construes pursuit of self-interest, so long as it does not do direct harm to others, as morally neutral if not morally good. In chapter 2 Jennifer Herdt tracks several of the historical influences in the development of this ethic, including Albert O. Hirschman's account of the evolution of that moral proj-ect in his book *The Passions and the Interests*.[4] The early moral defense of cap-italism arguably led to a shift toward evaluating capitalism by means of the outcomes it generated, rather than due to the moral quality of individual acts.

As Jonathan Haidt and Anthony Randazzo suggest, the modern debates about capitalism can be understood in light of competing moral narratives that serve to interpret the goods delivered (or not delivered) by markets.[5] One of these narratives sees capitalism as exploitation, focusing on the impact capitalism has on the poor and the marginalized. The other sees capitalism as liberation, focusing on the widespread economic prosperity produced by free markets. The debate between these two paradigms is reflected in the peren-nial question in economics about how to trade off the efficiency generated by profit-seekers in the marketplace against the resulting unequal distribution of wealth and income. Both narratives share the premise that under capitalism, individuals will pursue their narrow self-interest. The debate is about whether the resulting fruits are good or rotten. Few economists or other social sci-entists take extreme positions in this debate. Those who are inclined to the capitalism-as-exploitation narrative typically acknowledge that free markets produce economic prosperity; and those who are inclined to the capitalism-as-liberation narrative typically acknowledge that not all market outcomes are good. Thus the participants in these debates see a role for both free mar-kets and governmental intervention, differing primarily on questions of how much weight should be given to each.

Since the beginning of his pontificate, Pope Francis has used rhetoric that places him within the narrative that sees capitalism as exploitation. He has written about an economy that kills and the idolatry of money; he has tweeted that inequality is the root of social evil.[6] In a subsequent document released by the Vatican under his pontificate, there is an acknowledgment that "global economic well-being appears to have increased in the second half of the twentieth century with an unprecedented magnitude and speed"; yet this acknowledgment is immediately qualified with the concern that "at the same time inequalities proliferate between various countries and within them."[7] Pope Francis's encyclical on the environment, *Laudato si'*, yokes concerns about environmental degradation to concerns about widespread economic poverty in a way that heightens the sense that his pontificate underappreciates the role of markets in lifting billions of people out of poverty.

A quick reading of *Laudato si'* can give rise to the concern that the pope is offering little more than naive cheerleading for the moral narrative of capitalism as exploitation. Unlike his more academically sophisticated predecessors, the pope does not seem to acknowledge the good outcomes that are produced by free markets. In particular, he seems to have a dour view of profit-seeking. His analysis, then, might seem to have little to contribute to discussions about how to calibrate public policy to minimize the ill effects of markets while retaining the good outcomes they generate.

But a more careful reading of *Laudato si'* suggests that Francis is not entering into a preexisting secular debate about the strengths and weaknesses of modern capitalism. Rather, in *Laudato si'*, the pope offers a fundamental critique of tendencies in modern culture, which he dubs the *technocratic paradigm*. It is a critique that challenges premises that are shared by the left and the right in their debates about economics and the environment. For Francis, to the extent that market participants are shaped by the technocratic paradigm, most notably by embracing the goal of maximizing profits, the fruits of the tree must ultimately be bad fruits.

There is no tinkering with policy or regulation that will ultimately address the twin problems of environmental degradation and economic injustice. The way to break free from the technocratic paradigm is to reflect on the fact that the world is created. In other words, what is required is a conversion to a new way of thinking about the goods we seek and the way we seek them. It is a profound argument, and my aim in this chapter is primarily to explain it and to begin the work of putting it into a conversation with the modern defense of profit-maximization.

THE MORAL DEFENSE OF PROFIT-MAXIMIZATION

The primary reason for wanting to bring the concept of the technocratic paradigm to bear on the subject of business ethics is that the idea that profits should be maximized turns out to be a good exemplar of what the pope means by the term "technocratic paradigm." The concept gives us a new language for voicing concern about whether and how profits can be ethically pursued. Before exploring this critique of profit-maximization, however, it is worth rehearsing the ethical defense of profit-maximization proffered by economists like Milton Friedman.

The discipline of economics has elaborated on Adam Smith's basic insight that self-interested behavior, most especially the pursuit of profit, induces self-interested individuals to act in ways that bring about socially beneficial results. Friedman gives, perhaps, the most robust articulation of the ethical claim. According to him, in a free economy, "there is one and only one social responsibility of business—to use its resources and engage in activities designed to increase its profits so long as it stays within the rules of the game . . . without deception or fraud."[8]

One can base that ethical claim on the obligation business managers have to maximize returns to shareholders. But that argument competes with arguments that business also has obligations to other stakeholders, most notably their employees. The stronger ethical argument, advanced by Friedman, is that profit-maximization leads to the efficient use of economic resources, which should be understood as allowing the economy as a whole to reach the highest level of general prosperity possible, given the resources available to it.

This view is grounded in economic models that assume that there is "perfect" competition, models into which Martijn Cremers looks deeply in chapter 10. If there are many firms (so that no one firm can individually influence the market price), perfect information, perfect mobility, and perfect contracting, markets will both efficiently allocate resources to their best productive uses and distribute the resulting goods and services to the individuals in the economy who most value them. On the production side, the logic is simple. If the market price is at a point that allows firms in a given industry to make greater-than-average profits, other firms will have an incentive to enter the industry. The resulting increase in supply of goods in that market drives the price down, lowering profits for all firms in that industry. Analogously, if profits are lower than average, firms will exit the industry. The resulting decrease in supply drives the price up. In the long run, a perfectly competitive market will tend toward a price that allows all firms in that industry to make the same profits they could make in other industries. A corollary of this result is that the industry as a whole will be producing at the lowest possible average cost.[9]

The economic logic of competition among profit-maximizing firms has been elaborated to show that efficiencies are thereby produced throughout the system. And, indeed, the same logic shows that consumers likewise efficiently allocate their scarce resources to achieve the best possible outcomes for themselves, concerning both the sort of work they pursue and the goods and services they end up consuming. Moreover, in this perfectly competitive model, this system works to a point where nobody could be made better off without making someone else worse off.[10]

The profit motive also has a dynamic effect extending beyond the equilibrating mechanism. Firms seeking to increase profits have incentives to innovate: to find more cost-effective modes of production and to develop new products or features of value to their customers. Successful innovations will be mimicked by their competitors, spreading these innovations throughout the industry. Although entrepreneurship is not well modeled by economists, the dynamism of markets is often cited as another virtue of a system that encourages firms to maximize their profits.[11] It is from this perspective that voices like Friedman argue that the most ethical thing a firm can do is seek to maximize profits. And historically, the spread of markets and capitalist logic has produced a sustained rise in standards of living that are unprecedented in the history of the world.[12]

However, there are essential qualifications to this view that profit-maximization produces socially optimal outcomes. As is widely known, the result that markets are efficient depends crucially on the assumption that there is perfect competition. Yet few individual markets even come close to meeting those assumptions. In many markets, firms enjoy a degree of market power—that is to say, they are large enough relative to the overall market to have a direct influence on market prices.[13] Many markets are characterized by asymmetric information, wherein either the buyers or the sellers know more about contemplated transactions than do their counterparts.[14] And many market transactions have spillover effects, or "externalities," that affect third parties.[15] In any of these circumstances, market outcomes are not efficient. Thus, according to standard economic analysis, there is room for government intervention to correct these instances of market failures.

The second critical limitation of standard economic analysis is that it can only argue that markets deliver efficient outcomes based on the given initial set of resource endowments—the current distribution of income and wealth. It is silent about the desirability of redistributing income, though economists are quick to observe that policies redistributing income tend to generate inefficiency. That tension leads to the thought that there is a trade-off between achieving more equitable outcomes and efficiency.

It is against this backdrop that the competing moral narratives about capitalism take their shape. Both sides would acknowledge that markets produce prosperity. The moral defense of capitalism as liberation stresses the efficiency of markets. It further argues that freedom itself is an intrinsic good. And because markets channel this freedom in ways that promote economic growth, they further generate the freedom associated with prosperity (the wherewithal to do as one wills). The moral criticism of capitalism as exploitation downplays the widespread prosperity generated by markets and focuses attention on those who have bad market outcomes.

In his encyclical *Laudato si'*, the pope writes from the perspective of the latter moral narrative. Strewn through the encyclical are a series of disparaging mentions of profits. Profit-seekers generate externalities that harm both the environment and the economically marginalized.[16] More generally, firms focused solely on profits systematically fail to consider costs and benefits that are not "measured by the market."[17] These failures are sufficiently large that we must reject "a magical conception of the market, which would suggest that problems can be solved simply by an increase in the profits of companies or individuals."[18] In making these claims, Pope Francis might seem to merely be asserting one narrative over against the other. If that were all there were to the encyclical, it would not advance the conversation in any meaningful way. However, the pope launches a more profound challenge to the moral defense of capitalism, one that undermines the premises shared by both narratives. He does this by advancing the concept of the technocratic paradigm that he gleaned from the writings of Romano Guardini.[19]

A TALE OF TWO PARADIGMS

Pope Francis argues that the twin problems of environmental degradation and economic injustice are rooted in what he calls the technocratic paradigm. Because the main subject of *Laudato si'* is the environment, one might think he is simply railing against technology. But, in fact, he praises technology, arguing that it "has remedied countless evils which used to harm and limit human beings. How can we not feel gratitude and appreciation for this progress, especially in the fields of medicine, engineering, and communications? How could we not acknowledge the work of many scientists and engineers who have provided alternatives to make development sustainable?"[20]

One might also wonder if the pope is simply making the argument that progress in human wisdom has not kept pace with progress in human technology. And he does suggest that this is a problem.[21] But he goes on to say that the basic problem lies much deeper. It is rooted in the fundamental way we moderns see the world. To fully appreciate the criticism implied in the pope's description of the technocratic paradigm, we should begin by paying attention to what he has to say about the paradigm he tacitly holds out as an alternative: the creation paradigm.

The Creation Paradigm

Before the chapters in *Laudato si'* on the technocratic paradigm, Pope Francis devotes a full chapter, titled "The Gospel of Creation," to set up the lens through which he will view the technocratic paradigm. As he suggests, there might be some question about whether it is appropriate to introduce an explicitly religious perspective into public discussions about the environment and economic justice that are of concern to all people, regardless of their faith commitments. He argues merely that science and religion can enter into an intense dialogue that is fruitful for both.[22] We will return to the question of how we should understand the religious grounding of the view Pope Francis develops at the end of this chapter. But for now, the aim is to enter into it on its own terms.

The pope develops a paradigm rooted in the fact of creation. For our purposes, there are four features of this paradigm worth considering. First and foremost, God created the world ex nihilo, out of nothing. That means that God is the source of everything: being, goodness, truth, and beauty. There is nothing else to be sources of those things. This means that the world is utterly dependent on God. We do not need to exist. We only do exist because God gives us being, or existence. Because all that exists is contained in God or depends on God, God has no need of us. He is self-sufficient. There is nothing so wonderful about the world that is not already in God. This means that God's choice to create was totally gratuitous. It is a free choice to create creatures who can share in and reflect His goodness. The fact that the world in which we find ourselves and our very beings come from God suggests that our actions should be rooted in humility and gratitude. We are radically dependent on God and cannot make claims on Him.[23]

Second, God's purpose in creation was to share His infinite goodness. And so we are creatures who seek this infinite goodness. For us humans, this desire for infinite goodness will only be truly satiated when we know God face to face, in the beatific vision.[24] But in the meantime, we have His goodness, as reflected to us in ourselves and in the world. Insofar as God created the world, and it reflects Him, it is good.[25]

The third point concerns diversity and oneness, two characteristics arising from how God reflects His infinite goodness in a finite creation. On one hand, God creates a diversity of creatures. No one finite creature could reflect the infinite goodness of God. But each creature can reflect one aspect of this goodness. The apple in its appleness tells us something about God that the orange in its orangeness cannot. As the pope puts it, citing the *Catechism*, "each creature reflects in its own way a ray of God's infinite wisdom and goodness."[26] To appreciate the gift of creation, then, requires that we respect the particular goodness of every creature.[27] To use technical jargon that will prove to be important for thinking about the technocratic paradigm, we need to respect the *form* of things. The form of an apple is the "whatness" that allows us to identify an apple as an apple. It is the distinctiveness of forms that lies behind the intuition that one cannot add two apples to two oranges and get four.

On the other hand, it is not enough for God to reflect His superabundant goodness through the diversity of creatures that make up the world. God is also one. God's unity is reflected through the interdependence of creatures, the thick web of relationships that saturate the world.[28]

These two features of creation are interconnected because the only way to fully see the essence of each distinct creature is to see it in the context of the web of relationships that enfold it. Diverse individuality occurs in pervasive relationship. The theme of relationship permeates the entire encyclical. In addition to cultivating appreciation for the web of relationship we find in nature, we must also root our understanding of the world in the three "fundamental and closely intertwined relationships"—between humans and God, within the human community, and between humans and the rest of creation.[29]

The fourth and final feature of the creation paradigm is that we humans reflect God in a special way. Rocks reflect God in that they exist. Plants reflect God more deeply because they both exist and live. Animals reflect God yet more deeply because they exist, and live, and perceive. We humans reflect God even more because we not only exist, live, and perceive but also know and love. Our minds can rise to the knowledge of goodness, truth, and beauty in a way that animals cannot. We are persons, with all that this entails. Our special place in creation, issued in the biblical injunction given in Genesis, is that we humans would have dominion over creation. But as Pope Francis explains, dominion needs to be understood in light of the creation paradigm as a whole. We must exercise it in a way that is mindful of our relationships with God, each other, and the other creatures in this world. We must remain mindful of the intrinsic good of each creature, each singing its own distinctive song in praise of God through the manifestation of its being.

Unfortunately, our relationships with God, each other, and the rest of creation are all ruptured as a consequence of sin. In the modern world, these ruptures are manifested in two views about nature that are fundamentally mistaken. First, we tend to look at creation instrumentally, coming to see it as mere "nature," a system that can be "studied, understood, and controlled." In doing so, we forget that creation can only truly be understood as a gift from God, a "reality illuminated by the love which calls us together into universal communion."[30]

Second, we misunderstand our proper stance toward creation. Whereas God did intend for us to exercise dominion over nature, the exercise of dominion is distorted when we forget that creation is ultimately God's dominion. We shift from a stance of stewardship of God's creation—a stewardship that implies we have a responsibility for nature—toward a stance that sees nature as so much raw material to be disposed of according to our will. What drops out in this shift is recognition that each creature is good in its own right as a reflection of God.[31]

In our fallen state, we forget that God is God, not us. Having forgotten God, we are led to worship earthly powers, which in turn underlies a more exploitative stance toward nature.[32] This exploitative stance, in turn, ends up being extended to other humans as well. Thus, the pope sets the table for his account of the technocratic paradigm, which is rooted in the modern view of the world that is only plausible to us in our fallen condition.

The Technocratic Paradigm

Armed with that background view of the world, we are in a position to understand the force of the pope's critique of what he calls the technocratic paradigm, which he describes as follows:

> The basic problem goes even deeper: it is the way that humanity has taken up technology and its development *according to an undifferentiated and one-dimensional paradigm*. This paradigm exalts the concept of a subject who, using logical and rational procedures, progressively approaches and gains control over an external object. This subject makes every effort to establish the scientific and experimental method, which in itself is already a technique of possession, mastery and transformation. It is as if the subject were to find itself in the presence of something formless, completely open to manipulation. Men and women have constantly intervened in nature, but for a long time this meant being in tune with and respecting the possibilities offered by the things themselves. It was a matter of receiving what nature itself allowed, as if from its own hand. Now, by contrast, we are the ones to lay our hands on things, attempting to extract everything possible from them while frequently ignoring or forgetting the reality in front of us. Human beings and material objects no longer extend a friendly hand to one another; the relationship has become confrontational. This has made it easy to accept the idea of infinite or unlimited growth, which proves so attractive to economists, financiers and experts in technology. It is based on the lie that there is an infinite supply of the earth's goods, and this leads to the planet being squeezed dry beyond every limit. It is the false notion that "an infinite quantity of energy and resources are available, that it is possible to renew them quickly, and that the negative effects of the exploitation of the natural order can be easily absorbed" (emphasis in the original).[33]

The paradigm, thus described, denies each of the four key features of the creation paradigm. First, God has dropped out of the picture entirely. All that remains is us, subjects who have "exalted" themselves, confronting a world that is devoid of any intrinsic meaning. There are stars and rainbows and puppy dogs and black holes and hurricanes and spiders. We like some of these things, we are awed by some of them, and we are threatened by some of them. Any meaning these things have is meaning they have *for* us. There is nothing intrinsically bad about a hurricane, but they are bad for the people whose houses get flattened by them, so we generally do not like them. There is nothing intrinsically good about a puppy dog, but we find them to be charming (albeit often annoying) companions, so we like them.

The tendency is to see the world as so much raw material, available (subject to the limits of our technological powers) to be manipulated as we like.[34] We beat back the spiders and breed more puppy dogs. In other words, we see the world mostly in a utilitarian light. How do things (and animals and plants) serve us? How can they be made to be of use to us? Although the ecology movement often tries to remind us we should value biodiversity for its own sake, most of the arguments that feel persuasive are utilitarian. We need to maintain biodiversity because a cure for cancer might be lurking in some beetle in the Amazon. We need to fight global warming because it will destroy our way of living. The moral stance of humility and gratitude has been supplanted by one of pride and mastery.

Second, the technocratic paradigm blinds us to the "reality right in front of us." It does this by inviting us to see through the form of things, reducing them to quantifiable values that we can manipulate. One of the keys to the spread of the technocratic paradigm was the discovery that if we focus on particular features of objects in the world, we can better manipulate them. Looking at an apple as an object with dimension and mass allowed Newton to discover the law of gravity, for example. This technique of reducing objects to particular, preferably measurable, features has spread. Now when we see an apple, we might see its mass, or its nutritional value, or its market value. What we tend not to see is the apple itself, as an apple.

The problem is that in reducing the apple to quantifiable measures we miss the fullness of the apple. Consider the problem of explaining to a Martian what an apple actually is. There is something we recognize about it that just is "apple." That is the form. And though "form" sounds empty, in this context, it is actually fullness. You can try to describe it as a fruit that is sweet, that has a color (red or green), that is generally round, that has a stem, and a core. You can add in all those measurements we focus on. It is about the size of my fist. It weighs so many ounces. It has so many calories, so many vitamins, and so on. But if I described a fruit you have never seen before in such terms, you still would not really know what that fruit is until you saw it. I can read a description of an ackee, but a picture tells me more, and actually holding it, smelling it, and tasting it tells me even more.

Our habit of reducing things to various measurable components—and treating these reductions as the things that are "real"—ends up impoverishing us. We miss the fullness of the things that are around us. The "what" of things—their form—is a source of a deep goodness, and we tend to be blind to it, seeking the good we imagine around the next corner, rather than encountering the good right here, right now. The reminder that we should stop and smell the roses captures this point.

We can see the problem most readily when we consider what happens when we reduce *people* to various measurable features. I can see the people around me as part of the congestion on the freeway, or as potential customers for my store, or as mouths that need to be fed. In doing so, I miss the treasure that they are. I do not hear their stories, or marvel at the goodness they bring about in themselves and the world. The business person might be tempted by the technocratic paradigm to see an employee as a salary line, thereby failing to see him or her as the particular human person they are.

Third, the technocratic paradigm blinds us to the thick web of relationships that constitute creation. The essence of the technocratic paradigm is the effort to gain mastery over the external world by reducing objects to quantifiable measurements. But the result is a fragmentation of knowledge. We specialize according to those particular measurements on which we want to focus. The economist sees the price of the apple and the costs of producing it. The nutritionist sees its nutritional value. The physicist sees its mass and dimension. We become experts on those aspects of reality that we "know" about, but there is no science that fits that knowledge together. As Pope Francis puts it,

> The fragmentation of knowledge proves helpful for concrete applications, and yet it often leads to a loss of appreciation for the whole, for the relationships between things, and for the broader horizon, which then becomes irrelevant. This very fact makes it hard to find adequate ways of solving the more complex problems of today's world, particularly those regarding the environment and the poor; these problems cannot be dealt with from a single perspective or from a single set of interests.[35]

Moreover, as this specialization in knowledge has proceeded apace, fields like philosophy and theology that would allow us to integrate knowledge have receded in importance. Modern habits of knowing, then, make it difficult to see creation as it really is—a web of relationships between distinctive creatures.

Fourth, the technocratic paradigm invites us to exercise a distorted sort of dominion over creation, one where we see the world around us as so much formless material to be exploited for our own ends. From the perspective of the creation paradigm, it embodies our fallen state. Our relationships with God, the world, and each other are all ruptured.

Taken together, we can begin to see why the technocratic paradigm is likely to create a world filled with environmental degradation and economic injustice. We move through the world without seeing its value. We do not fully see the values of other people. We do not recognize our essential relatedness with each other and with the world around us. As a result, our desires can never really be satiated because we tend to look through the actual goods around us. This mind-set leads us to prioritize maximizing the means that enable us to fulfill our desires (or at least as many of them as possible). So more money is always better. More power is always better.

But this relentless drive means there will always be pressure to push past limits. This is the ultimate tragedy. Economic growth promises us riches, but the technocratic paradigm leaves us feeling unfulfilled. And we end up damaging or destroying the real goods around us in nature and in our communities and in other people around the world.

Armed with these insights, we are in a position to evaluate the moral defense of profit-maximization.

PROFIT-MAXIMIZATION AND THE TECHNOCRATIC PARADIGM

The pope explicitly connects the technocratic paradigm with the economic mind-set, and especially with profit-maximization:

> The technocratic paradigm also tends to dominate economic and political life. The economy accepts every advance in technology with a view to profit, without concern for its potentially negative impact on human beings. Finance overwhelms the real economy. The lessons of the global financial crisis have not been assimilated, and we are learning all too slowly the lessons of environmental deterioration. Some circles maintain that current economics and technology will solve all environmental problems, and argue, in popular and non-technical

terms, that the problems of global hunger and poverty will be resolved simply by market growth. ... Their behavior shows that for them maximizing profits is enough. ... We fail to see the deepest roots of our present failures, which have to do with the direction, goals, meaning and social implications of technological and economic growth.[36]

The model of behavior proffered by economists—wherein individuals seek to maximize their utility and firms seek to maximize profits—formally fits Pope Francis's description of the technocratic paradigm. In these models, the sovereign agent confronts a world outside her and seeks to act in the world to best fulfill her desires, which are unbounded. Her aim is not to encounter a good external to her, but rather to bend the world to satisfy as many of her desires as possible. The model further posits that in making her decision, she collapses the diverse goods she seeks by trying to maximize a one-dimensional vector of "utility" or "profit" (depending on whether she is a consumer or a producer). Finally, although one can include goods that have a relational quality into these functions, the mathematical functions themselves make it difficult to embrace the relational dimension that defines the various goods one might put into them. Thus the economic models of human agencies are merely models of decision-making within the technocratic paradigm. The identification of profit-maximization with the technocratic paradigm allows us to make the following criticisms of profit-maximization from the perspective of the creation paradigm.

True Self-Interest and the Technocratic Paradigm

The moral defense of profit-maximization argues that profit-maximizing behavior generates good social outcomes. Yet beneath this belief lies the assumption that this process is also good for profit-maximizers themselves. That is, we assume that people are made better off by getting as much wealth for themselves as they can. From the perspective of the creation paradigm, this is a misguided understanding of human happiness. The unbounded desire for more wealth (or more power) is in service of desires that are unbounded. These unbounded desires, in turn, are rooted in the broken relationships that stem from our fallen nature. The individual no longer sees himself as part of the web of creation. If he did understand himself as part of a web of relationship, then his desires would have more of the character of seeking fittingness than seeking extension (i.e., constantly seeking more).

Romano Guardini offers an image of this in his reflections on the aesthetic quality of the villages that surround Lake Como:

Everywhere it was an inhabited land, valleys and slopes dotted with hamlets and small towns. All nature had been given a new shape by us humans. What culture means in its narrowest sense struck me with full force. The lines of the roofs merged from different directions. They went through the small town set on the hillside or followed the windings of a valley. Integrated in many ways, they finally reached a climax in the belfry with its deep-toned bell. All these things were caught up and encircled by the well-constructed mountain masses. Culture, very lofty and yet self-evident, very naturally—I have no other word.[37]

In the creation paradigm, humans creatively interact with the given-ness of nature, turning it to human purposes, but in a way that respects and amplifies what is already there. It is an approach to building a life that is inherently bounded.

The creation paradigm can also offer a diagnosis of the source of the illusion that more is always better. In our effort to bend nature to our will, we have adopted a view that does not allow us to see the intrinsic good in the world around us. We see through the appleness of the apple. As a result, our desires never can be truly satisfied; we restlessly seek after more. We are like children who are excited to see all the packages under the tree on Christmas morning but who are then vaguely dissatisfied with the actual goods that reveal themselves on opening. And so we quickly put all our hopes on the new packages that will appear next Christmas. We have lost the ability to fully receive the good that presents itself, and thus we mistakenly think that more wealth will finally lead us to the imagined goods for which we hope.

True Agency and the Technocratic Paradigm

The moral defense of profit-maximization also gives weight to the freedom or agency that markets allow us to exercise. As Milton Friedman puts it, freedom is a good in and of itself.[38] But as echoed in Gregory Beabout's treatment of agency for "the business person as moneymaker" in chapter 4 of this volume, this sort of agency is conceived of as the ability to exercise control over the world. The sovereign agent confronts a world that exists independently outside her. Again, what is missing is the essential relatedness of all things, including us. From the perspective of the creation paradigm, true agency is exercised in light of the reality that we are embedded in relationships. We aim to act on the world, but we are also open to receiving it. That is, agency is more like a dance that aims at harmony rather than mastery. In chapter 4

Gregory Beabout provides an alternative account of human agency that is consistent with the creation paradigm.

From the perspective of the creation paradigm, it is not simply that the freedom involved in maximizing profits (or utility) is incomplete; it is illusory. In particular, the utility or profit functions are taken as given. Because our aim is to maximize utility or profits, our choices are essentially a matter of mathematical calculation, a mistake criticized by Andrew Yuengert in chapter 3, on practical wisdom. But if choices are only calculations, an external observer armed with data—about the functions we are trying to maximize and the array of prices (both monetary and nonmonetary) that we confront—can predict what our choice will be. Indeed, as Gary Becker argues, this is the whole aim of economic science.[39]

Moreover, the point of developing models that predict human behavior is to use that information to tweak the array of prices confronting an individual in order to induce them to act as we would like. In other words, to the extent that one really does act to maximize profits (or utility), one is subject to manipulation by others. The technocratic paradigm thus invites us to see others as objects to be manipulated for our own gain, while we, in turn, are subject to their attempts to manipulate us for their gain. What is missing is recognition of the relationality that paradoxically is necessary for us to exercise genuinely human creativity and freedom.

The Case Against Profit-Maximization

That brings us to the claim that profit-maximization is morally good because it produces socially desirable results, most notably by enhancing efficiency and promoting economic growth. Even those who are most staunchly in favor of this moral defense of profit-maximization recognize that some limits need to be imposed. Most obviously, firms are expected to stay within legal limits—that is, to not engage in fraudulent practices and the like. Further, as noted above, there is an ample body of economic literature on market failures and a corresponding openness to government intervention to correct markets in instances when the market, left to itself, will not generate socially desirable outcomes.

The pope expresses open skepticism of the idea that markets by themselves will lead to good outcomes:

Some circles maintain that current economics and technology will solve all environmental problems, and argue, in popular and nontechnical terms, that the problems of global hunger and poverty will be resolved simply by market growth. They are less concerned with certain economic theories which today scarcely anybody dares defend, than with their actual operation in the functioning of the economy. They may not affirm such theories with words, but nonetheless support them with their deeds by showing no interest in more balanced levels of production, a better distribution of wealth, concern for the environment and the rights of future generations. Their behavior shows that for them maximizing profits is enough. Yet by itself the market cannot guarantee integral human development and social inclusion.[40]

To some extent, the pope is overstating his case; few people think that markets should be completely unregulated. Nonetheless, from the perspective of the creation paradigm, it is natural to think that markets are as likely to produce bad results as good ones. If creation really is shot through with relationships, then externalities are likely to be pervasive.[41] If, erroneously, we really do view ourselves as sovereign subjects confronting a formless world, we are unlikely to see any limits to what we can do. We are more likely to view others as objects within this formless world, equally available to be manipulated for our own good. Those who succeed in obtaining market or political power are not likely to curb their behavior, even when it harms others or the environment. The assumptions that underlie the model of perfect competition are very far from reality, which means that the market's ability to channel profit-seeking activity in productive directions is less powerful than the conventional economic view would suggest.

In this way, the pope's argument is a left-leaning one. For theological reasons, he believes that markets must be subject to cultural and political control because the imperative to maximize profits simply does not conform to a world that was created, and therefore is likely to be damaging. One could argue that the pope does not fully appreciate that the same self-seeking behavior that can lead business to generate significant social and environmental harm is also likely to attempt to co-opt government to pass regulations that are unjustly beneficial to themselves.[42]

However, it seems to me that in light of the larger critique, the pope's argument is best seen as a call to conversion. The goods of profit-maximization are illusory; the agency it posits is not genuine human freedom; and though it does produce economic growth, much of it is of a "wasteful and consumerist" sort.[43] More importantly, it generates significant harm to the genuine goods we find in the created world and in the human world. We are destroying the planet and each other in a vain quest to sate our infinite desires in a finite world, all while seeing through the genuine goods that are present to us.

GOOD PROFIT IN A FALLEN WORLD

If that call is a good one, there are still some hard questions to be asked. In this final section, I take up two of them.

First, the pope's account does not do full justice to the genuine goods that businesses do produce. (He would do well to talk with the CEOs like the ones interviewed by Regina Wolfe in chapter 1.) The critique of the excesses and deformities that attend a mind-set that is aimed at maximizing profits would be more compelling if a meaningful alternative were present. There are a few scattered mentions of that more compelling view in *Laudato si'*. The pope does refer to profits in a few places that give the sense that there is such a thing as "good profits," which take into proper account the goods and types of harm that are not measured in market terms and that therefore do not show up on the bottom line. That said, elsewhere the Magisterium has offered a more robust account of the sorts of genuine goods that are proper to business. In *The Vocation of the Business Leader*, the Pontifical Council for Justice and Peace offers a paradigm captured by the phrase "good goods, good work, and good wealth."[44] This perspective informs many of the chapters in this volume.

The notion of "good goods," which is explored in detail by David Cloutier in chapter 7, reminds us that the primary task of business is to provide goods and services that are of value to the community. We can see this priority reflected in the attitudes of the business leaders interviewed by Gina Wolfe, all of whom think first of the goods or services provided. From the perspective of the creation paradigm, this reflects a vision of the world that sees qualitative goods themselves as primary, rather than collapsing them into quantitative metrics about revenues or sales. It also maintains a sense of relationship because the aim of producing good goods and good services is to benefit one's customers or clients. In other words, business activity is primarily relational.

This sense of relationship extends to the concept of "good work" as well, where business is also seen as of value insofar as it creates space for employees to develop and exercise their own agency. The CEOs interviewed by Wolfe all think in terms of the community created within their own workforce and of developing the human excellence of their workers. Again, the focus is on both relationship and cultivating genuine human goods. As the interviews suggest, firms that are working from this sort of perspective are pursuing a series of qualitatively distinctive goods (producing goods and services that benefit their customers, maintaining relationships with customers and suppliers, building community within the firm), a set of concerns that is not well captured by the intention to maximize profits.[45] In chapter 3 Yuengert explores the kind of practical wisdom needed, and regularly employed, in business that comprises far more than profit-maximization.

This leads to the question of the "good wealth" referred to in the *Vocation of the Business Leader*. If firms aimed at good goods and good works are not maximizing profits, what role do profits play in such firms? Firms do have to make money in order to stay in business. So business leaders operating out of the creation paradigm must also be concerned about maintaining "good profits." The key is that profits should be ordered to the higher goods served by businesses. That is, profits are what allow firms to produce the goods and services they offer to their customers and provide their employees and other stakeholders with just returns to their work. The profits *serve* these ends. In the technocratic paradigm, by contrast, goods are produced and employees are hired with the end of serving the bottom line.

In the creation paradigm, profits rightly serve as a signal about how to allocate resources well. Consider Thomas Holloran (a CEO interviewed in chapter 1) and the medical device industry. If, for example, Medtronic's profits start to go down because it is no longer able to sell a given product at a price that can cover expenses, this is a signal that it might want to shift its attention to a line of products that would better serve the community. This is among the real advantages of markets examined by Martijn Cremers in chapter 10 of this volume. Firms that attend to profits without aiming to maximize them can still produce the good outcomes touted by those who defend profit-maximization by referring to the efficient outcomes generated by markets. At the same time, firms operating out of the creation paradigm would be less likely to engage in the sorts of behavior that generate negative externalities because their ultimate aim is not the bottom line. It is, instead, the set of genuine human goods proper to business, advocated by Kenneth Goodpaster and Michael Naughton in chapter 6 under the name of the common good.

This leads to a second hard question about what the good firm should do when it is forced to compete in markets dominated by the technocratic paradigm. Pope Francis talks about the destabilizing effects of financial markets. Financial markets amplify the ills associated with the technocratic market because in them the focus is on the abstraction of money rather than the real goods produced by the real economy. Kathryn Tanner offers a good account of the distorting effect financial capitalism has on good business practice.[46] As the interviews conducted by Gina Wolfe suggest, it is possible for firms operating out of the creation paradigm to compete effectively enough to remain in business. But surely the competitive pressure from firms that aim solely at maximizing profits makes it more difficult for firms to fully live out the "good goods, good work, good profits" paradigm. As the pope suggests, what is needed is a cultural conversion.

CONCLUSION

The creation paradigm laid out by Pope Francis, and the corresponding critique of the technocratic paradigm, offer a vocabulary for distinguishing between ethical and unethical business practices. Although profit-maximization can produce some good outcomes, an entire culture oriented toward maximizing profits would upend environmental balance and thwart economic justice. The analysis thus suggests that in order to think well about the ethics of business in general, and profit-maximization in particular, we need to reflect more deeply about the nature of the world we inhabit. Our conception of the human good depends critically on how we understand the nature of the world. As Iris Murdoch has suggested, ethics does, indeed, depend on metaphysics.[47]

The framework offered by Pope Francis is rooted in a religious view of the world. We can ask what role such an analysis should play in a pluralistic culture that brackets questions about the nature of the world in favor of pragmatic discussion about the ordinary goods on which we can all agree. But as the pope's critique suggests, *any* discussion of pragmatic concerns is necessarily rooted in tacit assumptions about metaphysics. It is our unthinking adoption of the premises of the technocratic paradigm that makes our struggles with economic justice and environmental sustainability seem intractable. Yet as the contributors to this volume also suggest, the idea that we should focus on the human goods that are typically pursued by business is not itself obscure. There is a deep yearning for more meaningful work and a more meaningful economic life. It thus would seem that Pope Francis has opened the door to a conversation about removing the blinders imposed by the technocratic paradigm in favor of rearticulating the role of business in promoting authentic human goods.

NOTES

1. Friedman, *Capitalism.*
2. See, e.g., Aquinas, *Summa Theologica,* I-II, 2.1; II-II, 32.6.
3. Smith, *Wealth of Nations.*
4. Hirschman, *Passions.*
5. Haidt and Randazzo, "Moral Narratives."

6. Pope Francis, *Evangelii gaudium*. See Tornielli and Galeazzi, *This Economy Kills*, for a defense of Pope Francis against the charge that he is a communist, which nonetheless identifies him as a critic of financial capitalism. See Schlag, *Business Francis Means*, for an account of Pope Francis's thought that argues that his economic thought is in continuity with his predecessors and thus can accommodate a positive role for markets and for business.

7. Congregation for the Doctrine of Faith and Dicastery for Promoting Integral Human Development, *Oeconomicae et pecuniariae quaestiones*, 5. My understanding from Father Martin Schlag is that this document should be regarded as part of the body of Catholic social thought.

8. Friedman, *Capitalism*, 132.

9. Mankiw, *Economics*, 302. Essentially, whenever the price is above the average cost, firms will enter; and when the price is below the average cost, firms will exit. The equilibrium occurs when price equals average cost, and this can only happen when average costs are at the minimum point for individual firms.

10. Arrow, "Extension"; Debreu, "Coefficient."

11. Kirzner, *Competition*.

12. McCloskey, *Bourgeois Virtues*, 1–53, offers an extended encomium to the power of markets.

13. Mankiw, *Economics*, chaps. 15–17.

14. Mankiw, 484–90.

15. Mankiw, chap. 10.

16. Pope Francis, *Laudato si'*, 36, 82.

17. Pope Francis, 195. See also 187.

18. Pope Francis, 190.

19. Guardini, *End*, I; see also Guardini, *Letters*.

20. Pope Francis, *Laudato si'*, 102.

21. Pope Francis, 105.

22. Pope Francis, 62.

23. Pope Francis, 72–74.

24. Saint Thomas Aquinas, *Summa Theologica*, I-II, 2.8.

25. Pope Francis, *Laudato si'*, 65.

26. Pope Francis, *Laudato si'*, 69, citing the *Catechism of the Catholic Church*, 339.

27. Pope Francis, *Laudato si'*, 69.

28. Pope Francis, 86.

29. Pope Francis, 66.

30. Pope Francis, 76.

31. Pope Francis, 67–68.

32. Pope Francis, 75.

33. Pope Francis, 106.

34. Guardini, *End*, is a major influence on this section of the encyclical. In his words, the technocratic paradigm "sees nature as an insensate order, as a cold body of facts, as a mere "given," as an object of utility, as raw material to be hammered into useful shape" (p. 55).

35. Pope Francis, *Laudato si'*, 110.

36. Pope Francis, 109.

37. Guardini, *Letters*, Kindle location 109.

38. Friedman, *Capitalism*, 8.

39. Becker, *Economic Approach*.

40. Pope Francis, *Laudato si'*, 109.
41. Wilbur, "Contributions."
42. Zingales, *Capitalism*. See Acemoglu and Robinson, *Why Nations Fail*, for a discussion of the dynamic between economics and politics.
43. Pope Francis, *Laudato si'*, 109.
44. Pontifical Council for Peace and Justice, *Vocation*.
45. See also Hirschfeld, *Aquinas*, chap. 5, for a more complete elaboration of the goods pursued by a firm that is rooted in the creation paradigm.
46. Tanner, *Christianity*.
47. Murdoch, *Metaphysics*.

PART III

THE WIDER RESPONSIBILITIES OF BUSINESS

CHAPTER 6

The Institutional Insight Underlying Shareholder/Stakeholder Approaches to Business Ethics

Kenneth E. Goodpaster and Michael J. Naughton

At the center of any organization is its purpose, and so one of the most significant responsibilities of leaders in an organization is to articulate, cultivate, and execute that purpose. The history of institutions points to the importance of this leadership task. Whether businesses, governments, universities, or families, these institutions have a raison d'être, a reason for their being—an account of why they exist and what they are designed to do.

An institution's purpose clarifies what goods it is to pursue and how it orders such goods for the good of the whole. It is precisely such purposes that give institutions meaning as well as legitimacy in the communities where they reside. As we will explain, the content of this purpose is best understood in terms of an "institutional insight" informed by the common good. The conventional models focusing on the shareholder or stakeholder are inadequate for describing the purpose of business.

The articulation and pursuit of institutional purpose is not as easy as it may seem. One challenge is the significant cultural debate over the institutional purposes of business, universities, religion, marriage, government, health care, and the like. Because of the increasing pluralism of society, we have difficulty agreeing to a common understanding of the good in life generally, so we tend to go to the least debatable, "thin" approach to the good. This move flattens or dilutes the good of institutions by reducing them from a vibrant set of integrated goods to one emotive or instrumental good—business to shareholder wealth-maximization, universities to career credentialing, religion to emotive experience, marriage to sentiment between autonomous individuals, and so forth. We believe that this reductionist trend deprives institutions of a vertical or transcendent dimension—leaving only motives that are self-interested, knowledge that is empirical, and rationality that is instrumental. Deeper institutional thinking is required.[1]

As we step into this debate, we need a basic understanding of institutions. For leaders, this understanding can lead to what we call the "institutional insight"—with its underlying foundation in the common good. The business corporation is clearly an important institution in modern society, but polls indicate that people are losing trust in the leaders of business corporations as well as in the institution itself.[2] Business leaders, along with leaders in the media and in politics, are the least trusted institutional leaders in the United States. There are many reasons for this, of course, but we believe that when business ethics reduces itself to either the maximization of shareholder wealth (shareholder model) or to the balancing of stakeholder interests (stakeholder model), it runs the risk of severing itself from its most significant principle as an institution—the imperative to pursue the common good.

If business leaders are to ground themselves in a deeper purpose, they must, in the words of the sociologist Philip Selznick, move from "administrative management" to "institutional leadership."[3] In our view, administrative management is informed by one of the two predominant views of business mentioned above—the shareholder or stakeholder models. These are useful models because they identify important realities of business decision-making, but they are not robust enough for institutional leadership, which needs to draw from deeper roots.

The first section of this chapter focuses on what we mean by the institutional insight in relation to the shareholder and stakeholder views of business. At the heart of this insight is the realization that one's own institution—like all institutions—is part of the larger endeavor of seeking to improve the well-being of humankind. Those who do not grasp this institutional insight run the risk of dysfunctional decision-making, rooted in too narrow an understanding of their purpose. One of the consequences of such narrow decision-making is a loss of trust on the part of consumers, suppliers, employees, and local communities.

The chapter's second section builds upon the institutional insight by clarifying the common good as a principle that gives specific content to the institutional role of business in society. This content allows us greater detail in defining the purpose of business and illuminating what good business does. Functionally for leaders, institutional purpose serves as a guiding compass that orders institutional decision-making: setting strategies, allocating resources, and managing structures and systems. This has been a major theme throughout the management literature, counseling leaders to move beyond setting only strategy and tactics to building a framework for the purpose of the institution. Only through a robust and deep sense of purpose will employees become committed and dedicated to operationalizing their strategy. Purpose is frequently drawn from an institution's founding narrative, which is often derived from something that is noble and transcendent. It taps into the more profound convictions of the institution that give it meaning and direction.[4]

In particular, we will be drawing from Catholic social teaching, which has a long and vibrant tradition on the common good. Yet the message of this chapter is not intended only for Catholic or Christian business leaders. We are addressing all leaders who can discern the institutional insight defined below—essentially, all leaders who have the conviction that business must be accountable not only to stockholders and stakeholders but also to the common good that undergirds all forms of business responsibility.

THE INSTITUTIONAL INSIGHT: ENGAGING THE SHAREHOLDER/STAKEHOLDER DEBATE

This volume focuses on morality in business, but to address the purpose of the business firm, we must begin with two notions that apply not only within but also beyond economic life. The first is the philosophical concept called "the moral insight," which opens the way for a consideration of the focus of this chapter, the "institutional insight."

The Moral Insight: Beyond Focal Awareness

The nineteenth-century Harvard philosopher Josiah Royce believed that all ethics was grounded in the moral insight (a precursor to the "moral point of view").[5] He described it this way:

> The moral insight is the realization of one's neighbor, in the full sense of the word realization; the resolution to treat him unselfishly. But this resolution expresses and belongs to the moment of insight. Passion may cloud the insight after no very long time.... We see the reality of our neighbor, that is, we determine to treat him as we do ourselves. But then we go back to daily action, and we feel the heat of hereditary passions, and we straightway forget what we have seen. Our neighbor becomes obscured. He is once more a foreign power. He is

unreal. . . . Moments of insight, with their accompanying resolutions; long stretches of delusion and selfishness: That is our life.[6]

Many aspects of Royce's idea of the moral insight merit our attention, but for present purposes, let us highlight his view that morality for individuals depends for its practical significance on maintaining a kind of dual awareness—self-awareness plus "the realization of one's neighbor."

It is a long-held view among philosophers and theologians that human nature includes both self-interested and social aspirations. It is as if our inner lives can be represented by a camera that, when zoomed in on ourselves as subjects, displays an inadequate picture of who we are. Zooming out displays the reality of our neighbors, contemporary, historical, and future. Zooming out, we are still in the picture, but the image now gives us a broader perspective, a second kind of awareness, that supplements and enriches our perception of reality.[7]

The moral insight, then, complicates personal decision-making, which might otherwise be more straightforwardly self-interested. It introduces a larger perspective and therefore potential conflicts between self-interested behavior and respect for the other as other. This second kind of awareness asks each of us to see our own interests as part of a larger social good. But Royce believes that the moral insight—and so the second kind of awareness—is fragile because it is susceptible to a kind of "forgetting."

So when Royce refers to the moral insight, he is saying that it consists in realizing one's neighbor, appreciating the underlying truth of his or her reality and dignity, equal to my own. My awareness of my own reality is a departure point, but the moral insight enlarges my world to include my neighbor. This insight is the foundation of the oldest and most widely shared ethical precept known to us—the Golden Rule. Now, let us turn to an analog to the moral insight, what we call the "institutional insight."

Hugh Heclo, a professor of government and public affairs at George Mason University, in his book *On Thinking Institutionally*, offers a rich interpretation of institutions and institutional thinking. He observes that "amid the perpetual perishing that marks our individual existences, institutions are weathered presences."[8] In other words, institutions are ways to achieve a measure of permanence and continuity for what we value despite our mortality. They are a vehicle through which we inherit the goods and values of those who came before us and are a vehicle through which we pass on those goods and values to those who follow us.

As we think about the institutions in our lives (families, churches, schools, associations, businesses, and governments), it is essential to keep two truths in mind at the same time—a form of dual awareness. First, according to Heclo, institutions by their nature have a normative dimension: "by virtue of participating in an institutional form of life, there are more and less appropriate ways of doing things. These obligations are a kind of internal morality that flows from the purposive point of the institution itself."[9]

This normative dimension of institutions should be understood as creating what W. D. Ross called prima facie obligations concerning our participation in multiple institutions—for example, the norms of business, family, government, and voluntary associations. But one prima facie obligation can override or be overridden by another one.

Second, in addition to the prima facie obligations of the "internal morality" of institutions in relation to one another, there are more comprehensive obligations to which all institutions must be subject. To quote Heclo again, "Since people are not created for the good of institutions but institutions for the purposes of people, any call to the intrinsic worth of an institution is a lie if it does not ultimately recognize and serve the moral and ontological primacy of human persons and their well-being. To repeat, that means institutions exist for people, and for serving their good. People do not exist for institutions."[10]

Heclo, like Royce before him, is identifying two levels of awareness for institutional leaders—awareness of the immediate needs of the business in the foreground (zooming in), and awareness of the normative context in which the business before me must be managed (zooming out).[11] Martin Schlag, in chapter 8 of this volume, draws attention to this larger "ecology" of business as well. And as with Royce, this insight can be obscured or forgotten if it is not reinforced and practiced regularly.[12]

The institutional insight is part of a comprehensive perspective that business leaders must cultivate, concurrent with their narrower, firm-centered perspective ("internal morality"). This dual awareness ensures that the ultimate purposes of institutions themselves are not overlooked or ignored in the decision-making of their leaders.[13]

The institutional insight contrasts with Royce's moral insight, in that it applies not so much to our moral lives as individual persons as to the cultural lives of institutions. But it is also quite similar, in the sense that it requires a dual awareness that can be lost despite "resolutions" on the part of senior leadership. This dual awareness is evident in the viewpoints of the three executives interviewed for chapter 1, by Regina Wolfe. Wolfe concludes by observing that her three interlocutors "see in business a way of providing purpose and meaning to people's lives while at the same time contributing to the common good of the communities—local or global—in which the business operates."

One of Heclo's primary concerns is that Americans are increasingly losing touch with ("forgetting") this institutional insight, even to the point of some becoming anti-institutional. While institutions are for persons, the flourishing of persons calls for relationships with others, both now and across time. As the African proverb goes, a person is a person because of other persons. The good of the person is found through the goods that are held in common with other persons, what the Catholic social tradition calls a "community of persons."

The patterns of language and thought in modern culture, however, conceive of our freedom and individual identity outside institutions, not through them or because of them. Our cultural moral center is increasingly an individualistic one. In chapter 5, Mary Hirschfeld provides a fuller analysis of this individualistic view. Heclo articulates this new cultural redefinition of institutions as a "balancing act" of allowing individuals "to live out their life projects as they wish but limited by the interests of others to do the same. Individuals do not have the right to judge another person's chosen life project except if it harms another."[14] This balancing act becomes a procedural principle for solving most social problems. A politically expedient principle becomes a moral-cultural principle. In this mistaken contemporary view, institutions become collections of individuals that negotiate and bargain based on self-interest. Stakeholder subgroups emerge as interest groups laying claim to prima facie normative authority. What is lost is a community of persons bonded together by goods held in common.[15]

Problems with Shareholder and Stakeholder Accounts

Let us now examine the implications of the institutional insight for the conventional understanding of business ethics as a choice between shareholder-centered norms and stakeholder-centered norms. Goodpaster has argued that there are two "provisos" needed in business ethics rather than the single shareholder proviso that is commonly insisted upon: "The Shareholder Proviso: Corporate responsibility rests upon a fiduciary obligation to stockholders, shareholders, or owners, but this responsibility is provisional. It can be limited by other non-fiduciary obligations: to employees, to customers, to suppliers, to local communities, and even to the environment."[16]

This proviso is often presented as a challenge in discussions of agency theory, in which there are empirical and normative debates over a business leader acting out of self-interest or as a fiduciary agent for stockholders, shareholders, or owners.[17] The agency relationship is often invoked to provide a kind of immunity from wider ethical concerns: "My personal ethical principles lead me to do X, but I have an obligation to the stockholders, so I can't."

In contrast to shareholder thinking, stakeholder thinking is often presented as a more ethical alternative, insisting on the accountability of business organizations to a larger set of affected parties. Nevertheless, stakeholder thinking is also subject to a moral proviso: "The Stakeholder Proviso: Corporate responsibility rests upon a fiduciary obligation to stockholders, employees, customers, suppliers, and local communities, but this responsibility is provisional. It can be limited by other fiduciary obligations required by the common good."

Just as the shareholder proviso warned us about reducing ethical decisions in business to fiduciary duties to stockholders alone (not to mention the self-interest of the agent), the stakeholder proviso warns of another kind of reduction and invites a more comprehensive approach to our ethical thinking about business.[18]

The primary reason that business ethics must countenance two provisos and not just one is G. E. Moore's classic "open question argument."[19] The intuition that the following two questions are meaningfully "open" questions should tell us that each of the conventional business ethics norms must be taken as provisional:

Question 1: "This corporate decision serves the stockholders best, but is it right?"

Question 2: "This corporate decision most satisfies our stakeholders, but is it right?"

What is it about these questions that lies beneath their openness? Is it just an intuition, full stop? Here is where a discussion of the institutional insight can be helpful.

One explanation for the open question is that the shareholder and stakeholder views are shallow views, leaving undiscussed the deeper justifications, the moral roots, underlying the two provisos.

In the case of shareholders, it is the fiduciary responsibility to respect and protect a vulnerable party (the patient in health care, the client in legal advocacy, and the stockholder in financial affairs). Alexei Marcoux argues quite persuasively that the root of the fiduciary obligation of managers to shareholders lies in the vulnerability of those to whom the obligation is owed.

Thus, one explanation for the openness of Question 1 is that partiality to the vulnerable is the deeper moral justification beneath it. This way of thinking echoes Catholic social teaching in its emphasis on human dignity and solidarity with the vulnerable and the disadvantaged. It also highlights for shareholders the social nature of the property they hold in the form of shares, which is often ignored by advocates of the shareholder model. Edward Kleinbard helpfully addresses the "social mortgage" on property in chapter 9 of this volume.

In the case of stakeholders, the underlying moral justification is different. R. Edward Freeman generalizes the shareholder fiduciary view to all stakeholders.[20] He offers a "multi-fiduciary" account of corporate responsibility[21]—a view that Marcoux finds incoherent: "To be a fiduciary for someone is to be partial to that someone's interests and to promote them within a certain domain, but the stakeholder theory demands impartiality among and between the admittedly competing interests of stakeholders. Therefore, the stakeholder theory demands that managers be fiduciaries to no one."[22]

Others have argued that the underlying intent of stakeholder thinking (and the interests of stakeholders) can be rescued by appealing to "market failures" that call for regulations, as Martin Schlag also notes in chapter 8, where he discusses the views of the economist Jean Tirole.[23] Both the stakeholder view and the market failure view ultimately invoke deeper sources of moral obligation: they appeal to the interests and well-being of those affected by business behavior. The underlying justification of stakeholder thinking seems to lie in a social obligation to take into account the good of all affected parties in society.

Thus, an explanation for the openness of Question 2 is that we must be impartial when we look at the implications of business behavior for human freedom and well-being. This way of thinking gestures in the direction of (but is not equivalent to) Catholic social teaching. This tradition emphasizes the importance of virtues such as justice, understood not only as an external constraint through contracts and regulations but also as an internal excellence in the form of right relations with others. It also draws upon social principles like the common good to give moral roots to institutional life, which we explore in the next section.

Debates about corporate responsibility between proponents of shareholder fiduciary duties and concern for stakeholders reveal the possibility of deeper moral roots—and it is in the realm of these deeper convictions that we find the institutional insight. Only in this realm can corporate responsibility be understood in a comprehensive way, as the locus of normative business ethics.[24] To make progress, we need to dig deeper, and in this sense we can appreciate the comparison that the sociologist Philip Selznick makes between institutional cultures and individual personalities: "The study of institutions is in some ways comparable to the clinical study of personality. It requires a genetic and developmental approach, an emphasis on historical origins and growth stages. There is a need to see the enterprise as a whole and to see how it is transformed as new ways of dealing with a changing environment evolve."[25]

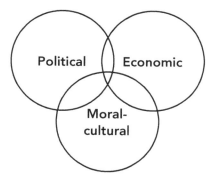

Figure 6.1 The Three Sectors of Society

Categorizing Institutions

So where do these deeper moral roots come from? What are the more fundamental—or transcendent—sources of ethics for business? Essential to appreciating the institutional insight described above is the recognition that institutions are dependent upon a more comprehensive notion of the good, which is found in the relationship among society's three main sectors. Michael Novak, in his book *The Spirit of Democratic Capitalism*, echoed Alexis de Tocqueville when he offered a description of American society as an intersection of three broad subsystems or "sectors": the economic, the political, and the moral-cultural, as depicted in figure 6.1: "Democratic capitalism is not a "free enterprise system" alone. It cannot thrive apart from the moral culture that nourishes the virtues and values on which its existence depends. It cannot thrive apart from a democratic polity committed, on the one hand, to limited government and, on the other hand, to many legitimate activities without which a prosperous economy is impossible."[26]

According to Novak, the economic sector accounts largely for the wealth of a nation (its production of goods and services and its provision of work). The political sector aims, in the words of the preamble to the US Constitution, to "establish justice, insure domestic tranquility, provide for the common defense, promote the general welfare, and secure the blessings of liberty to ourselves and our posterity." The moral-cultural sector shapes and articulates our virtues and moral principles through the basic elements of civil society, including the family, educational institutions, churches and other religious institutions, the media (print and electronic), and various nonprofit associations. Each of these three sectors represents an "institutional bundle" that complements the other two in overlapping ways.

In view of the three larger spheres of culture, politics, and economics, we begin to see the deeper roots of business as an institution. The business philosopher Charles Handy seems to have intuited the dual awareness needed for the institutional insight in his *Harvard Business Review* article "What's a Business For?" In his words, "We cannot escape the fundamental question, 'Whom and what is a business for?'" Handy adds: "The purpose of a business . . . is not to make a profit, full stop. It is to make a profit so that the business can do something more or better. That 'something' becomes the real justification for the business."[27]

Handy, echoing Heclo and Novak, implies that institutional leadership must be anchored not merely in the achievement of profits for stockholders—or even in simply advancing the interests of stakeholders—but in an awareness of the institution's true contribution to the life of the human community. Profits may be a reward for this contribution. Failure to recognize this fundamental justification of business, says Handy, is what leads to "suspicions about capitalism [that] are rooted in a feeling that its instruments, the corporations, are immoral in that they have no purpose other than themselves." Martijn Cremers makes a similar argument in chapter 10 of this volume when he explores these themes, calling for increased transparency, accountability, and social responsibility, characteristics that help prevent market participants from directly benefiting at the expense of others.

Summary of The First Section

The institutional insight may be defined as the realization that one's own institution—like all institutions—is part of a larger enterprise of seeking to fulfill its sector purposes (economic, political, or moral-cultural) and ultimately the dignity of human persons and the well-being of humankind. Leaders need a dual awareness: both foreground vision (zoom in) and concurrent peripheral vision (zoom out) in guiding their efforts, regardless of the sector in which they find themselves.

So, we must press the "mission question" at four distinct levels: about the purpose(s) of a business, of its industry, of its sector, and ultimately of all institutions taken together. We eventually arrive at the institutional point of view and why the common good is critical to making sense of institutions, as outlined in figure 6.2.

If business leaders settle for a limited, one-level measure of success (like return to stockholders), without the deeper levels, they deny themselves,

Mission level	The goal at this level	ABC Bank	JKL Automotive	XYZ Hospital
1. This business	The good served by this company	Banking services to a city	Parts for an automaker	Hospital services to a region
2. This industry	Role of this industry in society	Banking "services that truly serve . . ."	Automobiles: "Goods that are truly good . . ."	Health care: "services that truly serve . . ."
3. This social sector	Political, economic, or moral-cultural goals	Economic well-being	Economic well-being	Economic and moral-cultural well-being
4. The ultimate purpose of all institutions	The Common Good: The good of all persons and every person	Human need for resources and saving	Human need for transportation	Human need for health care (body, mind, and spirit)

Figure 6.2   What Is a Business For? Getting to the Moral Roots
of Business as an Institution

their employees, their customers, and their society the full benefits of the institution that is business. Similarly, if leaders focus only on the multidimensional purposes of stakeholders, they deny themselves and their shareholders the moral bonds that the culture and the common good afford. Both groups settle for less and increasingly depend upon either market incentives or procedural rules and contracts to carry the good of the business. Mary Hirschfeld makes an analogous argument in chapter 5, in distinguishing the creation paradigm from the technocratic paradigm. Similarly, in chapter 7 David Cloutier addresses the character of "good goods," pointing to the more fundamental issues at stake.

The deeper our awareness of the moral roots of our institutions in the common good, the sounder our moral outlook will be. As our awareness increases, we include not only the foreground of particular goods but also the background, the common good. The institutional insight then serves as an "integrative force." Here we see the importance of practical wisdom, as Andrew Yuengert explores in chapter 3, which assists in concretely connecting the good of a business to its industry, to the goods of the economic sector informed by the cultural and political sectors, and finally to the common good of our larger society. Both shareholder wealth-maximization and stakeholder interest-balancing are too weak to connect the good of a business to the good of society. What we need are not simply discrete particular goods defined in terms of interests but also common goods that belong to us collectively. It is this idea to which we now turn.

THE COMMON GOOD AS BASIC
TO HUMAN INSTITUTIONS

The common good as the moral foundation of all institutional forms answers the persistent question: "What's a business (or industry or sector) for?"

The "common good" is one of those ubiquitous terms that is often invoked but rarely defined. People are attracted to the phrase because they intuitively know that the common good, as an institutional principle, describes the way institutions work when they are at their best. For leaders who see themselves as institution builders, the common good articulates the unity of their diverse gifts and endeavors.

Yet the phrase "common good" is in danger of dissolving into an empty slogan if it is regularly repeated without content. The challenge of the phrase, like most noble phrases, is whether we can properly describe and define it and give it meaning for the institutions in which we find ourselves. To avoid the snare of generic and platitudinous use (which allows people to use the phrase to justify practically any action or ideology), we must locate, focus, and clarify what we mean by the common good, both in terms of a specific societal sector (i.e., moral-cultural, political, or economic) and a specific tradition (e.g., utilitarianism, Catholic social teaching, etc.).

Such a "sector-plus-tradition" framework is not optional. Whether explicitly or not, whatever one's definition of the common good, the use of the phrase invokes one or more of the three societal sectors, with their normative purposes, and arises out of a tradition of interpretation, even if the tradition is simply the secular humanism of our age. The common good is unavoidably a normative concept.

In the Catholic tradition, the common good is the principle that underlies all three sectors of society. In this chapter, we look primarily at economic sector institutions, including for-profit and not-for-profit organizations. Moreover, we speak of the common good from a distinct social tradition. This is important because we need to know what our terms mean and where they come from.

In the case of the common good, many tend to default to an individualistic, utilitarian tradition often expressed as "the greatest good for the greatest number." This is often how both shareholder and stakeholder views of business ethics are parsed. The greatest good, in this utilitarian tradition, is typically composed of goods that can be allocated through the market (incentives) or the state (regulations and contracts), so a larger number of people can benefit. These goods are often material goods involving production and consumption—interpreted as interest or preference satisfaction, with little attention given to the relationship between those satisfactions and human fulfillment. This utility-maximization approach, however, is not the understanding of the common good in the Catholic social tradition, which has worked out a formulation of the common good that is premised upon a distinct understanding of the human person and the relationship of the person to community.[28]

The Good of the Whole Person and of All Persons

Catholic social teaching, especially over the past sixty years, emphasizes the importance of "integral" or "authentic" human development—understood as the good of the whole person and of all persons (figure 6.3). Benedict XVI (like several popes before him and Pope Francis after him) affirms this conviction: "The truth of development consists in its completeness: if it does not involve the whole man and every man, it is not true development."[29]

Two dimensions of integral human development undergird the view of the common good in Catholic social thought, which can be defined as including both the good of the whole person (respecting the person in all the dimensions of his or her being) as well as the good of all persons (seeking, over time, through institutions, human fulfillment in community).[30] The good of the whole person cannot fully develop unless he or she exists with others and for others.[31] The common good must be both personal, with attention to the social (institutional), and social (institutional), with attention to the personal.

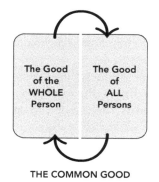

THE COMMON GOOD

Figure 6.3 The Inner Dynamism of the Common Good

Integral human development offers a window on the common good that is distinctive, in that it eschews the vocabulary of maximizing interests, for it insists on the dignity of each person and the dignity of the human community without compromise or trade-off. This is, of course, difficult to do in a fallen world, but it should be the fundamental hope of every leader. It is an understanding rooted in faith and reason, seeing humankind as truly a family with a shared Father: "As society becomes ever more globalized, it makes us neighbors but does not make us brothers. Reason, by itself, is capable of grasping the equality between men and of giving stability to their civic coexistence, but it cannot establish fraternity. This originates in a transcendent vocation from God the Father, who loved us first, teaching us through the Son what fraternal charity is."[32]

As these ideas apply to business and the economic sector, Benedict is drawing upon his predecessor, John Paul II, who in his encyclical *Centesimus annus* reminded us that

> of itself, an economic system does not possess criteria for correctly distinguishing new and higher forms of satisfying human needs from artificial new needs which hinder the formation of a mature personality. Thus, a great deal of educational and cultural work is urgently needed, including the education of consumers in the responsible use of their power of choice, the formation of a strong sense of responsibility among producers and among people in the mass media in particular, as well as the necessary intervention by public authorities.[33]

John Paul went on to insist that economic systems must be guided by "a comprehensive picture of man which respects all the dimensions of his being and which subordinates his material and instinctive dimensions to his interior and spiritual ones."[34] Whereas the Catholic perspective draws heavily upon the cultural sector of family and religion, shareholder thinking draws principally upon market-sector incentives and stakeholder thinking draws principally upon political-sector regulations.

Unlike utilitarianism or a generic relativism, Catholic social teaching offers a substantive perspective on the nature and ordering of human goods (from material and instinctive to interior and spiritual), as Martin Schlag offers in chapter 8, and a substantive perspective on the nature of human community. Without these substantive normative perspectives, there can be no meaningful understanding of the common good. Again, in chapter 5 Mary Hirschfeld provides the philosophical and theological background for these observations. Leaders in all sectors who embrace institutional awareness (as part of their dual awareness) must work toward what the *Catechism of the Catholic Church* describes as the common good, creating "social conditions which allow people, either as groups or as individuals, to reach their fulfillment more fully and more easily."[35]

There are two perspectives from which we can think about "social conditions" in relation to the common good.

First, from a cross-sectoral and developmental perspective, it takes many institutions in healthy relationships with one another to foster the common good.[36] No one social sector—whether political, economic, or moral-cultural—can embody the fullness of the common good. We need a network of relatively autonomous but interdependent and collaborating sectors (each with many institutions within it), and we must recognize their unique roles and contributions, for example:

- In the moral-cultural sector, family, education, and religion provide the initial formation on which the notion of the common good is introduced and grounded.
- In the economic sector, businesses and not-for-profit organizations provide many goods and services necessary for persons and communities to flourish.[37]
- In the political sector, government decisions—from Congress to the city council—provide "the juridical framework" (as John Paul II called it) within which daily life unfolds.

If a society does not have vibrant and relatively autonomous but collaborative social sectors, the conditions for social living suffer. When the structure or culture of moral-cultural life disintegrates, severe social and economic problems plague a community. Without a dynamic entrepreneurial economy, communities stagnate. Without prudent political decisions, neither the economy nor personal life will flourish. In other words, the common good emerges from a collaboration between the three sectors of culture, economics, and politics, each producing a set of common goods for the growth of people ("the good of the whole person and of all people").

Second, from a specific sectoral perspective, we can understand the social conditions necessary for the common good as the set of goods to which each social sector aspires, for itself and the wider society. Instead of focusing only on the particular interests of shareholders or stakeholders, we need to articulate the "common goods" that the institutions within each sector seek.

Because the focus of this volume is business, we can ask: What is the good to which business organizations in the economic sector aspire?[38] The Vatican document *Vocation of the Business Leader* speaks about three goods that business contributes to the common good of society:[39]

- Good goods: Making goods that are truly good and services that truly serve;
- Good work: Organizing work in which employees develop their gifts and talents so as to serve the larger community; and
- Good wealth: Creating sustainable wealth so that it can be distributed justly to the institution's contributors.

When all three goods are present, business contributes positively to the social conditions that engender integral human development, the flourishing of persons and communities.

Allocated and Participative Goods

Although the three goods identified above are critically important to business, by themselves, they are not sufficient to capture what we mean by the integral human development of those who have access to such goods. The goods of the economic sector contribute to but do not constitute the fullness of the common good. And this is true of the institutions in the other two sectors (political and cultural) as well.

The common good consists not merely in having good goods, good work, and good wealth. It also consists in the quality of relationships among people—the goods held in common that bind people in relationships leading to the integral development of each. These relationships will be at their core formed by all three sectors: the culture people come from (family, religion, education, etc.); the quality of the juridical framework (from local to national); and, the focus of our attention in this chapter, the specific organizational culture of the business in which people work. The local culture of a business affects not only what occurs there but also, because so many people, for most of their lives, spend more time at work than anywhere else except at home, it shapes the moral character of all who work there.

William O'Brien, the former CEO of Hanover Insurance Group, explained that even in workplaces where good goods and services are generated for customers and clients, where good work is fostered by enlightened human resource practices that treat people well, and where good wealth is created and distributed, people still can be dispirited because their work lacks relationships and meaning.[40] Companies can have the proper social conditions in place but still lack community and, ultimately, fail to contribute to integral human development.

An allegory from Chinese literature on the surprising difference between hell and heaven can help us with this point of relationships and culture:

> Hell is a room with a big table full of bowls of delicious steaming rice. People sit around the table, and each has chopsticks in his or her hands to eat the rice. However, the chopsticks are so long that nobody is able to eat, and instead pokes the others in the eyes and face. There ensues a constant and bitter fight, and consequently people starve in front of the bowls of food.
>
> Heaven is quite different. The room is the same, the table with the rice bowls is the same, even the chopsticks are just as long and cumbersome. However, instead of fighting, the diners feed each other in sublime harmony. They have a real common good.[41]

In hell, people have the things—chopsticks, bowls, rice—but their only interest is in feeding themselves. Hell is the clash of individual preferences and interests. What makes heaven different from hell is not the things, but the purpose: to feed the other, the arts of cooperation, the bonds of communion—in a word, a love that produces relationships that build authentic community.

Business leaders and owners who are self-interested maximizers—who instrumentalize relationships—are calculators of interests rather than protectors and nurturers of the good. Their calculations may for a time generate the goods of the business, but they will not foster organizational culture that cultivates trust and deep relationships among employees. The reason for this can be expressed in an important distinction within the common good tradition between allocative and participative goods and the relationship between the two.

Allocative goods diminish when shared. Participative goods grow when shared. Allocative goods are material goods. They are divisional and represent a sum zero reality; participative goods are relational, typically immaterial, and cannot be parsed into pieces. When a group of people shares a pizza at a meal, the pizza as a material good diminishes through the division. But if good conversations are occurring, with a sense that each person wants others to have their share of pizza, relationships among the group start to develop. This group is not only sharing pizza that is diminishing; they are also expanding relationships and community. The more they share the good conversation, the more they are concerned that others have enough to eat, the more they build a community among themselves. This is why the Catholic social tradition considers the common good to be more than the sum of individual goods (those goods that are allocated). The key is how the allocation serves to build a community of persons where relationships are strengthened.

Within business, the allocation of resources is a central task of leaders. Resources are limited, and when they are distributed, one group will get more and another less. When a business makes a profit from the prices they charge to the consumer, there is a limited amount they can distribute to bonuses, dividends, capital investment, future wage increases, training and development for employees, charitable contributions to the civic community, and so on. This distribution of wealth, however, is never a value-neutral activity. This is why solidarity and justice are so important as they relate to the distribution of goods.

When a business distributes its resources justly, it participates in justice. But when a business fails to pay a living wage or when it gouges vulnerable customers with higher prices, or when it manipulates smaller suppliers by delaying their payments, the lack of justice prevents the development of a community of persons. Such a business is only concerned about allocating the maximum economic goods to itself. In chapter 2 of this volume, Jennifer Herdt helpfully traces the historical development of this distorted view of interest.

The second kind of allocation—the sharing of participative goods—happens without diminishment. When a candle lights another candle, it loses nothing. When the vibrant moral purpose of a company is shared throughout the organization, nothing is diminished, and great power is generated throughout.

When someone is treated with justice, he or she is more prone to respond with justice; and when two people treat each other justly, they trust each other more with each succeeding decision. They have less need for onerous contracts that specify obligations in great detail. They spend less time checking up on each other, and they are more willing to make sacrifices for the good of the other. Employees are more likely to stay at their company despite challenges and tensions, reducing turnover. All these qualities contribute to the organizational culture and morale of the business. They make business more meaningful, usually more enjoyable, and in most cases more effective.

Shared purpose is a critical success factor for world-class companies because it is one of those qualities where the lights start to go on throughout the whole firm. Justice, love, and moral purpose increase the more they are shared. The interviews with CEOs presented in chapter 1 demonstrate this sort of commitment from business leaders.

THE CHALLENGE OF TELEOPATHY

Our analysis of the common good provides a richer and "thicker" normative description of what we call good business. To describe business only in terms of shareholder and stakeholder categories is to describe a morally impoverished space. A similar argument is made by Gregory Beabout in chapter 4, where he explores the value of the Neo-Aristotelian "grammar" for helping business professionals (and students who plan to be business professionals) to articulate their motivations and desires in a more socially nuanced manner.

Shareholder and stakeholder categories constrain our thinking because they typically focus on allocative goods that diminish when shared, and they ignore or discount participative goods that do not diminish when shared. The shareholder model, with its thin normative framework, sees the common good as shareholder wealth-maximization. This, it is claimed, provides the greatest amount of wealth for the greatest number of people. The stakeholder model, with a similarly thin normative framework, sees the common good as a more just distribution of allocated goods to the various stakeholders based on their rights and interests. The value of these models is indisputable: if a business does not create wealth, it cannot distribute it—and it needs to find ways to distribute allocated goods to its contributors justly. But their "thinness" results from failing to draw upon the primary institutions of the cultural sector, defaulting to a utilitarian view of ethics that sees businesses as collections of individuals. Leaders need more if they seek to create and sustain a good business.

The institutional insight and its foundation in the common good remind us of what is too often lost in an individualistic and consumeristic culture, a culture that is preoccupied with the choices and interests of the consumer, the employee, the shareholder, and the like.

The moral insight offers a corrective: I cannot achieve my good except by ordering it toward your good in such a way that we develop a community. Writ large, the moral insight reveals the institutional insight: if a business fails to order its particular goods to its industry and its sector, and ultimately to a common life of desire and action—a common good—its particular goods or services will lead to a thin corporate purpose that lacks moral and spiritual roots. The development of a business is and should be integrally connected to the development of a community. No doubt, in a fallen world, this is extremely difficult to do; but it is the vision that leaders must bring to their institutions if they are to flourish.

We saw earlier in this chapter the importance of our ordering lower and higher goods. For social conditions and goods to encourage the development of the whole person, we must order them in relation to the good of others. Thomas Aquinas made this point more than seven hundred years ago: "A man's will is not right in willing a particular good, unless he refer it to the common as an end."[42] It is precisely in this willing that people form bonds of connection and create authentic community. In other words, the common good is not only about doing good and achieving the three goods of business, it is also about being good. And at the heart of being good are relationships and the development of a community of persons. The common good calls for concern about the deep relational structure of our actions and not just about their overt consequences that dominate the shareholder and stakeholder approaches.

Forgetting the Institutional Insight
by Fixating on the Foreground

A significant impediment to the dual awareness of the institutional insight anchored in the common good is a kind of fixation on the foreground that we might call "teleopathy" (from the Greek "telos," or goal): the disordered "pursuit of purpose in individuals or institutions."[43] The US Department of Defense has identified a hazard in the training of fighter pilots that also applies to institutions: "Channelized attention is a factor when the individual is focusing all conscious attention on a limited number of environmental cues to the exclusion of others of a subjectively equal or higher or more imme-diate priority, leading to an unsafe situation. It may be described as a tight focus of attention that leads to the exclusion of comprehensive situational information."[44]

When a business fails to be the best version of itself, it creates a small moral world, typically built around balancing interests and instrumental rationality, and the people within it lose the capacity to sacrifice and suffer for the good of the institution. The firm manifests a tight focus of attention that leads to the exclusion of comprehensive situational [institutional] information.

Leaders who fail to draw upon the ultimate, institutional reasons for their being are prone to multiple disorders. On one hand, they can default into procedural and instrumental reasons to explain why they exist. When leaders ignore or forget the moral and spiritual purpose of their institutions, they often capitulate to bureaucratic and procedural forces, focusing on either instrumental goods—such as efficiency, rewards, growth, margins, market share, and rankings—or on values that are so generic and slogan-like that they inspire little loyalty or conviction. On the other hand, leaders can err in overemphasizing the institutional background to the point of not serving the needs of the business. In the end, business leaders need to exercise steward-ship in two ways (zooming in and zooming out), not just one.

The fixation on the foreground implied by teleopathy obscures the insti-tutional purpose in the background. This is made worse by the hesitation within a pluralistic culture to address religious and spiritual questions in rela-tion to work. The result can be an evasion of discourse about the transcendent in discussing historical roots (recall chapter 2 by Jennifer Herdt) and the contemporary challenges of business. This illustrates the importance (and inevitability) of interpreting the common good through the lens of a tradition.

It is possible, as we have observed, to parse the common good in strictly secular terms. But these terms, especially within an increasingly technological and secular culture, make it difficult to understand the common in common good as more than responsiveness to the individual preferences of the majority of people in a society. A faith-based understanding of the common good sees it more like the good of a family, in which preferences are not the most important moral "data." The good of a family includes but also transcends the particular goods of its members and attends to the *integral* development of each person.

Institutionally, the common good is reflected in the way we share goods in common that build up a community of persons, whereby the person has access to a deeper integral development. Some in the tradition have called this "communitarian personalism." This is radically different from the shareholder and stakeholder views that largely see business as a collection of individuals held together by an aggregation of interests (what some have called a "liberal individualism.") The Catholic social tradition speaks of a business as a community of persons, as a metaphysical reality that predates outcomes, that frames them. This highlights not only the moral but also the spiritual roots of the common good within business.

CONCLUSION

The common good in Catholic social teaching presupposes that the community of persons found in business has a basis within the cultural institution of the family and religion, which is ultimately grounded in human nature because we are created in the image of God who is Trinitarian—a community of persons. We as humankind can have a common good because of this divine "We." Faith lies in the background of the "We"—our (common) Father. It is in this spiritual dimension of the common good that we begin to grasp our vocation at work, the universal destination of material goods, the created order of the natural environment, and the virtue of love—all of which guide us in creating a good business and making the world a better place.

Finally, we must remember that in the Catholic social tradition, the common good is not some kind of unending evolutionary social progress. Instead, the common good culminates in an identity—a family (our Father), a "kingdom," the reign of God that diminishes for no one when it is shared.

As Max Scheler and Werner Stark put it, "the final goal of all human restless-ness is calm meditation on the divine majesty, instead of a kind of unending improvement—as it was for nearly every modern thinker."[45] In its ultimate articulation, the goal is not work but calm, expressed through a contempla-tive outlook that not only achieves but also receives. Although not all people will agree on this ultimate resting place, this end has enabled the Catholic social tradition to articulate its understanding of the common good and sup-port what we have called the institutional insight that should ground every business.

NOTES

1. Heclo, *On Thinking Institutionally*, 101.
2. Kennedy, "Most Americans Trust the Military."
3. Selznick, *Leadership*.
4. Bartlett and Ghoshal, "Changing the Role."
5. Frankena, *Ethics*, 69–70.
6. Royce, *Religious Aspect*, 155–56.
7. Nagel, *What Does It All Mean?*
8. Heclo, *On Thinking Institutionally*, 127.
9. Heclo, 85.
10. Heclo, 154.
11. Walsh and Donaldson. "Toward a Theory of Business."
12. Moss Kanter, "Managing Yourself."
13. Goodpaster, "Human Dignity."
14. Heclo, *On Thinking Institutionally*, 33.
15. Naughton, *Logic of Gift*.
16. Goodpaster, "Corporate Responsibility," 140.
17. Eisenhardt, "Agency Theory."
18. Goodpaster, "Corporate Responsibility."
19. Moore, *Principia Ethica*.
20. Freeman, "Stakeholder Theory," 126.
21. Goodpaster, "Business Ethics."
22. Marcoux, "Fiduciary Argument."
23. Heath, "Business Ethics."
24. Walsh and Donaldson, "Toward a Theory of Business."
25. Selznick, *Leadership*, 141.
26. Novak, *Spirit*, 56.
27. Handy, "What's a Business For?"
28. See Maritain, "Person"; and De Koninck, "Primacy."
29. Benedict XVI, *Caritas in veritate*, para. 18.
30. Pontifical Council for Justice and Peace, *Compendium*, section 165.
31. Pontifical Council for Justice and Peace.
32. Pontifical Council for Justice and Peace, 19.

33. John Paul II, *Centesimus annus*, para. 36.
34. John Paul II.
35. *Catechism of the Catholic Church.*
36. Lewis, "Is the Common Good an Ensemble?"
37. Habiger Institute for Catholic Leadership, *True Leadership.*
38. Kennedy, *Good That Business Does.*
39. Pontifical Council for Justice and Peace, *Vocation.*
40. O'Brien, *Character*, 104.
41. From an unpublished paper by Father Martin Schlag.
42. Aquinas, *ST*, I-II, q. 19, a. 10.
43. Goodpaster, *Conscience*, chap. 1.
44. US Department of Defense, *Inspector General Report*, 3.
45. Scheler and Stark, "Thomist Ethic."

CHAPTER 7

How Consumers and Firms Can Seek Good Goods

David Cloutier

This volume addresses the morality of business, and the most basic thing firms do is to produce and sell goods—and services—to their customers. The question naturally arises: Are those products actually good for the people who ultimately use them? Are they good goods? The classic answer to this question was provided by Adam Smith and centered on the interests of those producers.

Smith famously intuited that "it is not from the benevolence of the butcher, the brewer, or the baker that we expect our dinner, but from their regard to their own interest."[1] Out of self-interest, those merchants produce "good goods"—or else their customers will leave and buy from a competitor. Thus, markets align the interests of producers and consumers to produce high-quality goods that people actually want. Evidence for this confidence in markets ranges from the bad effects of suspending markets (e.g., the defective cars and televisions produced by Soviet regimes) to the positive effects of market competition (e.g., the exposure of the American auto industry of the 1970s to higher-quality Japanese competition). As Jennifer Herdt notes in chapter 2 of this volume, although Smith is not an antigovernment libertarian, he was struck by "the unintended effects of human actions." In this case, the seeking of private gain in business in small, competitive markets leads to better-quality products and more of them.

Many businesspeople have no difficulty identifying the self-interest of their business with providing quality goods that consumers want. Gina Wolfe's interviews with three business leaders, described in chapter 1 of this volume, confirm it: "Without exception," she writes, they defined the purpose of business as "meet[ing] real needs of their customers and clients" through "providing quality goods and services." Even the controversial libertarian Charles Koch defends his approach in terms of "good profit," which he defines as "creating superior value for our customers while consuming fewer resources and always acting lawfully and with integrity. Good profit comes from making a contribution to society—not from corporate welfare or other ways of taking advantage of people."[2] Koch's argument for his unique management approach is that it ultimately delivers for customers: "No one can decide which products and services a customer values better than the customer. Dedicating ourselves to satisfying what she values is showing respect for her."[3]

Yet markets do not automatically lead people to value the right things. The Vatican document *The Vocation of the Business Leader* states that business leaders must "serve the common good by creating goods that are truly good and services that truly serve," ones that "meet authentic human needs" and contribute "to human development and fulfillment."[4] The implication is that some businesses do not do this.

Of course, even Charles Koch rejects forms of rent-seeking that "improves the welfare of someone at the expense of the welfare of someone else," instead of by creating value for society.[5] Criticism of rent-seeking transcends ideology. For example, Joseph Stiglitz explains that the backlash against "big banks" during the Great Recession happened because it became "clear that it was *not* contribution to society that determined relative pay" but rather the ability to set the rules of the game to favor their interests. Stiglitz and Koch disagree about much, but they agree that rent-seeking is the antithesis of what good businesses should do: create real value for the consumer.[6]

This chapter thus asks: to what extent does this creation of real economic value correspond to what the Catholic tradition means by the responsibility of a business to produce "good goods"? It is only the start. The more extensive answer will proceed in four stages. First, I outline the general principles regarding "good goods" in Catholic social thought in a way that develops more explicit norms for judgment about such goods. Second, I engage these norms in dialogue with standard accounts of how consumers actually make choices in advanced economies. Third, I examine the ways the agency of firms, presumably acting out of self-interest, attempt to shape consumer agency, paying particular attention to how this shaping can contradict Catholic social thought. Fourth and finally, I raise questions about the collective character of consumption, which require attention to broader structures within which consumers and firms exercise their respective agencies.

GOOD GOODS: FROM GENERAL PRINCIPLES
TO NORMS FOR JUDGMENTS

Paul VI indicated that Catholic social thought consists of three categories: general principles, norms for judgment, and directives for action.[7] The middle category is least developed yet most crucial. Without norms for judgment, competing arguments over specific choices or policies can each plausibly appeal to the same general principles. For example, the principle of work as central to human dignity can be used to support pro-union policies (unions protect worker rights) or to weaken such policies (unions can protect irresponsible workers). A clearer discussion requires norms for judgment about what the general principle of the dignity of work is supposed to mean—for example, John Paul's norm that the "subjective value" of work is more important than its "objective value."[8]

Thus, the first task for the chapter is to develop a more detailed set of criteria for deciding what are good goods. To begin, it is helpful to distinguish three categories of goods that are questionably good.

The first category is "defective" goods. Little need be said about this. No consumer actively seeks shoddy goods or bad service; and in theory, firms subject to market competition will fail if they supply such goods. In Gina Wolfe's interview with Joan Wrenn, recounted in chapter 1, Wrenn criticizes firms that make parts that do not last. Carelessness and deception by firms are not in their self-interest, especially if an appropriate juridical framework is in place.[9] Of course, there are still plenty of instances of poor service and badly made goods, but (1) the moral categories for criticizing firms that act in these ways are undisputed, and (2) the exercise of market-driven self-interest ought to penalize the producers and solve these problems.

A second category consists of "harmful" goods. John Paul cites drug use as an instance of "artificial consumption" that "implies a materialistic and ... destructive 'reading' of human needs" in which product innovation comes "to a one-sided and inadequate conclusion" because products "exploit the frailty of the weak."[10] The Vocation of the Business Leader offers a list of examples: "the sale of non-therapeutic drugs, pornography, gambling, violent video games, and other harmful products."[11] More is said about harmful goods below.

Finally, a third category can be labeled "futile" goods.[12] These entail confusion between genuine goods and "mere wants." These goods involve "a demand for quality" that is "of itself legitimate" but that "must be guided by a comprehensive picture of man which respects all the dimensions of his being and which subordinates his material and instinctive dimensions to his interior and spiritual ones."[13] It is wrong, John Paul suggests, to desire to "have more, in order to spend life in enjoyment as an end in itself."[14] Although not obviously harmful in themselves, futile goods are not properly ordered to higher ends. This third category requires the development of further norms for appropriate ordering—especially in affluent economies whose productive potential far exceeds mere subsistence.

When developing norms for judgment about good goods, authors have typically focused on "harmful goods." This raises challenging questions. Consider gambling. In the quotation above, "gambling" is harmful; a few sentences further, the document refers to a "hierarchical order" in which "the need for nutritious goods . . . clearly outweighs the wants of gambling entertainment." True enough, but what if a family or a society has sufficient nutritious goods? Can gambling then be a legitimate desire for recreation, if satisfied in modest ways? Or is it still definitely "harmful"? What about riflery, when connected to the widespread, sometimes-unintentional harm done by privately owned guns? What about the recreation of extensive leisure travel, which depends heavily on harmful fossil fuel consumption?

An example of this unclarity is presented in chapter 1, where Joan Wrenn (whose firm makes precision parts for a whole range of uses, including bombs) notes that even bombs can be understood as protective, so it is "a double edge." Simultaneously, she states a second, quite different defense: that *someone else* would produce these bomb parts if her firm did not. Wrenn's honorable if unresolved wrestling with this question depicts how little clarity we have on the question of "harmful" goods. In chapter 4 Gregory Beabout examines the "divided" account of agency produced when the language of business self-interest prevents the development of a more robust "grammar" for deliberating about the relative worth of different ends in situations less straightforward than those envisioned by Smith.

In developing this grammar, some scholars have focused their discussion of "good goods" on businesses' responsibilities toward less-obvious instances of direct harm. This is a helpful step. For example, Gene Laczniak and his collaborators suggest that companies must prioritize product safety, helpfully identifying a norm for judgment.[15] Recent debates about gun regulation note that the technology exists for manufacturing "smart" guns that would only work for specified users; this would eliminate a major category of gun deaths due to accidental discharge, as well as minimize the possibility that others in a household could use the guns.[16] Gun manufacturers are reluctant to do this and thereby tolerate significant harm that could be prevented.

In a similar vein, Kenneth Goodpaster also argues that businesses have a responsibility to account for the *full* effects of their products, including harmful environmental effects "from production through recycling" and harmful effects that "reinforce dysfunctional consumer habits."[17] In the latter category, he cites things like texting and driving and tobacco advertising.

Laczniak also calls for firms to avoid ultimately harmful pricing schemes "that take advantage of information asymmetries and/or buyer weakness."[18] The consumer advocate Bob Sullivan chronicles countless business strategies he dubs "gotcha capitalism," which intentionally play on the weakness of some consumers. Sullivan cites a pair of economists who distinguish between "sophisticates" and "myopes." The former will pay every bill on time, think of every possible surcharge, shop around when an introductory rate disappears, and the like, whereas the latter will in effect subsidize the former by making predictable mistakes in consumption decisions.[19] Although some of these "sneaky fees" may represent legitimate incentives or deterrents, many are part of an overall business plan that is in effect a (concealed) part of the product being sold.

It is tempting to stop the discussion of "good goods" at this juncture. As Laczniak notes, "most products can be used (as well as promoted and distributed) for good or evil."[20] However, the question of appropriate criteria for identifying "futile" goods is left undeveloped. Yet, given that Catholic social thought insists that there is an "objective order" of some sort, there must be *some* norms for judgment that can help both consumers and businesspeople of goodwill direct their decisions in accord with that order.[21]

NORMS FOR JUDGING FUTILE GOODS

John Paul II claims that "of itself, an economic system does not possess criteria for correctly distinguishing new and higher forms of satisfying human needs from artificial new needs which hinder the formation of a mature personality."[22] Here especially is where the initial market claim to "create value for customers" needs supplementation. Paul VI, in *Populorum progressio*, outlines an order, which is carried through John Paul II's encyclicals, as the proper subordination of "having" to "being":

> Conditions that are more human: the passage from misery towards the possession of necessities, victory over social scourges, the growth of knowledge, the acquisition of culture. Additional conditions that are more human: increased esteem for the dignity of others, the turning toward the spirit of poverty, cooperation for the common good, the will and desire for peace. Conditions that are still more human:

the acknowledgment by man of supreme values, and of God their source and their finality. Conditions that, finally and above all, are more human: faith, a gift of God accepted by the good will of man, and unity in the charity of Christ, Who calls us all to share as sons in the life of the living God, the Father of all men.[23]

Paul VI's sketch clarifies the content of John Paul's "formation of a mature personality." The first level would be goods that met basic material needs, in efficient ways, for all. Beyond the importance of food, clothing, shelter, and routine medical care, Paul VI also rightly includes some level of education and culture as basic. These claims about basic needs are embedded throughout Catholic social thought: the principles of a just wage and of the universal destination of goods both require a specification of "necessity" along these lines. Basic needs are "first level" not because they are less important, but rather because they are "foundational," in the sense the term is used by Helen Alford and Michael Naughton.[24] These ends are essential, and yet they are properly ordered as a means or instrument for the sake of achieving higher goods.

This understanding can shape norms for judgments for meeting basic needs themselves. For example, the food necessary is food that would be healthful—or if not healthful, then of a celebratory quality that serves to mark a special occasion. Thus, an ongoing expansion of basic needs—fancier food and housing, for example—would suggest the possibility of "futile" goods: these elaborations would not direct their possessor to higher levels of human flourishing.

However, this ordering depends on the claim that *alternative* higher goods ought to be pursued instead. How do we name those levels? In *Populorum progressio*, Paul VI states that "every life is a vocation."[25] Every life—not just those in wealthier nations—deserves "integral human development." This is the language of "having more" in order to "be more" that John Paul II adopts in his discussion of inappropriate superdevelopment.[26]

This notion of personal vocation can serve as a powerful norm for judgment about worthwhile and futile consumption beyond necessities. It is developed in some detail in the moral theology of Germain Grisez. Although he is best known for his rigorous defense of certain moral absolutes, Grisez's project is more deeply animated by Vatican Council II's call for "integral human fulfillment." He quotes the council's claim that we "will find again . . . all the good fruits of our nature and enterprise" in the final Kingdom of Christ.[27] For Grisez, this means that all choices, including consumer choices, must be subject to our destiny in the Kingdom of God. For individuals, this destiny is in part the fulfillment of our "personal vocation," realized through our choices over time. Specifically, such choices should increasingly reflect our commitment to the Kingdom. He contrasts a life in which one seeks to *make commitments* with a life that seeks to *satisfy preferences*. This is especially true in our choices relating to all sorts of material goods and even of leisure activities. "Christians should subordinate possessions to the Kingdom," which means that "an individual's personal vocation or a group's proper mission provides the standard for judgments about acquiring, holding, and disposing of things."[28] Any other "having" simply gets in the way.

Of course, Grisez also acknowledges that there is an obligation to share with others.[29] Thus, Grisez's idea of personal vocation must be connected to a notion of "having" that also aims at "the dignity of others" and "cooperation for the common good."[30] The common good and personal vocation are not competing but complementary criteria. Catholic social thought is careful to avoid collectivism, in which persons subordinate themselves to social systems, but at the same time it avoids individualism, by recognizing that the person's nature and destiny are intrinsically communal.[31] While there are extensive debates about the meaning of "common good" in Catholic social thought, especially in relation to the modern state,[32] the *Catechism* insists that, once basic needs are met, one's possessions should "allow for a natural solidarity" to develop in which such ownership "can benefit others as well as himself."[33] For the purposes of this discussion, "common good" can refer to any and all associations in which the consumption of goods aims at "natural solidarity," rather than exclusively private benefit.

Corresponding to Grisez's narration of "futile" consumption as preference satisfaction unrelated to vocation, "futile" ownership in relation to the common good is captured by John Paul II's powerful reappropriation of the Marxist idea of alienation. Marx did not understand what real alienation was because he did not have a proper conception of the human person. The human person, for John Paul, is ultimately aimed at the gift of self. Therefore, genuine alienation "happens in consumerism, when people are ensnared in a web of false and superficial gratifications rather than being helped to experience their personhood in an authentic and concrete way." He explains that "a person is alienated if he refuses to transcend himself and to live the experience of self-giving and of the formation of an authentic human community oriented towards his final destiny, which is God. A society is alienated if its forms of social organization, production and consumption make it more difficult to offer this gift of self and to establish this solidarity between people."[34] Similarly, Benedict XVI's core argument is that market transactions themselves should not simply maximize economic value but allow for "quotas of gratuitousness" that enact John Paul II's claims about the necessity of self-gift.[35]

Beyond and above the pursuit of personal vocation and natural solidarity, Catholic social thought's vision of even higher goods aims at "the infinite bond which unites" the person to their Creator.[36] This bond applies to all, thus generating "a recognition that the human race is a single family working together in true communion."[37] The Church is a "sacrament" of this shared human destiny in communion with God.[38] And it is within the mystery of Christ that persons are "fully revealed" to themselves, including their "one and divine" vocation.[39] Thus, "being more" is ultimately a matter of life in the Spirit, in which material goods and services foster the "special relationship with the Creator, who is [the person's] sole end."[40] Therefore, a good that enabled both individuals and community to improve on a temporal level but that somehow obscured human transcendence could be "futile." More pointedly, the temporal, nonbasic goods into which we pour our deepest dreams and energies—things like sport or fine arts—must somehow direct us to this transcendent end, rather than tacitly substitute for or actively marginalize it.

HOW DO CONSUMERS EXERCISE AGENCY?

This explication of norms that order "having" to "being" takes us some way toward a richer ability to pinpoint concerns about futile goods. But what does this have to do with business? Is not such an ordering simply a matter of consumers choosing rightly? Or, following Martin Schlag's argument in chapter 8 of this volume, do firms have a responsibility for the social context within which they operate?

The answer to these questions is obviously complex. In chapter 4 Gregory Beabout helpfully investigates the character of human agency; we need to bring these philosophical insights about agents properly ordering goods into dialogue with the literature on how consumers actually choose in the marketplace. After that conversation, we will be in a better place to assess how businesses affect this agency.

Those who criticize "consumerism" and consumer agency in affluent societies sometimes make sweeping claims; these often insightfully identify a particular pattern or process but overgeneralize. In order to be more precise, three approaches to consumer agency can be distinguished, in varying answers to the question "why is Mr. X buying/using Y if he doesn't need it?" One is ancient; two others arise from the literature on consumer society in the twentieth century.

The first is what might be called the "luxury account," the dominant explanation in Western philosophy going back to the ancients. It depends on a sharp distinction between consumption to meet basic needs and "luxury consumption," which is typically understood as an inordinate attention to bodily pleasure and comfort.[41]

The papal encyclicals assume something like the "luxury" account of futile consumption. As Colin Campbell notes, most critiques of consumer society still assume that a core problem with consumerism is that "want-driven consumption" is "unnecessary" insofar as it is "contrasted with 'real,' significant activities such as work, religion, or politics."[42] This is certainly true of the encyclicals in their ordering of lower goods to higher goods. Thus, the tradition rightly retains some distinction between necessities and luxuries.

Still, this distinction is challenging. It seems reasonable to assume that many goods and services people now find basic—from household refrigeration to an Internet connection—are not problematic even though these were once luxuries. But where is the line drawn? The theologian Craig Gay suggests that much consumer culture is not very hedonistic but is "highly risk averse and geared largely toward relatively mundane and antiheroic creature comforts."[43]

In my own work on luxury, I drew on Adam Ferguson's careful recognition that commercial society is problematic because it produces people "who shrink from small inconveniences" and may even come to see "these conveniences as the principal object of human life" in comparison with "friends, to a country, or to mankind."[44] The danger is not with luxury items themselves, but with our becoming preoccupied with them in ways that block higher goods. Many distracting habitual comforts might fit these descriptions; and as I emphasize in my book, the concern is not with occasional use but with a habitual attachment to them.[45]

This appeal to limiting luxury, however, is just a start. As William Cavanaugh has pointed out, "most people do not simply choose material goods over spiritual values." Rather, consumerism is a matter of the "commodification" of everything—even religion—rendering everything "a way of pursuing meaning and identity" via the ongoing rituals of buying.[46]

Thus, the second answer to the question "Why is Mr. X buying/using Y?" involves consumption that is too closely tied to one's identity. This identity-through-consumption recognizes that "having" is oriented to "being," but it is mistaken about what "being more" really means. Included here are variations on Thorstein's Veblen's thesis about "conspicuous consumption" as status signaling.[47] Other examples explain consumption as a form of Romanticist identity creation and self-expression.[48]

This is no ivory tower critique. Marketing professionals and marketing textbooks themselves lay much stress on this element of consumer behavior.

For example, one text explains at length various "psychographic" profiling systems for different lifestyle niches. A lifestyle, the book explains, "is more than the allocation of discretionary income" but rather "a statement about who one is in society and who one is *not*" (emphasis in the original).[49] Another text explains "the intimate link between products and self-identity" via a concept of "the extended self," especially in light of the constant reconstruction and maintenance of visible identities in the virtual world.[50] Linking a good or service with a particular sort of lifestyle identity can be done in many ways: through advertising imagery, through demographically savvy celebrity product endorsement, through the specific refinements of customer experience associated with the good or service (e.g., Apple stores), and increasingly through peer-driven endorsements on social media.

Is this construction of identity through consumer choices "futile"? The answer is complex. For example, Allan Kimmel notes a study in which buyers of the Toyota Prius most frequently described their purchase in terms of identity, one stating straightforwardly, "I really want people to know I care about the environment."[51] This statement might be read in two ways: as self-serving status signaling or as a real commitment to make a significant consumer choice that is best for the environment *and* to communicate that choice in order to strengthen others' commitment. Thus, even the signaling function could be understood as oriented correctly to personal vocation and the common good. Moreover, identity formation through consumption does create real community—not by itself, of course, but by drawing together a group of people with similar interests or commitments that may foster genuine friendship.

The third answer to the question "Why is Mr. X buying/using Y?" involves a final distortion that is more clearly problematic: consumption as one's goal. Consumption of goods and services itself *becomes* the end of life. "Being" ultimately serves "having." Other identities (worker, citizen, religious adherent) either become instrumentalized toward sophisticated consumption or become crowded out entirely. Especially in a society where, as Charles Taylor puts it, it becomes possible and even common to see life entirely within an "imminent frame," this reversal can, gradually yet thoroughly, take over life.

I emphasize "gradually" because the description of "living to shop" conjures up cartoonish images of the frenzied consumer whose whole life is about finding the latest product. This seems rare. But more readily envisioned might be the "bucket list" person, whose life ambitions have to do with a set of ongoing travel experiences, constantly enhanceable housing, or an entrenched set of novelty-seeking leisure habits (e.g., new restaurants, the latest craft beer)—without any sense of this activity having any significance beyond the consumption of the experiences themselves. People may choose jobs because of the geographical attractiveness of consumption goods or even because of the "perks," from travel to in-house gourmet cuisine. Alternatively, they choose retirement in a state where one can pay little to no tax, even though one has no civic connection to the place. Or they seek out religious communities based on "getting something out of it." All these examples can be qualified in different ways, but they involve an implied reversal about what is important in life. For those in the middle of life, taken up with work and family commitments, this may not be easily seen. Yet especially for younger digital natives and relatively well-off retirees, this vision of a good life of novel, stimulating consumption may be quite powerful, taking much time and money. Moreover, especially when these bucket lists tend toward consuming "experiences," and experiences that can *seem* very social, one can miss the way in which this is just another form of "having."

FIRMS AS AGENTS: NAMING HOW BUSINESSES SHAPE THE HIERARCHY

I have portrayed three forms of consumer agency—luxury consumption, identity-driven consumption, and consumption as de facto life goal—as different ways in which a proper ordering of goods can become distorted, rendering consumption futile. Although I have named specific goods and services as examples of how this can happen, one cannot easily identify specific goods and services themselves as *inherently* futile. Instead, it is in the way that goods and services are used. In principle, markets and firms simply respond to well-ordered or badly ordered consumers. If drinking alcohol is sometimes acceptable and sometimes futile, it cannot be that the liquor store bears responsibility for ascertaining which of its customers has a drinking problem and which are using alcohol temperately. If consumers pursued "self-interest" properly—in terms of one's personal vocation, local communities, and religious commitments—markets mechanisms could serve them efficiently.

Yet this picture is too simple, in two ways. First, markets assume interaction of self-interest between consumer and producer, and so the definition of "self-interest" on the side of the business cannot be neglected. Largely through marketing their products in certain ways, businesses use their agency in part to shape the agency of consumers—and in doing so, communicate either a proper or distorted hierarchy of goods. Second, markets always exist within structures of state and culture. The banker David Bochnowski, interviewed in chapter 1, faces the Community Reinvestment Act, which requires his bank—and, importantly, his competitors also—to forgo maximum profits

and invest locally. Few industries face a similar requirement, but both structures and culture can themselves be examined, critiqued, and reformed in line
with some account of what a proper ordering of goods looks like. Thus, I first
examine the point about the agency of firms, and then, in the next section, the
structures within which consumers and firms operate.

Shaping Consumer Choices

As I noted at the outset, the most common defense of business is that good
businesses generally create good goods and services that "deliver value for
their customers" because it is in the firm's self-interest to do so. The common
objection to this claim points to the ubiquitous role of advertising and marketing in driving consumption. Are not businesses also in the "business" of
defining what is valuable for their customers? Yet the standard reply to this
objection suggests that marketing exists "to create awareness that needs exist,
not to create needs," and that the failure rate of new products proves that
"advertisers simply do not know enough about people to manipulate them."[52]

Although this is literally true—advertising does not *coerce*—it is striking that the same textbook, after its initial chapter titled "Consumers Rule,"
spends most of its time telling readers all about how these consumers have
certain tendencies, lifestyles, and identities, knowledge of which should be
used to convince some group of people that they need your product. In its
first pages, the book gives the example of the fact that fast-food "heavy users"
make up "only one of five customers" but account "for about 60 percent of all
visits," and then notes that "Taco Bell developed the Chalupa, a deep-fried
and higher-calorie version of its Gordita stuffed taco, to appeal to its heavy
users."[53] The company is not just passively reacting but is exercising agency
and intention, in this case on a segment of consumers who are the ones using
the product problematically.

According to Catholic social thought, a firm's agency in offering an implied
vision of flourishing connected to the product need not be nefarious . . . so
long as it is shaped by a correct picture of the human person. But tellingly,
the textbook does not offer anything like a natural human anthropology, but
rather slices and dices consumer behavior based on changing cultural norms
that firms must somehow capture. Indeed, there are sections on "values," but
they involve things like a marketing instrument that "identifies nine consumer segments based on the values they endorse and relates each value to
differences in consumption behavior."[54] This may still seem "responsive,"
except the extent to which the marketing segments are self-fulfilling proph-
ecies is never clear. Is the marketer simply responding to a link? Perhaps in

some cases. But in other cases the marketer is actively creating the link, trying to lock in their good or service to the "value segment."

Consider another example of a taxonomy of consumer agency: in Kimmel's typology, "usability" and "utility" are two important consumer motivations involving functionality. Successful products must meet a real need that consumers have (utility) and must do so in efficient and effective ways (usability). He notes, for example, that many people seek products that are mobile or timesaving, but only insofar as they truly deliver what they promise. Some devices may promise benefit but be too difficult to use or include useless features, while others may be more well received because they combine logically related functionalities.

All well and good. But the simple functionality of the product is insufficient to sell it. Kimmel helpfully explains how this works when he notes that "consumers are moved to acquire things that go beyond the capacity to perform promised functions effectively and efficiently" (emphasis added).[55] This description nicely shows that functionality, while essential to selling products, is not sufficient. To sell a purely functional product is to sell a pure commodity like gasoline. In such a case, it is unsurprising that the primary "advertising" involves large signs touting prices down to the penny—and competitive strategies based on things like the location of stations and non-gas-related goods and services.

Two other key motivating factors go beyond functionality. One is the already-mentioned lifestyle aspirations, in which a product is linked to "the distinctive or characteristic ways of living adopted by consumer segments."[56] The other, which Kimmel treats in great detail, is the "emotional allure" of the product, the evocations of product design and packaging, but also the "brand engagement," made possible especially by new media. One marketer notes that "content is no longer something you push out" but "an invitation to engage with your brand."[57] A thorough illustration is offered via two hugely successful DEWmocracy campaigns by Pepsico to develop and market new Mountain Dew flavors. The first "interactive, story-based online game" was targeted toward "a consumer-generated beverage innovation" by enlisting over 200,000 registered users, and the second campaign built on that via an elaborate online competition between three "Flavor Nations," involving peer-to-peer promotion of the competing new possible products.[58] Given the huge profit margins on soft drinks, companies have long invested a great amount of effort to invest their products with "emotional allure," and it is no surprise that they would lead the way in this kind of interactivity.

Whether in terms of lifestyle or emotional resonance, firms clearly try to shape consumer agency. How might we distinguish between good and bad shaping? Advertising a "tough" pick-up truck may have a lifestyle appeal evoking emotional allure, but it could also target hard-working, independent contractors who understandably may develop affection for their resilient vehicles as tools of their trade. And what about advertising that directly appeals to how a product can legitimately be an occasion for family bonding or neighborhood camaraderie?

I want to suggest two key considerations for evaluating the intentions of the firms selling the products. These will determine the difference between marketing that makes genuine goods more attractive and other approaches that draw on and reinforce distortions in consumer agency.

The first is somewhat obvious: how legitimate is the *connection* between product and lifestyle? Or product and emotion? On one hand, tourism ads for out-of-the-way places that tout peace and quiet are making a plausible emotional appeal and might legitimately suggest lifestyle connections that would attract people with particular interests to their location. On the other hand, the lifestyle and emotional connections with car brands are largely "manufactured." As I explain at length elsewhere, "luxury marketing" is oriented to creating brand mythologies far removed from the product's core functionality.[59] In these manufactured connections, firms often actively encourage the problematic ordering explained above, focusing their appeals on luxury, status, and identity.

A second issue concerns whether the identity or emotion evoked is itself in line with *authentic anthropology*. Appealing to an authentic view of the person is not an impossible fantasy. There is a considerable body of literature suggesting that firms respond to increasing consumer demand that their products be "ethical" in some way. An example is a recent volume displaying the rise of "goodvertising"—products that are promoted specifically through linkages to good works. The author highlights examples such as Chipotle's investment in an elaborate web video (with an original soundtrack featuring Willie Nelson) depicting a farmer who pursues industrial practices of production, only to find them disheartening. He then returns to practices "where he is closer to the animals and more in tune with Earth"—the very practices Chipotle requires from its suppliers.[60] Another book investigates the rise of what it calls "ethical chic," looking at companies in traditional areas of business that clearly foreground an ethical mission in their business practice.[61] The six companies surveyed are subjected to a good bit of criticism, but the author does recognize in each case that the companies try to shape both their products and their marketing with reference to higher goods.

An interesting approach for Catholic business schools would be to develop marketing textbooks that would be guided by the appropriate ordering of goods, rather than simply by the psychological and demographic measures typically used. For example, Jim Wishloff suggests that marketing, in addition to transparently supplying information that actually helps consumers "make prudent decisions," must "do even more today" to "encourage people to simplify their lives" and "help people find a place for contemplation and prayer."[62] Laczniak suggests marketing inclusively to the poor but "without exploitative intent."[63] Poor consumers are often either neglected by marketers because they have less disposable income or exploited by business models that provide substandard goods and services. In marketing to wealthier consumers, alternative business models that better fit the Catholic conception of the person could be emphasized. For example, my own experience as the board president for a $20 million/year consumer food cooperative allowed me to witness the importance and value of marketing "mutualist" or "cooperative" enterprises in order to attract dollars into a local and sustainable food economy.[64]

STRUCTURAL ASPECTS OF CONSUMPTION

The agency of consumers and firms does not exist in a vacuum but in a social context and, as Martin Schlag's rightly argues in chapter 8 of this volume, businesses have some responsibility for this "moral ecology" of structures and culture. I cannot analyze all the forces at work here, but three areas and a key example illustrate their impact on how consumers and firms act.

First, the recent work by Cass Sunstein and others explains how all choices are made within a "choice architecture," defined as the "background against which choices are made" that "effectively makes countless decisions for us" and "influences numerous others, by pressing us in one direction or another."[65] Sunstein's "libertarian paternalism" designs choice architecture with "nudges," which are "initiatives that maintain freedom of choice while also steering people's decisions in the right direction (as judged by people themselves)."[66] Critics seize on Sunstein's claim to know what is "right." His response is to emphasize an admittedly ambiguous distinction between ends and means: libertarian paternalists allow agents freedom in choosing their ends but shape the choice architecture for means, in order to counteract empirically substantiated biases known to behavioral economists. Whether for ends or means, Sunstein's insights could encourage people of faith to design choice architectures in the direction of good goods, rather than futile ones.

A second key factor is the structure of investment capital. Especially in advanced economies, new or improved goods and services usually do not simply emerge from an inventor's garage. Neglected by ethicists, the structure of capital markets has a great deal to do with what sorts of goods and services are developed.[67] A specific problem—perhaps one of many that could be named—is the dominance of speculative, short-term-return oriented capital. This bias of investment capital generates a very important set of restrictions and opportunities that firms face when trying to develop and market products. Pope Benedict explicitly raises a concern about "the human consequences of the current tendencies toward a short-term economy— sometimes very short-term," and he insists that long-term considerations must be introduced because of "the earth's state of ecological health" and "the cultural and moral crisis of man."[68] Given that many Catholic institutions possess large amounts of investment capital, a direction toward "truly good goods" could be valuable. One of the few Christian attempts to do this uses a "logic of gratuitousness" to distinguish between "additive" and "extractive" practices in three cases—pharmaceutical patents, the monetization of personal data, and the financialization of debt—all of which would fall in the area of investment.[69]

The economist Fred Hirsch's work raises a third, general problem of the collective effects of individual decisions. In his key paragraph on consumerism, John Paul II writes that "a given culture reveals its overall understanding of life through the choices it makes in production and consumption."[70] But Hirsch helps us see that this may be more complicated than the pope thinks. He explains that, in advanced economies, more and more consumers are given resources beyond what they need for basic goods, and so enter into competitions for what he calls "positional goods."

The problem with such competitions, as Robert Frank notes, is that they are "smart-for-one" but "dumb-for-all."[71] It is smart for one car to try to cut in line or one fan to stand up to see better at the game (both "positional" in the literal sense), but nothing is gained if all try to do so. As Hirsch explains it, "the market provides a full range of choice between alternative, piecemeal, discrete, marginal adjustments, but no facility for selection between alternative states. . . . Choice in the small does not provide choice in the large."[72] Thus, for example, individual decisions about the best housing or the best transportation can only be made among immediately available choices, but individuals making what appears to be the better choice, given their own position, may drive the community in a direction that they would view as undesirable. Yet no agent ever confronts a discrete choice of "what sort of community overall" one might desire. A related problem, of adverse selection (where low-quality goods can drive higher-quality goods from the market), is examined by Martijn Cremers in chapter 10.

ELECTRONIC CONSUMPTION

All these insights prompt reflection on what might be considered the central example of an emergent set of "good goods": the virtual consumption economy, fueled by various corporate platforms and the radically innovative good: the smartphone.[73] This has now generated an enormous literature on anxiety, especially concerning children.[74] Both Benedict and Francis reinforce this concern, a theme Mary Hirschfeld investigates in chapter 5 of this volume. Although not "against technology," Francis warns strongly against "the technocratic paradigm." He rightly notes that "we have to accept that technology is not neutral" but creates "a framework which ends up conditioning lifestyles and shaping social possibilities along the lines dictated by the interests of certain powerful groups." So he concludes that "decisions which may seem purely instrumental are in reality decisions about the kind of society we want to build."[75] This claim echoes Benedict's concern that "the reduction of cultures to the technological dimension" is a key part of the bias toward short-termism, which "requires further and deeper reflection on the meaning of the economy and its goals."[76]

Such reflection often gets caught in a trap between criticizing users and demonizing corporate behemoths that dominate the tech sector. However, questions about collective context loom large. For example, much technological innovation involves choice architectures that companies deploy and manipulate in problematic ways. Tim Wu points out in great detail how technologies are designed in ways that are meant to *emphasize* the various distortions in use people *decry*.[77] For example, the "always present" element of defaults in technology is decried in ways as diverse as laments over never truly being away from work emails or innovative apps designed to limit the amount teens check their phones, and yet the tools are designed to be more and more integrated into every aspect of everyday life. In a recent, can't-make-this-up example, the chairman of Netflix, in an earnings call, tried to explain how his business model would expand: "When you watch a show from Netflix and you get addicted to it, you stay up late at night. We're competing with sleep, on the margin. And so, it's a very large pool of time."[78] It is true that new apps such as Screen Time are meant to alter the choice architecture of device use by imposing limits—but only as a user-programmed extra, not as a default setting.

Capital markets also distort the agency of firms. Douglas Rushkoff points out how financing new tech ventures has been "gamified" such that the "playbook" emphasizes eventually selling a company that is on its way "to owning its entire marketplace, presumably forever," through platform monopolies.[79] That is to say, inventors and entrepreneurs are more likely to get capital for their idea if they can demonstrate how their idea can create a monopoly in a given marketplace, able to generate the correspondingly high revenue. This affects not only which ideas get funding but also the nature of the goods and services developed in the first place. Rushkoff contrasts this typical strategy with seemingly "better goods" like Meetup, whose founder "aims for Meetup to be a civic platform rather than a platform monopoly," and so seeks only a reliable, long-term revenue stream while avoiding monopolizing tactics or exploitation of "captive" users to *maximize* revenue.[80] Quite strikingly, Rushkoff, a secular writer, suggests "digital distributism" is the answer to the problem, extensively discussing the early-twentieth-century popes and the English Catholics who developed their thought!

Finally, Hirsch's insight into positionality indicates that consumers—and even many businesses—never actually face *overall* choice about the technological world. David Bochnowski reports in chapter 1 that consumer attitudes toward new technologies push his business to adopt novelties like electronic check deposits. Businesses often have little capacity to actually do what the encyclicals call them to do. Individuals considering what Facebook or Twitter might do to help or distort personal lives, or businesses considering the ethics of "mining" social media data to target consumers, never face the choice of a world with or without these technologies. They only face individual, piecemeal choices that often run contrary to their convictions about the kind of society they would prefer.

In fairness, some commentary suggests that this analysis is one-sided. For example, Brad Stone's study of the rise of Uber and Airbnb, two of the biggest novel products of the last decade, illustrates how complicated these judgments are.[81] In one sense, neither Airbnb nor Uber is a "product" per se. Rather, they take advantage of connectivity and data sharing in order to provide distinctive user experiences. They each began small, with far more modest goals than they eventually achieved, and each faced substantial investor resistance because they seemed to propose services—having strangers stay in your home or getting into a private car with a stranger— that people would actively resist. Yet both ended up providing services that a lot of people started feeling passionately about—both on the provider and the consumer ends. For many, Uber and Airbnb are services that make possible hitherto impossible "quotas of gratuitousness." Conversely, both Uber and Airbnb have raised hackles for the social "externalities" they produce— reckless drivers on smartphones or irresponsible mini-landlords who care nothing for their neighbors next door. And economic analyses have suggested the real economic beneficiaries of the "gig economy" are the companies that control the business model. Such are the detailed questions that must be confronted in discussing whether the smartphone and the services it spawns are "good goods."

CONCLUSION: GOOD GOODS AND GOD

To conclude, I return to a final consideration that, from *Rerum novarum* to *Laudato si'*, is the actual anchor of the ordering of goods: the human orientation to a transcendent destiny. The social encyclical tradition is emphatic that the ultimate destiny of union with God must properly order society, including an intentional openness to this "transcendent dimension." As Saint John XXIII writes, "The moral order has no existence except in God; cut off from God it must necessarily disintegrate. . . . Advances in science and technology frequently involve the whole human race in such difficulties as can only be solved in the light of a sincere faith in God."[82]

Paul VI insists on a "new humanism" formed "by embracing the higher values of love and friendship, of prayer and contemplation," furthering aiming at a "brotherhood that is at once human and supernatural."[83] And the entire papacy of Francis is dedicated to his call for a "missionary option," in which Christians are "liberated from our narrowness and self-absorption" in order to "see God's word accepted" by everyone we encounter.[84] Thus it is not only Benedict XVI who believes that "without God man neither knows which way to go, nor even understands who he is."[85]

This presents a particular challenge in a social order where material considerations are taken as legitimate objects of public debate and decision but where religious ones are excluded. Some forms of secularization can critique such religious talk about "good goods," claiming that it simply seeks religiously committed companies. In teaching seminarians social ethics, I have found that their first answer for a company that is "following the encyclicals" is Chick-fil-A because of its countercultural practice of closing on Sundays. Given the encyclicals' insistence on Sunday rest and the freedom of religious exercise,[86] this is not surprising—and yet it does not address many other considerations about "good goods."[87] Perhaps most importantly, limiting the implications in this way neglects the consistent call for the evangelical cultivation of a "spirit of poverty,"[88] and of "sobriety,"[89] which only makes sense in the light of a communion with God, or at least a relation to some transcendent destiny.

In this chapter, I have sought to flesh out the general principles of the Catholic social tradition that firms and consumers have a responsibility to produce and consume "good" goods and services. Beyond the usual examples of clearly harmful things, I have sought to highlight systematically the norms for judgment that would guide both consumers and firms to avoid the futile pursuit of goods also explained in the encyclicals. The norms discussed here inevitably require prudential application—the sort of "practical wisdom" that Andrew Yuengert encourages managers to develop in chapter 3. Yet these norms can help businesses see beyond "value creation" for the consumer and instead shape their products with a deeper vision of selling not just bread but a truly better life.

NOTES

1. Smith, *Wealth of Nations*, book I, chap. 2, 14.
2. Koch, *Good Profit*, 4.
3. Koch, 7.
4. Pontifical Council for Justice and Peace, *Vocation*, 42.
5. "Rent-Seeking Behaviour," in *Penguin Dictionary of Economics*, by Bannock, Baxter, and Rees, n.p.
6. Stiglitz, *Price*, xv. See also this same emphasis in a later essay: White, "Stiglitz."
7. John Paul II, *Octogesima adveniens*, 4; John Paul II, *Sollicitudo rei socialis* 3, 8; Benestad, *Church*, 6–7; Pontifical Council for Justice and Peace, *Compendium*, 7.
8. John Paul II, *Laborem exercens*, 5–7. This norm by itself does not decide the prior argument, but it does force the competing parties to analyze more closely the particular case or law being discussed.
9. The typical failures here would involve the exercise of monopoly power to exclude competitors, regulatory capture, and situations where it is difficult for a purchaser to see or understand defects.
10. John Paul II, *Centesimus annus*, 36.
11. Pontifical Council for Justice and Peace, *Vocation*, 42.
12. Here I adopt a term from Oswald von Nell-Breuning, quoted by the Pontifical Council for Justice and Peace, *Vocation*, 42; von Nell-Breuning, *Reorganization*, 115–16.
13. John Paul II, *Centesimus annus*, 36.
14. John Paul II.
15. Laczniak, Santos, and Klein, "On the Nature of Good Goods," 71.
16. See, e.g., *Time*, "Invest," 34.
17. Goodpaster, "Goods," 14.
18. Laczniak, Santos, and Klein, "On the Nature of Good Goods," 71.
19. Sullivan, *Gotcha Capitalism*.
20. Laczniak, Santos, and Klein, "On the Nature of Good Goods," 67.
21. Pontifical Council for Justice and Peace, *Vocation*, 42.
22. John Paul II, *Centesimus annus*, 36.
23. John Paul II, *Populorum progressio*, 21.
24. Alford and Naughton, *Managing*, 42–49.
25. Paul VI, *Populorum progressio*, 15.
26. John Paul II, *Sollicitudo rei socialis*, 28.

27. Vatican Council II, *Gaudium et spes*, 39.

28. Grisez, *Living*, 803.

29. Grisez, 800.

30. Paul VI, *Populorum progressio*, 21.

31. This rejection of the "double danger" of "individualism" and "collectivism" is stated by Leo XIII, *Quadragesimo anno*, 46. The communal nature and destiny of the person is emphasized by the Vatican Council II, *Gaudium et spes*, 24–25; and Benedict XVI, *Spe salvi*, 10–15.

32. For more detail, see the illuminating discussion by Benestad, *Church*, 81–112, as well as that by Cloutier, "What Can Social Science Teach," 170–207.

33. *Catechism of the Catholic Church*, 2402, 2404.

34. John Paul II, *Centesimus annus*, 41.

35. Benedict XVI, *Caritas in veritate*, 39.

36. Francis, *Evangelium vitae*, 34.

37. Benedict XVI, *Caritas in veritate*, 53.

38. Vatican Council II, *Lumen gentium*, 1.

39. Vatican Council II, *Gaudium et spes*, 22.

40. Francis, *Evangelium vitae*, 53.

41. For an extensive study of the history and continuing normative significance of this view, see Cloutier, *Vice*.

42. Campbell, "Consuming Goods," 20.

43. Gay, "Sensualists," 30.

44. Ferguson, *Essay*, 286–94; cited by Cloutier, *Vice*, 180.

45. For more on these prudential judgments, see Cloutier, 253–71.

46. Cavanaugh, *Being Consumed*, 36.

47. E.g., see "Why is he buying that car? Because he is keeping ahead of the Joneses." See Veblen, *Theory*.

48. For example, "Why is he buying that car? Because it fits his lifestyle; it expresses who he is" For this basic contrast, see Campbell, "Consuming Goods," 19–32.

49. Solomon, *Consumer Behavior*, 198.

50. Kimmel, *People*, 7–22.

51. Kimmel, 11.

52. Solomon, *Consumer Behavior*, 22–25. This marketing text illustrates this point with a 1970s ad from the advertising industry itself, showing a woman shaving her face and explaining that ads cannot create needs. It also adds another defense: advertising is a useful service because it "reduces search time."

53. Solomon, 9.

54. Solomon, 135.

55. Kimmel, *People*, 145.

56. Kimmel, 101.

57. Kimmel, 141.

58. Kimmel, 224–25.

59. Cloutier, *Vice*, 108–13.

60. Kolster, *Goodvertising*, 27. For the video, see Vimeo, "Upload." One might question whether the video paints a too-rosy picture of its required practices (or a too-bleak picture of corporate farms), but this is a matter of whether its appeals are true. It is clear that the values of treating creation well is consistent with an authentic anthropology.

61. Hawthorne, *Ethical Chic.*

62. See Schlag and Mercado, "Freedom," 129.

63. Laczniak, Santos, and Klein, "On the Nature of Good Goods," 74.

64. For a recommendation of these models, see Benedict XVI, *Caritas in veritate*, 38, 66. For more on these forms of business from an author who happens to be a fellow member of the same cooperative, see Flynn, "Global Capitalism," 239–55.

65. Sunstein, *Why Nudge?* 14.

66. Sunstein, 17.

67. Keynes, e.g., envisioned a market economy where investment was nevertheless increasingly "socialized." This was in part because he believed that "at all times the key to the economic problem" was "the weakness of the inducement to invest"—Keynes, *General Theory*, 348—but also because the eventual abundance of capital and decline in its rate of return would require "a somewhat comprehensive socialization of investment" (p. 378).

68. Benedict XVI, *Caritas in veritate*, 32.

69. Baker, "Free Markets," 92–112.

70. John Paul II, *Centesimus annus*, 36.

71. Frank, *Luxury Fever*, 146–58.

72. Hirsch, *Social Limits*, 18.

73. Kimmel, *People*, titles one of his last sections "The End of Products?"

74. See especially Twenge, *iGen*, noting remarkable rises in delayed maturation and mental illness among the first "digital native" generation.

75. Francis, *Laudato si'*, 107.

76. Benedict XVI, *Caritas in veritate*, 32.

77. Wu, *Attention Merchants.*

78. Sweetland Edwards, "Masters," 36.

79. Rushkoff, *Throwing Rocks*, 184–88.

80. Rushkoff, 196.

81. Stone, *Upstarts.*

82. John XXIII, *Mater et magistra*, 208–9.

83. Paul VI, *Populorum progressio*, 20, 43.

84. Francis, *Evangelii gaudium*, 8, 27, 24.

85. Benedict XVI, *Caritas in veritate*, 78.

86. Leo XIII, *Rerum novarum*, 41.

87. However, the company's humorous anticow advertising does drive consumers to prefer chicken, which is far better for the environment!

88. Paul VI, *Populorum progressio*, 21.

89. Francis, *Laudato si'*, 222–23.

CHAPTER 8

Are Businesses Responsible for the Moral Ecology in Which They Operate?

Martin Schlag

Most of the chapters of this volume address issues internal to the business firm. Aiming to assess the moral legitimacy of business in Catholic social thought, they investigate the role played in business by such things as agency, autonomy, interest, and practical reason. Although each of these has implications for how business *interacts* with persons and institutions outside the firm, this chapter focuses directly on the obligations of firms *for* the external conditions in the society within which they operate. In chapter 1, the banker David Bochnowski identifies the importance of those outside conditions when he reports that some potential clients worry about the stability of small banks like his; these are businesses that might not survive the next financial crisis, even though the big banks would be bailed out. Another interviewee, Thomas Holloran, explicitly argues that businesses have an obligation to improve their social, political, and economic environments.

To sort out the issues, this chapter investigates the role of morality in markets, the importance of a first-person perspective, the superiority of a "Benedict Project" over the "Benedict Option," and the significance of institutionalizing morality in everyday institutions.

THE MORAL ECOLOGY OF A BUSINESS

The title of this chapter is inspired by Daniel K. Finn's work *The Moral Ecology of Markets*.[1] With this concept, he expresses the insight that "any analysis of the morality of markets should begin with the recognition that no human institution—not even one as broad as the market—can be adequately understood without reference to its context."[2] He borrows "a concept from biology, where it is universally recognized that no single species of plant or animal can be understood without reference to its ecology, the pattern of relations between organisms and their environment."[3] Analogously, it would be "futile to analyze markets as either moral or immoral, just or unjust, without attention to the social, political, and cultural context within which any particular market exists."[4]

Finn lists four elements that make up the moral context—the moral ecology—of markets: the character of markets themselves, the provision of essential goods and services, the morality of individuals and groups, and civil society.[5] The first and most crucial element for Finn is the nature of markets, which he defines as "arenas of freedom defined by fences.... Markets are highly complex institutions that vary widely in their history and operation depending on social, cultural, religious, political, and economic factors."[6] Therefore, "for any moral assessment of markets, it is far more productive to understand most arguments about economic policy as debates over where to construct the fences than as disputes about the merits of capitalism or socialism."[7]

From a philosophical point of view, Michael J. Sandel, some years after Finn, claimed that "markets crowd out morals";[8] more precisely, that extrinsic market incentives tend to crowd out intrinsic, nonmarket motivation.[9] What Sandel observed was the encroachment of markets on fields of life that are not meant to be up for sale (political votes, academic titles, human organs, gratuitous public entitlements) that, however, increasingly are commercialized. Sandel argued that we have "drifted from *having* a market economy to *being* a market society."[10] Market reasoning, according to Sandel, does not pass judgment on the preferences the markets satisfy. This nonjudgmental stance toward values lies at the heart of market reasoning and is part of its appeal.[11] However, markets are not ethically neutral: "What begins as a market mechanism becomes a market norm."[12] Market norms tend to "corrupt, dissolve, or displace,"[13] to crowd out morals, and "commercialism erodes commonality."[14]

Why? This occurs because commodifying a good—putting it up for sale—alters its character. Commodification changes the reason *why* we do something, and thus profoundly changes the character of the goods in question: "When people are engaged in an activity they consider intrinsically worthwhile, offering them money may weaken their motivation by depreciating or 'crowding out' their intrinsic interest or commitment."[15] An example for this phenomenon would be blood donations. Blood donations often diminish when blood is bought for money instead of being the fruit of a voluntary sacrifice for persons in need.

Thus, Sandel encourages us to ask when financial incentives are useful and when they are not. His own response is that "to answer this question, market reasoning must become moral reasoning. The economist has to 'traffic in morality' after all."[16] Disappointingly, Sandel did not spell out this project in more detail, but instead called for a public debate on what should be for sale and what not, because this is a debate on values, on what we hold sacred (outside economic life). It would invigorate politics if competing notions of the good life were welcomed into the public square.[17] In other words, instead of himself developing a proposal for a moral form of economy or pointing out the epistemological consequences of morality for economics, he delegates this task to public discourse.

Recently, Jean Tirole, the Nobel laureate for economics in 2014, rebutted Sandel's analysis.[18] Tirole states that the real question we should be looking at is the failure of markets. Tirole chides Sandel for "ignorance of economists' work, . . . ignorance of the interdisciplinary studies undertaken over the last twenty years, both theoretical and experimental."[19] What Sandel described as an encroachment of markets into other fields of human life is, in Tirole's view, a market failure, an indication that incentives are not properly aligned. Tirole points out that extrinsic incentives (reward in the form of money or monetary value) do not always replace intrinsic motivation; but more basically, his position is that "individual and collective objectives [need] to be aligned" in order to further the common good.[20]

I find neither of these two positions completely satisfactory.

Despite his fleeting suggestion that the whole of market reasoning be subject to an overarching moral evaluation, Sandel does not go beyond the notion of "moral limits of markets." His argument seems to presuppose that the market sphere is an amoral (i.e., morally neutral) or immoral field of human action that ends where morality begins. For this reason, he demands a public debate about where that line should be drawn. To say that "markets crowd out morals" seems to set markets and morality in opposition. But why should this be the case? Why should we submit to the dominant paradigm by reducing the morality of markets to restrictions imposed from the outside? Why should we refer to ethics as something external to markets? Markets need to be intrinsically ethical in order to be free.

For Thomas Aquinas, it would be inconceivable to affirm that markets are amoral in their operations. How could they be, if they are free human activity? The decisive question for us is whether it is possible to conceive of moral markets today in the prevailing ethical paradigm of modernity. As we shall see, authors like Alasdair MacIntyre deny this. But I affirm it, because I think there is an internal good in market mechanisms even in advanced capitalism (e.g., the price mechanism, purchasing power as allocative instrument, and the economic freedom of consumers to satisfy their wishes within the general laws) that comes from the common good as the end of social ethics through an institutional analysis.

Tirole's position, conversely, is too descriptive and normatively diluted: it does not tell us what the common good is, or which objectives really are conducive to the common good. He echoes John Rawls's veil of ignorance and Rousseau's *volonté générale*, both of which rely on formal rules of coexistence without creating the freely shared core of moral convictions needed for social cohesion.[21] Tirole's argument thus falls under the indictment of liberalism provided by Sandel (and other communitarians): it is foolish to assume that whatever alignment arises from individual and collective choices will automatically promote the common good. This liberal misconception of social life goes beyond the idea of the invisible hand in Adam Smith because the founder of modern economics knew exactly what larger outcome he aspired to.

Tirole does reflect extensively on the institutions that we would need for the common good, but he attempts this without sufficiently providing the normative basis upon which his requirements could be established. Instead, he simply refers to the idea of aligning private and collective incentives. As Mary L. Hirschfeld has pointed out, speaking of incentives: "If we work from the economic paradigm, there's no good explanation for why bribery is not merely a matter of 'incentivizing.' . . . To articulate the evil of bribery, we need to appeal to higher goods that lie outside the economic paradigm."[22]

THE FIRST-PERSON PERSPECTIVE IN BUSINESS

Fundamental to the Catholic view of life is the conviction that the many goods that make for a fulfilling life exist within a hierarchy of lower and higher goods. The groceries we buy are goods, but subordinate to the meal they make possible. Both the nutrition and the good taste of the food at the meal are goods but are subordinate to our health and the family unity the meal promotes. In an integrated life, each of our actions contributes to the highest aim to which we aspire, whether that is our own glory, wealth, power, or pleasure, or God's glory. It is this ultimate aim that defines our morality. Everything we do is a means to achieve it. David Cloutier, in chapter 7 of this volume, addresses this issue by investigating how the higher ends of business present the question of whether the firm is producing good goods.

Such higher ends, and indeed the ultimate end of our actions, are a question of an ongoing subjective intentionality (which is more than mere intention or motive) of the acting person, and this intentionality is not easily verifiable from the outside. If a mother comes home for lunch and finds her son, who is usually in school at this hour, lying on the couch in the living-room, she will ask, "What are you doing here at this time of the day?" An answer such as, "I am lying on the couch," will not satisfy her. Even though it is descriptively accurate, her son's answer does not explain the moral signifi-cance of his action. The boy could have come home because he was sick or because he had been expelled from school for dangerous behavior or because school had been canceled that day. The moral significance of an action is basi-cally defined by its moral object—that is, the meaningful action the person wills to do. His mother may guess at the unspoken meaning, but she will not know until he discloses it. In every action, there is an important moral differ-ence between the physical action (e.g., my arm goes up) and the inner world of intentionality (I raise my arm for a reason).

Because of this fact of the moral life, we need to adopt a first-person per-spective, not the third-person vision typical of a judge or impartial spectator. We can, of course, describe the structure of human intention and action theo-retically, as Thomas Aquinas did, but we cannot know intentionality with cer-tainty from the outside.[23] The first-person perspective grasps this difference, based as it is on the moral object of an act.

In the third-person perspective, the first step of analysis consists in establishing, for example, whether an act in its physical reality qualifies as a transgression of law. In the first-person perspective of moral analysis, the focus is on intentionality, a combination of intention and physical reality. The first-person perspective is important for business ethics because it presses us to address fundamental questions about the various goods we pursue there and whether the lower goods at which we aim will actually promote the higher goods we hold to be more important. We pursue some goods as means, others as ends. This requires a debate about what is good in itself, a true end.

In an earlier publication, Mary L. Hirschfeld (and also David Cloutier) distinguished between two traditions of Catholic social thought that in differ-ent ways responded to the Machiavellian challenge against premodern politi-cal philosophy: it had not described reality adequately and, for that reason, had not produced public welfare.[24] One Catholic tradition on the common good concentrates on the necessary means that set the stage for human flour-ishing without asking about what constitutes this flourishing or happiness. Food, shelter, health, education, and so on, in this tradition are to be given to as many people as possible in order to lift them out of poverty and so grant them the possibility to achieve their goals and pursue happiness in freedom of choice. The other, older Catholic tradition considers the virtuous life as constitutive of happiness and of the common good. In other words, it focuses on the ends. It is not enough simply to have the basic essentials for survival and moderate comfort (the means) but also to "order those basic goods to the transcendental goods of truth, beauty, goodness, and communion. The social conditions necessary to promote the pursuit of such fulfillment would then include not only political and economic arrangements that help us to secure and equitably distribute the basic goods but also cultural norms that encourage pursuit of those higher goods."[25]

Hirschfeld shows how each of the virtues, as pursuit of the right ends, affects the common good, especially the virtues of prudence and justice. As Andrew Yuengert details in chapter 3 of this volume, on practical reason, prudence is the virtuous counter piece to rational choice in the economic paradigm: it centers our decisions on the aims that are really worth the means (money, time, etc.) we employ to achieve them.[26] Justice makes community constitutive of the pursuit of happiness.

As a result, it is a mistake to call an action a "good" means or a "technically good" action if the action is not also good in an ethical sense. Are there business skills that can be called "good" in an economic sense but not in an ethical sense? I deny this because the goodness of a means is derived from the goodness of the end. The expression Aquinas employed for a means—"*quae sunt ad finem*" (what leads to an end)—makes clear that the essence of a means is its contribution to the end.

Our language today fails us here. We may hear things like "he is a technically excellent manager but an immoral person." However, if we understand moral intentionality, this is not possible. Would a good chess player ever call a successful move to capture an opposing knight a "good chess move" if it simultaneously led to his losing the game? Every person in a business firm has a multiplicity of ends, both lower and higher. In an integrated life, an action that contributes to a lower end such as one's salary or the firm's profit must also contribute to that person's higher ends in order to be a "good" action. Economic "success" achieved with immoral means is a loss of human excellence, the paramount measure of all human life and behavior. Such an outcome constitutes an economic defeat, not a victory.

In chapter 4 of this book, Gregory Beabout distinguishes between the "moneymaker" and the "businessperson concerned with promoting a positive social impact." He uses this distinction for his analysis of the different types of human agency. Here, I refer to its implications on the meta-ethical epistemological level. The formal aspects of business as an institution and of managerial agency as an art or skill are defined by and ordered toward the higher ends. What "business" means is conditioned by ethics, not the other way around. Even though a burglar possesses an effective skill at breaking and entering, it would not make sense to refer to him as a "technically excellent professional."

I am not rejecting the legitimacy of the discipline of economics and its use of models in describing business as profit-seeking. The Second Vatican Council accepted the autonomy of earthly affairs and the legitimacy of specific sciences and arts. But a mistake arises when persons in businesses assume their goal is merely the seeking of profit, instead of realizing that profit is an intermediate goal, and it must promote their ultimate goal.

Morality is not an extrinsic, after-the-fact evaluation of business activity that alienates business from its own nature. Morality is intrinsic to any human action, including actions in the field of business and the economy. Moral intentionality vitalizes business as human business practice. Because of this intentionality internal to business that extends outward to more ultimate ends, business professionals need to attend to their moral ecology, the culture and structures that exist outside business and within which firms operate. Without this, we will not be able to strengthen social cohesion in times of growing inequality and the centrifugal forces that seem to be ripping apart the institutional consensus in the Western world.[27]

REJECTING THE "BENEDICT OPTION"

The philosopher Alasdair MacIntyre has applied the insights of Aquinas (and Marx) to business and the economy. He is highly skeptical of advanced capitalism. He considers ethics not only as irrelevant to business in modern financial capitalism but also to actually be incommunicable in the modern moral order: "Just as the successful training of a boxer will destroy his prospects as a violinist, so the inculcation of qualities of moral character is no way to prepare someone for a rewarding career in the financial sector. Ethics is not just irrelevant. It is a probably insuperable disadvantage."[28]

MacIntyre hastens to clarify that he is not calling all traders and financial analysts immoral people but that "the financial sector as a whole ... [is] a school of bad character."[29] His concern is with the institutional setup and the moral tradition from which these activities and institutions have emerged. Modern capitalism and finance have become separated from growth and integral human development in a way that MacIntyre described in his later book, *Ethics in the Conflicts of Modernity.*

Capitalism, according to MacIntyre, "is not only a set of economic relationships. It is also a mode of presentation of those relationships that disguises and deceives."[30] His criticism of advanced capitalism is that it inculcates a vice as the basis of what is (erroneously) described as rational behavior:

> So they learn to want more and then more and then more and become consumed by their own desires. Moreover, it is by how good they are at increasing their stock of money that others measure their success or failure, admire them or withhold their admiration. So the trait that the Greeks called *pleonexia*, acquisitiveness, a trait that both Aristotle and Aquinas took to be a vice, comes for the first time to be treated as a virtue by large numbers of people and money becomes an object of desire, not only for what it can buy, but also for its own sake.[31]

This distortion, according to MacIntyre, infects the whole system of capitalism that has become distorting: it instills the wrong desires. MacIntyre seems to feel oppressed by the existing social order and proposes a strategy of opposition and antagonism: "The exploitative structures of both free market and state capitalism make it often difficult and sometimes impossible to achieve the goods of the workplace through excellent work. . . . We therefore have to live *against* the cultural grain, just as we have to learn to act as economic, political, and moral antagonists of the dominant order."[32]

I agree with MacIntyre on his underlying conviction that virtue is at the center of morality and with his assessment of the *true* nature of business as directed to human growth and development. But I do not agree that there is not also a good form of modern capitalism.[33] I think that most of the time (though not always!) it is possible to pursue an external, intermediate good and at the same time as a higher, internal good. The victorious soldier has won victory (external good) but has also shown valor (internal excellence). The line is fine, as Aristotle wrote in the *Politics*: "They think that the coveted prizes of life are won by valor more than by cowardice, and in this they are right, yet they imagine wrongly that these prizes are worth more than the valor that wins them."[34]

In an analogous way, a businessperson can, in a morally authentic way, acquire personal wealth, beat competitors, conquer market share, and achieve other economic successes. The interviews with CEOs that Regina Wolfe presents in chapter 1 illustrate real-world efforts to live this out. Doing so requires that the business leader seek moral excellence in a virtuous life and abide by the natural law, both individually and in promoting the common good, as Kenneth Goodpaster and Michael Naughton expand upon in chapter 6 of this volume. This is admittedly difficult, but not impossible, in capitalist business, as John Paul II also thought.[35]

The radicalism of MacIntyre's criticism is surprising, especially if one considers that he himself has peacefully lived and taught several generations of students in the system of advanced capitalism and has received his salary from well-endowed academic institutions that enjoy the fruits of interest and investments of a capitalist kind. Such denunciation of existing systems can be dangerous. Certainly, denunciation is an important, even essential, feature of the prophetic vocation that every Christian receives in baptism together with the priestly office and the royal mission of oversight that make up the *tria munera* of Christ (to be priest, prophet, and king, in earlier language). In the name of God, prophets raise their voice to accuse the rich and powerful of the injustices they commit against the poor and underprivileged.

However, this denunciation needs to be complemented by the priestly call to holiness through the virtues and the constructive, "royal" work of communal oversight, building the institutions, structures, and culture required by the common good, both temporal and spiritual. The Church, especially under Pope Francis, is strong in her prophetic calling but frequently lacks feasible alternatives that construct society and show viable paths forward. This deficiency is especially harmful when political reform is urgently needed, as in Venezuela, where there is a strong Catholic majority but where Catholic social teaching should have more impact. A former student of mine in Rome, who came from Venezuela, pointed out to me that the leaders of the political opposition there hardly have constructive proposals that would be a credible alternative. Denunciation alone, whether from ecclesiastics or lay politicians, is not a motivating program.

I am therefore worried about the series of books that have been appearing in the United States that in the name of Christian morality and faith reject liberalism and the existing American culture in an undifferentiated way.[36] Here I refer to culture as the set of elements that shape our life in common and vary according to time and place.[37] We can also call the culture of society its "moral ecology," its "moral climate,"[38] or its "human ecology" or "integral ecology."[39] These notions are similar, and I use them as synonyms here.

Besides the culture of society as a whole, there also exist different cultures in corporations and other smaller units of human cooperation. Like social structures, culture and moral ecology constrain and influence our behavior in a morally positive or negative way. The above-mentioned books loosely gather around the promotion of what they call "the Benedict Option," striving "to build a Christian way of life that stands as an island of sanctity and stability amid the high tide of liquid modernity."[40] The concept harkens back to the closing remark in MacIntyre's book, *After Virtue*: "We are waiting not for a Godot, but for another—doubtless very different—St. Benedict."[41]

Joseph Ratzinger, in contrast, warned against the danger of feeling "disgust for what exists."[42] Permitting disgust for what exists in oneself or others is a dangerous game to play. Karl Barth and Carl Schmitt unintentionally helped pave the path for Hitler with their constant criticism of democracy and their call for strong political authority as the answer to the paralyzing party squabbles that beset the immature years of the fledgling European republics. I fear that similar criticism is taking place in the United States now. It is true that there are many negative and sinful phenomena in contemporary American culture. Some are in plain sight, others are of a more insidious nature and creep into academia under fine-sounding epitaphs but dissolve intellectual discourse and natural law like acid.

ENDORSING THE BENEDICT PROJECT

Cultural change always begins with the affirmation of what exists. Except in very rare cases of evident repression and persecution, as in North Korea or the former Soviet bloc, to reject what exists as totally evil would make impossible the process of cultural transformation that is essential to evangelization—because such a transformation always needs to begin by loving what exists. In order to evangelize a person or a culture, we need to love them first. False and oppressive "culture" that we cannot love because it turns against human dignity tends to disintegrate due to its self-contradictions and repulsiveness.

Of course, in a second step, we need to cleanse our culture of the sins and impurities that infect it. We need alternative lifestyles and a new "counter-anticulture."[43] However, it is essential to recognize that culture evolves only from preexisting culture. There can be no "completely new culture" because culture, like language, needs cultural expressions to develop, and these can only be expressed in the forms of the existing culture. It is like linguistic change: language can only evolve if it is spoken. Dead languages are conserved according to rules of grammar and orthography that we memorize and apply like computer programs. They cannot evolve anymore; they are fixed in time. Culture, too, can be dead, if we study it as an object of the past. Our culture is alive when we live, breath, and swim in it. Just as we cannot change a language without first understanding and speaking it masterfully, we can only change culture from inside as a living part of it.

We can thus reformulate the initial question that forms the title of this chapter: How can businesses change the culture in which they operate? If they cannot, they cannot be responsible for not doing so. Are there levers of cultural change that businesses can push or pull while "swimming" in the culture and structures of organizations and whole industries? A first practical step to achieve this aim is what Goodpaster and Naughton refer to in chapter 6 of this book as the "institutional insight": the comprehensive awareness of business leaders for their institution's contribution to the culture, life, and structures—in other words, to the ecology—in which they operate. Such an institutional insight is like the ability to see the water in which one swims and caring about whether it is clean or dirty.

True human culture is open to the transcendent; human nature is not earthbound. Pope Benedict XVI put it into these words: "Authentic cultures are not closed in upon themselves, nor are they set in stone at a particular point in history, but they are open, or better still, they are seeking an encounter with other cultures, hoping to reach universality through encounter and dialogue with other ways of life and with elements that can lead to a new synthesis, in which the diversity of expressions is always respected as well as the diversity of their particular cultural embodiment."[44]

This is also the reason why human cultures of all kinds are open to Christ, the incarnate logos. Being the Truth, he is not alien to any culture but revives culture and gives it its ultimate identity. The culture of philosophical liberalism—which gave birth to the United States and has evolved into the form of liberalism we have now—is not an oppressive or antihuman culture. Nor do I think it is a false culture; it would not have proven to be the victorious system of common life into which millions of people have immigrated and to which millions more still want to. Therefore, my approach is that of healing culture from within. We can accept the main structural elements, the institutional construction of society, and its ideals but supplement these with the Christian anthropology that was underlying it at its foundation but has been constantly resisted since the sexual revolution of the 1970s, or even earlier. This denial is a remote consequence also of an "original sin" of so many intellectuals of the Enlightenment—to want to maintain Christian values without Christ.

In order to heal our culture, I prefer the "Benedict Project" to the "Benedict Option." The "Benedict Project" is my name for the program of Benedict XVI to enlarge the narrow, modern rationalistic view of reason, and thus save the positive social achievements of the Enlightenment from self-destruction. The arguments of the other authors in this volume indicate that they share this aim. In his famous speech in Subiaco, Joseph Cardinal Ratzinger prayed that men like Saint Benedict will arise in our time. This future pope—who later took the name of Benedict, the patron saint of

Europe—spoke appreciatively of the important positive social values and institutions that the Enlightenment brought to us Christians, and to others. However, he goes on to say that the philosophies of the Enlightenment "are based on a self-limitation of positive reason, which is adequate in the technical domain but which, when it gets generalized, mutilates man. It follows from this that man no longer acknowledges any moral authority outside of his calculations, and, as we have seen, even the concept of freedom, which at first sight might seem to expand here without limit, leads in the end to the self-destruction of freedom."[45]

The advantage of the Benedict Project over the Benedict Option is that it enters into a direct and sustained dialogue with modern culture; it does not reject modernity completely. It certainly deplores many of its phenomena but affirms its basic goodness and achievements. The critique of the technocratic paradigm provided by Pope Francis and examined by Mary Hirschfeld in chapter 5 of this volume exhibits a similar aim.

The Benedict Project does not wish to replace the prevailing liberal culture emanating from the Enlightenment but to heal it from the inside. Such an attempt might seem less radical, less pious, less Catholic, and less religious than the more explicitly religious handbooks for culture wars provided by the Benedict Option. However, sometimes it is necessary to seem less religious in order to be more genuinely religious. We should recall that the Aristotelian Thomas Aquinas in his optimism for human reason seemed less religious than his Augustinian critics of the voluntarist Franciscan School, who instead prioritized obedience and submission of the heart to God and revealed Scripture.

The task of Catholic social thought is neither to be irenic nor cynical but realistic, with a realism that presents constructive, practical solutions not for the righteous but for reasonable people. Moreover, it does so knowing that the system must also cope with those few who are not even reasonable. This Benedict Project is undoubtedly difficult to put into practice, but it should be easier to accomplish than the Christianization of Roman pagan culture that was achieved in the early Church. For in the case of the Enlightenment, we need only help the system discover Christianity as its own parent. A child, who for whatever reason did not know its parents, is usually at least curious to discover them because the parents give it its identity—and love. So, too, the return to its roots in Christianity will bring new life and healing to the modern culture we live in. This I think is the way forward: Christian individuals and communities—including businesses—who are part of this world as the soul is inside the body. They must affirm and love what exists, see its positive sides, but cleanse it from evil.

INSTITUTIONALISM IN CATHOLIC SOCIAL ETHICS

How can we apply the Benedict Project to business and economy? Building on Mary Hirschfeld's insights, I wish to recur to Thomas Aquinas's justification of private property, and from there make inferences about the importance of institutions, also in the economy, and the incremental responsibility of collectives that are not united by a shared intentionality but only by a culturally mediated habitual intentionality.

In a nutshell: culture is a human product in which all our activities are embedded. Even though individual responsibility is highly diluted and hardly perceptible, individuals and corporations influence the culture or moral ecology in which they operate. They are therefore co-responsible for it.

Businesses have a collective responsibility for the moral ecology/context/culture in which they operate. In other words, the issue we need to tackle is not primarily the individual moral behavior of an agent but the collective structuring of society and the agency of those collective actors we call businesses.

In doing so, we cannot escape the challenge of the three Ms—Machiavelli, Mandeville, and Marx—that bad actions by an individual can have positive social outcomes, a challenge with a history that Jennifer Herdt helpfully documents in chapter 2 of this volume. Seen superficially, and not completely wrongly, Machiavelli's writings are only about conserving power for power's sake, encouraging politicians to *seem* good rather than to *be* good in order to deceive the masses cynically. Similarly, Mandeville's *Fable of the Bees* is about living out individual vices and reaping public benefit, and Marx's analysis urges the use of revolution, class struggle, and the dictatorship of the proletariat in order to achieve a new society. These must be rejected.

However, at a deeper level, there is a true insight underlying them all. What they grasped in their judgments, although imperfectly, was the different logic, focus, or aim of social ethics as the moral ordering of a collectively acting subject. What is good for an individual might not be good for the collective, and vice versa, because the aim of the individual is holiness, and for the political community it is the temporal common good. Saint Thomas, based on Aristotle, had fully realized this before Machiavelli muddied the waters. I will try to reconstruct an aspect of his teaching and to apply it to our issue in a different way than Machiavelli, building on the temporal common good as the last end of social ethics.

An analysis of the common good as a central concept of Catholic social thought would take us beyond the scope of this chapter. I thus refer to its meaning for Thomas Aquinas, for whom the common good was the structuring principle for our dealings with others, so much so, that it is one of the central elements in his definition of every law: "an ordinance of reason directed to the common good."[46] Put briefly, we can say that the substantive notion of Aquinas for the temporal common good of political human society is justice and peace. He refers to justice, virtues, and peace as the great aims of human society that require the protection of law from unjust actions that harm others.[47] The common good is also essential for his notion of private property.

For Thomas, the rational arguments brought forward in favor of private property are economic arguments formulated in terms of natural law. It is important to notice that he does not speak of individual natural human rights, as we moderns used to, but justifies property as an institution required for the common good of society. For Thomas, private property was *not* part of primary natural law but was something rational and highly convenient—a wise human invention of an institution that is indispensable for the common good.

Thomas employs the notion of natural law to define the set of rules that conform to social necessity or expedience.[48] He points out that the natural law could be changed through *addition* for the benefit of human life. Thus, something might not be natural (in the sense that nature does not provide it), but it could be a morally good addition to nature. For example, clothes are not natural: a human being is naturally brought into the world naked. The personal ownership of property is similar, Thomas argues. Personal ownership is not natural, as it was human decision that created it, but it is a prudent addition to natural law, "devised by human reason for the benefit of human life."[49]

There is nothing in the nature of a field (an area of land) by which it would belong more to one person than to another. But if we consider its cultivation and its peaceful use, then there is a good reason for ascribing the field to one person rather than to another. Such ascriptions are established by human reason, which considers the consequences of an institution.[50]

As can be glimpsed from what has been said so far, in determining the correct functioning of human institutions such as property, Thomas and the thirteenth-century Scholastics rely on a notion of final causality (a notion incompatible with that of modern natural science, which is based on mechanics[51]). For Thomas, Aristotle, and everyone with a teleological view, all creatures, animate or inanimate, are brought into being not only *by* an efficient cause (how they came to be) but also *for* a final cause (why they came to be). All creatures are directed toward an aim in which their perfection consists. From this explicitly teleological perspective, nature possesses finality and meaning. In the case of human law (including laws establishing personal property ownership), the common good is the end.

From Aristotle's arguments for property, Albert the Great and Thomas Aquinas developed three arguments: concerning efficiency, order, and peace.[52]

First, people tend to take better care of what is their own. Holding goods in common is inefficient because people leave the work to others. Second, without a division of property, there is confusion. If everybody knows exactly what things are in their care, things are treated better. Third, with private property, everybody has their own and can be content with it. Undivided communal goods among sinful men lead to frequent quarrels.

Following Aristotle, Aquinas grants a logical priority to the common over the individual good: the very concept of the individual good requires some notion of the common good, and the realization of that individual good, in practice, demands the presence of a common whole, society. These ideas apply to the institution of private property, so Aquinas's arguments for property aim at the better functioning of the whole.[53] If private people own things individually, then they will use them more efficiently, and that is better for us all.

In addition to the appeal to the common good in justifying the personal ownership of property, Aquinas also articulates a limit on that ownership, as he teaches that those who have more than they need should share with those who have less than they need.[54] Material goods themselves have a finality—to meet the material needs of all human persons, and so those who own material goods have an obligation, Aquinas argues, to respect that finality. Ownership entails obligations—and this included the ownership of business.

CONCLUSION

Contrary to the view of some who simply condemn contemporary capitalism, Catholic social thought aims to change it from the inside. This tradition unites two arguments concerning the hierarchy of goods, both of which affect the obligations of business and managers of businesses. The first concerns the moral necessity that every person act in a way that efforts to achieve lesser goals serve the higher and ultimate goals of that person. The second concerns the moral necessity that those who own material resources act in a way that respects the nature of those things, which have been destined by God for the good of everyone. Both of these open us to our responsibility—as individuals and leaders of businesses—to consider the goodness of our aims, the means to achieve them, and the consequences of our actions.

Businesses operate in markets where they compete and cooperate, buy and sell, act and interact incessantly and in multiple ways. Frequently, they do not share an intentionality—that is, they do not act together with a common purpose but are independent of each other. Businesses as a group are not one actor inspired by a common will but many actors with diverse and frequently antagonistic aims.

Nevertheless, by interacting, businesses create habits, structures, standardized behavior, and expectations. All this is an integral part of what we call culture. Businesses thus are co-responsible for the culture and the institutions in which they operate, a point also made by Edward Kleinbard in his treatment of the social mortgage in chapter 9 below. In the language of Catholic social thought, by so doing they exercise their royal office because we all are responsible for the common good. One cannot fully participate in a political community as a citizen, without love for the common good of the community to which one belongs. Leaders of business then exercise their royal office by shaping the institutions of business and society so that the larger moral ecology of economic life encourages human flourishing in the lives of everyone.

NOTES

1. Finn, *Moral Ecology*.
2. Finn, 104.
3. Finn.
4. Finn, 105.
5. Finn, 108.
6. Finn, 113.
7. Finn, 124.
8. Sandel, *What Money*.
9. Sandel, 64.
10. Sandel, 10.
11. Sandel, 14.
12. Sandel, 61.
13. Sandel, 113.
14. Sandel, 202.
15. Sandel, 122.
16. Sandel, 91.
17. Sandel, 14.
18. Tirole, *Economics*.
19. Tirole, 36.
20. Tirole, 39. On pp. 157–60, Tirole lists six types of market failure. He also decries failures by governments.
21. Tirole, 3.
22. Hirschfeld, "What Theology Should and Should Not Learn," 219.
23. See the beginning of Aquinas, *Summa Theologiae*, I-II.
24. Hirschfeld, "What Theology Should and Should Not Learn"; Cloutier, "What Can Social Science Teach."
25. Hirschfeld, "What Theology Should and Should Not Learn," 212.

26. Hirschfeld, 222.

27. This is something David Hollenbach showed years ago; see Hollenbach, *Ethics*. The facts since then have proven the accuracy of his analysis.

28. MacIntyre, "Irrelevance," 12.

29. MacIntyre.

30. MacIntyre, *Ethics*, 95.

31. MacIntyre, 109.

32. MacIntyre, 237–38.

33. Several authors have applied MacIntyre's principles to modern capitalism, showing that it is possible to pursue an internal good despite the deficiencies of our system; see Beabout, "Management"; and Moore, *Virtues*. See also Beadle, "MacIntyre's Influence"; Beabout, "Practical Wisdom"; Knight, "MacIntyre's Critique"; and Dobson, "Against MacIntyre."

34. Aristotle, *Politics*, II, vi, 23; 1271b 7–11, p. 147.

35. See John Paul II, *Centesimus annus*, 42.

36. Dreher, *Benedict*; Chaput, *Strangers*; Deneen, *Liberalism*. A positive exception is Reno, *Resurrecting*.

37. Schlag, *Handbook*, 355.

38. See Brooks, *Road*, 261.

39. See Francis, *Laudato si'*, 137–55.

40. Dreher, *Benedict*, 54.

41. MacIntyre, *After Virtue*, 263.

42. See Ratzinger, "Christliche Orientierung," 233.

43. Deneen, *Liberalism*, 192.

44. Benedict XVI, "Inaugural Address."

45. Ratzinger, "Europe." For interesting considerations on historical Catholic forms of Enlightenment, see Lehner, *Catholic Enlightenment*.

46. See Aquinas, *Summa*, I-II, q. 90, a. 2 and a. 4.

47. Aquinas, I-II, q. 95, a. 1; q. 100, a. 2. This is true also of the jarring topic of Aquinas's treatment of heresy. He justifies the persecution of heresy because, on his view, heretics harm others, not because it harms the individual heretic himself, whose interior act of faith cannot be touched by human laws; cf. *Summa*, II-II, q. 11, a. 3.

48. See Aquinas, *Summa*, I-II, q. 94, a. 5; II-II, q. 57, a. 3c.

49. Aquinas, I-II, q 94, a. 5.

50. Aquinas, II-II, q. 57, a. 3.

51. See Langholm, *Legacy*, 160.

52. Thus Aquinas renders two of Aristotle's arguments, adding one of his own (in order): Aquinas, *Summa*, II-II, q. 66, a. 2; Aquinas, *In Libros Politicorum*, book 4, lectio 4; cf. also Langholm, *Economics*, 171–73 (for Albert) and 210–16 (for Thomas).

53. See also Hollenbach, *Ethics*, 78: "A person is not free alone, but only in a community of freedom—a community in which freedom is shared with others."

54. Aquinas, *Summa*, II-II, q. 66, a. 2.

CHAPTER 9

The Social Mortgage
on Business

Edward D. Kleinbard

This volume sets out to examine the moral legitimacy of business in Catholic social thought. To this end, most of the preceding chapters have examined the moral character of internal business processes and the obligations inherent in them. This chapter, in contrast, begins by asking, "What are the obligations of wealth holders to society as a whole?" And because the wealthy are wealthy mostly because of their ownership claims on businesses, we need to ask, "What do these obligations mean for the activities of business?"

Christian thought has much to say about economic life, rooted in three thousand years of reflection. From the gleaning laws of Deuteronomy to Jesus's teachings, to Augustine, Aquinas, and Luther on the character of property ownership, the tradition has understood that personal ownership is a morally warranted but limited claim. In modern Catholic social teaching, Pope John Paul II encapsulated that teaching in the phrase "the social mortgage" on property. In this teaching, the aims of business, or capitalism more generally, are recognized as legitimate, provided one acknowledges that the assets so accumulated are held subject to a mortgage, not a financial lien, but a senior claim owed to all members of society.

This chapter begins with an exploration of this notion of a social mortgage in papal teaching. As the tradition has consistently said, the prosperous have an obligation to share from their surplus with those whose needs are unmet. It then presents an alternate, secular, rationale for endorsing this same sort of obligation: the fact that so much of the success of the prosperous must be attributed to luck. Recognizing that many of life's outcomes are dependent on luck, whether of birth or events later in life, can generate a gratitude that leads to a willingness to recognize a kind of social mortgage and to contribute to the common good through both private and governmental efforts.

But because this call, particularly for government action, often faces the response that such "redistribution" costs jobs and economic growth, the third section reviews recent research on "inclusive growth." Studies show that if social programs funded by taxation are targeted on education, health, and infrastructure, the result is not only good for lower-income citizens but also leads to higher economic growth. The fourth section examines the two-step claim that it is best to make the economy as efficient as possible (minimizing the restrictions on business), and thus any concerns about the moral obligations of firms should be transferred "up" from the businesses themselves to the owners of firms as individuals. There are several reasons why this argument makes less sense today than it did a generation ago. The fifth and final section proposes that we should understand these public policy efforts as a kind of insurance. In private insurance markets, many buy insurance policies so that money can be paid to the few who have disasters occur. Government programs that provide income support for the neediest or that invest in human capital—for example, in the health and education of those unable to pay for them—are a sort of insurance where all citizens contribute (taxes), and those facing potential disaster receive the help.

THE SOCIAL MORTGAGE ON PROPERTY

In his encyclical *Sollicitudo rei socialis*, Pope John Paul II offered an extraordinarily helpful metaphor to frame the question of the obligations of the prosperous. This was the idea that holders of wealth in a market economy hold their assets subject to a "social mortgage"—an obligation to apply their wealth not simply to the accumulation of more wealth but also to pay off the *senior* claim that society legitimately places on that wealth: "It is necessary to state once more the characteristic principle of Christian social doctrine: the goods of this world are originally meant for all. The right to private property is valid and necessary, but it does not nullify the value of this principle. Private property, in fact, is under a 'social mortgage,' which means that it has an intrinsically social function, based upon and justified precisely by the principle of the universal destination of goods."[1]

As is true of any other mortgage, the social mortgage ranks ahead of the equity holder in its claims on assets and income, but it is not ownership or control, which remain fully vested in the owner. The social mortgage thus neatly reconciles private property and the market economy to the larger obligations that each individual has to his or her community. It takes full advantage of the efficiencies of private markets, where prices seamlessly convey extensive information to producers and consumers, while reminding us that the returns captured in those private markets remain encumbered by larger obligations to the community, whose laws and norms have created the environment where those private markets can flourish. The theme of the social mortgage is a new way of expressing the integration of our participation in private markets with our obligations to our inner selves and to others.

The overarching purpose of *Sollicitudo rei socialis* is to promote the development of all peoples, where "development" is understood as encompassing far more than material gains: "Development which is merely economic is incapable of setting man free, on the contrary, it will end by enslaving him further. Development that does not include the cultural, transcendent and religious dimensions of man and society, to the extent that it does not recognize the existence of such dimensions and does not endeavor to direct its goals and priorities toward the same, is even less conducive to authentic liberation."[2]

This development is neither a materialistic concept nor an exercise in spiritual contemplation. Nonetheless, it presupposes access to the material goods of the world sufficient to enable the individual to live a life of dignity and reach his or her full potential:[3] "The motivating concern for the poor— who are, in the very meaningful term, 'the Lord's poor'—must be translated at all levels into concrete actions, until it decisively attains a series of necessary reforms. Each local situation will show what reforms are most urgent and how they can be achieved."[4]

For this reason, the encyclical considers the impact on the poor of numerous aspects of domestic economies and political systems, as well as international institutions and terms of economic exchange, down to foreign exchange rates.[5] The size of the social mortgage, and the instruments used to embody the abstract concept in daily life, are driven in substantial part by the extent of economic disparities within a society. Where those disparities are evidence of a society in which some individuals lack the material resources necessary to fully live lives of dignity in which they can pursue their own integral human development, the social mortgage is that much larger.

The circumstances required to promote the authentic development of the individual are not the exclusive purview of members of the Catholic faith, but rather are universal claims on all societies: "Collaboration in the development of the whole person and of every human being is in fact a duty of all towards all, and must be shared by the four parts of the world: East and West, North and South; or, as we say today, by the different 'worlds.'"[6]

Sollicitudo rei socialis maintains that Catholicism has a special role to play in promoting the authentic development of men and women; but again, the objects of this attention are all persons, not just those who are members of the Catholic faith:

> The Church is an "expert in humanity," and this leads her necessarily to extend her religious mission to the various fields in which men and women expend their efforts in search of the always relative happiness which is possible in this world, in line with their dignity as persons.... This is why the Church has something to say today, just as twenty years ago, and also in the future, about the nature, conditions, requirements and aims of authentic development, and also about the obstacles which stand in its way.[7]

In sum, the obligation described in *Sollicitudo rei socialis* to promote the authentic development of the individual is made real, in part, through concrete economic action. Its message applies to all members of society, and its reasoning rests on principles of moral philosophy that are not the exclusive province of one faith. This means that the social mortgage—indeed, the entire operation of promoting authentic development—can and must exist within the political sphere, even a secular political society: "For the decisions which either accelerate or slow down the development of peoples are really political in character. In order to overcome the misguided mechanisms mentioned earlier and to replace them with new ones which will be more just and in conformity with the common good of humanity, an effective political will is needed."[8]

The encyclical thus offers more direction on the scope and instantiation of the social mortgage than at first appears. The social mortgage is the senior creditor claim on the ownership of goods necessary to ensure that all members of a society possess the material circumstances necessary to pursue their own authentic development. The social mortgage does not interfere with the rights of ownership any more than a commercial mortgage does, but like a commercial mortgage, its claim comes ahead of the owner's ability to consume that wealth or the income it generates. The instruments by which the social mortgage is defined and applied exist as real and salient in the political sphere, not simply as hortatory calls in Sunday sermons.

In *Sollicitudo rei socialis*, Pope John Paul II was careful not to prescribe one particular set of economic reforms to satisfy the claims of the social mortgage.[9] Nor did he propose a metric to determine the size of that obligation. But he was clear that the mortgage increases with the wealth of a society and the inequality of its economic system. By every measure, then, the social mortgage that encumbers the US market economy should be large, and its existence and purpose should be universally acknowledged. Yet neither is true: the United States today is the richest large economy in the world, but it imposes uniquely small communitarian claims on private wealth.

This idea that the social mortgage takes visible form within the political system is necessary because the instruments through which the social mortgage can be embodied largely rest in the hands of the state—in particular, in its power to compel its citizens, who are subject in the United States only to constitutional protections. To move from the abstraction of a hypothesized social mortgage to making good on this social claim, we *must* invoke the power of the state.

The most important of these state instrumentalities of compulsion is fiscal policy, meaning here government taxing policies, which in turn are used to finance public spending on income security, investment, and insurance programs. For example, we—appropriately—cannot sell our future services in a binding way in order to raise money to fund our education today, so investment in the human capital of those without family access to money capital will always fall short of economically efficient and morally satisfactory levels, in the absence of some sort of public intervention. This intervention takes the form of assessing a social mortgage through taxation sufficient to ensure that comparably able kids receive comparable levels of investment in their human capital through education, regardless of family circumstances.

Taxing and spending policies directly affect citizens' income security, inequality, and opportunities for economic mobility in large and measurable ways that lead to obvious differences in social welfare across similarly affluent societies. The heart of the impact of the social mortgage lies here.

Government mandates are also important. For example, mandates can correct for private market externalities—places where the price mechanism at the heart of our market economy fails to send the right signal because a private actor can avoid shouldering the social costs of its private economic behavior. Environmental pollution is the classic example. Similarly, mandates can address fundamental information or power asymmetries—for example, where one side of a bargaining process (the average worker dealing with his or her employer, or the average lower-income household dealing with a payday lender) is forced to accept terms that would not be reached by two fully informed and autonomous parties, each under no compulsion and with a continuum of alternatives to consider. This is the motivation and economic justification for minimum wage laws. The focus of this chapter, however, is on the impact of taxing and spending policies.

LUCK AND GRATITUDE

Catholic social thought understands the social mortgage on property as founded on the providential destiny of the material world to meet human needs. The social mortgage is an obligation in justice and an instrument to instantiate this destiny. And yet we can also recognize the role of a personal sense of gratitude in living out this obligation, something apparent in some of Regina Wolfe's interviews of CEOs presented in chapter 1. The prosperous enjoy the bounty of creation, and gratitude makes their sharing with the needy humane and even gracious, rather than a begrudging response to a requirement.

There is a helpful, secular analogy to the gratitude arising from this religious tradition that provides a nonreligious rationale for supporting the social mortgage. That is to frame our social obligations to each other around the pervasive importance of brute luck in our lives. Brute luck orders—or, more accurately, disorders—everything we set out to do, and every aspect of our life that we believe we control. If those of us fortunate to be prosperous can recognize this fact, we have reason to be relieved, even grateful, at our luck, and we have further reason to acknowledge the bad luck of so many of the unfortunate.

Let me offer an analogy. I cycle regularly and have a standard 15-mile route that I follow a few times a week. On ordinary days my time around the course does not vary by more than a minute or two. On some occasions, however, there is a strong headwind blowing down from the mountains on that stretch of my journey that is most vulnerable to the wind. On those days, I push myself as hard as I can against the wind in my face, but despite my best efforts I finish the route far behind my usual time. But there are other, more fortunate, days when a meteorologist would note the existence of a wind in the opposite direction. Not I. All I notice is that I am barely touching the pedals, and yet I fly through that part of the route and finish at or near a personal record. Like every other cyclist, I have suffered through many tough headwinds but do not recall ever feeling a tailwind.

Life is like that. The winds of fortune buffet us, sometimes to our advantage and sometimes to our detriment. What is more, those of us who sail through life with the wind at our backs often believe that we can be distinguished from others entirely through our claims to superior talents or dedication, not because of the good fortune of a tailwind. Authentic self-reflection can lead us to acknowledge our good fortune and through this to recognize a social mortgage on our success.

Both the genetic attributes that define who we are and the resources that our parents could bring to bear to help us are wholly outside our control.

So, too, are many of the events throughout our lives that knock us off our intended course—for better or worse. Yet all these have profound effects on our material outcomes. Call it luck or the winds of fortune or serendipity—the inescapable fact is that our lives are far more contingent than most of us can comfortably accept. Our material outcomes and our happiness are shaped to a large extent by random events, both favorable and unfavorable.

When we think clearly about the pervasive role of luck in our material outcomes, we come to appreciate that when we employ well-designed government insurance and investment policies to mitigate the worst instances of brute luck, we give life to our aspirational values as a body politic and our current commitments to each other. At the same time, we increase our national prosperity. As we will see in the next section, the inclusive growth literature demonstrates that the path to greater economic growth, and a more equal sharing of that growth, lies through more muscular government spending policies in the form of insurance and investment.

Because brute luck is random, its impact on any one individual is entirely unpredictable. But when analyzed from the perspective of the group, the consequences of some forms of brute luck become highly predictable. The most important of these predictable instances of brute luck are our health and existential fortuities—where we are born, to whom we are born, and when we are born. All these leave their handprint on incomes, social mobility, economic inequality, and lifetime satisfactions. We do not choose or control these existential fortuities, or very much about our basic health—although when they act as tailwinds we are quick to congratulate ourselves on our moral superiority.

It is possible for a child born into poverty to rise to great wealth, but it is far more likely that he or she will remain for their whole life nearer to the bottom of the income distribution. When we ignore facts like this, we condemn millions of Americans who suffer at the hands of existential fortuities to lives that are less productive and less satisfying than they could be.

The aggressive contrarian view to the acceptance of brute luck as a powerful causal force of our material outcomes is market triumphalism. This perversion of moral philosophy rests on the systematic denial of luck and the assertion that markets give people what they deserve. It treats market outcomes as necessarily efficient ones, and then implies that unhappy market outcomes must reflect psychological or spiritual defects rather than headwinds.

The acknowledgment of the importance of brute luck brings with it an attitude of gratitude and humility. It leads to greater empathy toward fellow citizens because we feel their pain and understand their values, rather than simply assuming that the distance between them and us reflects their moral failing or some divine judgment. It leads to a recognition of a social mortgage on our prosperity.

INCLUSIVE GROWTH IS HIGHER GROWTH

The social mortgage is a powerful metaphor, but some will demean it as a simple exercise in redistribution from "makers" to "takers." This is a serious distortion, given that important recent economic research has demonstrated that careful expenditures generate "inclusive growth."

The social programs that can be funded through taxation—public education, public health, greater investment in infrastructure, and so on—all have large positive economic returns that are broadly shared. When the social mortgage is animated by this recent work in "inclusive growth," the idea of the social mortgage becomes more persuasive and more powerful. Its implementation turns out to lead not only to greater fairness—to more opportunities for authentic development of individuals—but also to a wealthier society overall in which those economic gains are more broadly shared.

Much traditional policy literature addressing economic growth starts from the premise that taxes in general, and taxes on capital (wealth) in particular, are bad for growth because those taxes reduce the capital stock or the incentive to work. At its extreme, this literature reduces to a bizarre cheerleading for the United States to prevail in an imagined Gross Domestic Product Olympics, in which more accurate measures of welfare (including social cohesion, environmental sustainability, and many other factors) are ignored in favor of a single, deeply flawed metric—gross domestic product (GDP)—determined without regard to any distributional implications.

The groundbreaking economic research undertaken in recent years by the International Monetary Fund, the Organization for Economic Cooperation and Development (OECD), and allied academics on the theme of "inclusive growth" stands in direct opposition to this mistaken but widely held view. The inclusive growth literature responds directly to these traditional models that posit a trade-off between efficiency and equity—without tumbling all the way down the hill to empirically questionable gross national happiness formulations. The first point is that the United States, along with most other advanced economies, is held back by weakness in demand, not capital supply. The second is that inequality hurts an advanced economy's most important capital stock: human capital. And this is before considerations of the corrosion of social bonds promoted by fiscal policies that emphasize lower taxes on capital supply and fiscal consolidation measures.

As the IMF, hardly a hotbed of Marxist economic thought, wrote:

> Income equality can lead to higher long-term growth through faster human and physical capital accumulation. . . . Recent studies indicate that high levels of inequality are, overall, harmful for the pace and sustainability of growth. Education and health outcomes of the poor tend to be better in a more equal society, due to higher personal income, larger transfers from the government, and/or better public services. This can lead to a faster accumulation of human capital. In addition, higher income equality can expand the size of domestic demand and support higher physical capital accumulation. (emphasis omitted)[10]

The IMF's institutional change of heart in large measure has been attributable to an important Staff Discussion Note that it published in 2014. The paper concluded: "Lower net inequality is robustly correlated with faster and more durable growth, for a given level of redistribution. . . . [Further], redistribution appears generally benign in terms of its impact on growth; only in extreme cases is there some evidence that it may have direct negative effects on growth. Thus the combined direct and indirect effects of redistribution— including the growth effects of the resulting lower inequality—are on average pro-growth."[11]

To the same effect, the OECD has released a series of book-length publications on the social and economic costs of inequality. One such publication summarized its findings as follows:

> Beyond its impact on social cohesion, growing inequality is harmful for long-term economic growth. The rise of income inequality between 1985 and 2005, for example, is estimated to have knocked 4.7 percentage points off cumulative growth between 1990 and 2010, on average across OECD countries for which long time series are available. The key driver is the growing gap between lower-income households—the bottom 40% of the distribution—and the rest of the population.
>
> A main transmission mechanism between inequality and growth is human capital investment. While there is always a gap in education outcomes across individuals with different socio-economic backgrounds, the gap widens in high-inequality countries as people in disadvantaged households struggle to access quality education. This implies large amounts of wasted potential and lower social mobility.[12]

Together, these conclusions reached by the IMF and OECD are remarkable, and they represent a virtual reversal of course from their standard analyses of a decade earlier. These policy statements stand in sharp contrast to neoclassical microeconomic models that still dominate much academic and policy discussion in the United States. The analyses by the IMF and OECD imply that capital taxes (which, by virtue of the concentration of capital income shares at the top end, fall mainly on the most affluent) can lead to higher growth if used to fund investment in the human capital of lower-income households.

Here we see the social mortgage made concrete. The social mortgage takes its principal form in our tax structures. The revenues so raised fund useful collective investment and insurance programs that not only make a society more equal but also make an advanced economy like the United States more affluent over the long term. This is what the OECD calls the "double dividend" of inclusive growth strategies.

The long-term stability, welfare, and income of an advanced economy depend on its investment in its largest single asset class: its citizens. They, in turn, have equal moral claims to the investments in their own human capital through education required to enable them to achieve their full potential. To the same effect, health is not only a moral imperative but also an economic one, and public investment in infrastructure and the like yields direct positive economic returns while at the same time opening job opportunities for thousands.

The social mortgage places a claim on national income sufficient to fund all these obligations, and, as a result, a healthier and more productive society emerges. The social mortgage is repaid, and, as a double dividend, society is more affluent than it would have been if unabated market incomes had dominated, and the bulk of the country's citizens had been starved of the human capital and good health they need to achieve their potential.

THE SOCIAL MORTGAGE ON FIRMS

Although the three CEOs interviewed in chapter 1 recognize a kind of social mortgage on their businesses, many standard economic frameworks reject the claim that firms have independent social obligations, beyond following any rules that explicitly constrain their behavior. In chapter 2 Jennifer Herdt details several strands of development of this view in history. In the hands of some authors, like Milton Friedman, this position marks the foundation of a libertarian theoretical framework aimed at denying the existence of a social mortgage at any level of society. In chapter 5 Mary Hirschfeld demonstrates how Friedman goes too far, but one can be sympathetic to a portion of his claim. That is, one can imagine encumbering business with only a modest social mortgage, while at the same time arguing that wealth holders—in practice, the owners of those firms—have large social mortgages to repay.

Standard economic analysis views the social obligations of business firms through the prism of economic externalities. It says that we should accept that business firms have a focus only on maximizing profits, and we should channel this impulse when necessary through rules that require firms to absorb *all* the costs associated with their business objectives, including those costs that otherwise would not be reflected in the market system.[13] Environmental pollution is the classic example.

A fundamental tenet of welfare economics is that competitive markets in which prices reflect all relevant social as well as private costs yield optimal allocative efficiency: the economy is as profitable as it can be, given the available resources of labor, capital, and the systems to put the two together. In short, profitability, and ultimately wealth, is maximized. This kicks upstairs (to wealth holders, and individuals more generally) the question of the fairness of any resulting income and wealth distribution. The distributive issue is then seen as the function of collective action through the intermediation of government, by means of an individual tax system that has the desired level of "redistribution" (a word I put in quotation marks because it, by itself, has an implicit moral dimension that often is unappreciated). In short, welfare economics divides aggregate social welfare into a two-step dance, in which aggregate wealth first is maximized (subject only to the discipline of the internalization of economic externalities), and then social debts are measured and collected from the resulting holders of wealth.

Legal analysis offers little by way of any counterbalance. The firm's principal duty is to its shareholders (owners), but courts allow firms, as instantiated in their board of directors, a tremendous amount of latitude in judging what is in the best long-term interests of the firm. Thus, a board is not liable for corporate waste if the board causes the firm to make a charitable contribution, so long as the board articulates its reasoning as more than just feeling good about it (or getting free tote bags for all the directors). Conversely, a board also can decide that charitable giving properly is the province of its owners in their individual capacity, which those owners express by deciding how to maximize their individual welfare through their decisions about how they will spend their wealth.

The two-step dance of welfare economics is a concise and salient story. What is not to like? I see five flaws in this simple argument neatly separating the obligations of firms from the obligations of their owners.

First, it shifts the issue of social responsibility within the firm's business cal-
culus to the question of which social costs should be internalized and thereby
reflected in the price mechanism. Environmental costs appear conceptually
easy, which is why they are the standard example (even though we have made
much less progress here than we should). Yet there are many examples of
social costs that are thought to be too attenuated to the operations of a firm
to require internalization. Adam Smith commented on the mental and emotional harm of the rote work demanded of employees in the factories of his
day, but we do not generally think of these sorts of harm to workers as a social
cost that should be internalized by taxing firms that do not offer intellectually
stimulating work environments.[14] Conversely, as a matter of national policy
the United States views private employers as the primary delivery mechanism
for the social good of health care; that is, we approach health care as a social
cost that should be internalized into market prices—in this case, the price of
labor. Is this the right place for this social cost to be borne?

Second, the two-step dance of firm wealth maximization and owner-level
"redistribution," where wealth creation and social obligations are viewed
as largely independent of each other, leads to the fundamental problem of
the stickiness of wealth: the firm maximizes its owners' wealth, and we then
"redistribute" from that point.[15] However, it turns out (mirabile dictu!) that
once business profits enter an individual's bank account, he or she develops
an extraordinary attachment to them. This, in part, explains the underlying
implications of the "re-" in "redistribution"—it implies a legitimate claim to
the wealth in question in the hands of whoever's bank account it first touches,
which in turn must somehow be overcome by a more compelling but second-
ary social objective of fairness (or, in the language of the most candid affluent,
"mob rule"). The reaction of owners would be different if more of the social
mortgage were incorporated into the first-step wealth creation at the level of
the firm.

Third, the classic welfare economics story, envisioning government's role
as establishing guardrails that internalize social costs not otherwise reflected
in prices, and then stepping back, is implicitly premised on an old-fashioned
view of corporate behavior, which is that firms are passive rule takers and not
rule makers. The *Citizens United* Supreme Court decision and the breakdown
of most campaign finance strictures have changed that. Today, firms clearly
understand that the rules under which they operate are highly malleable,
and they, therefore, spend tens of millions of dollars annually to bend these
rules in directions congenial to their owners' wealth. This phenomenon is
reflected not merely in electioneering but also in campaigns to form public
opinion, and (perhaps most effectively) in actively participating to shape the

administrative agency rules that in practice define the bulk of the framework in which firms operate.

One can see the double-headed agenda, for example, in the financial services industries' efforts to relieve themselves of the burden of the Dodd-Frank legislation passed by Congress in the aftermath of the financial crisis of 2008: their investments in lobbyists and campaign contributions have paid handsome dividends in revisions to the law and in relaxed regulatory standards. The externalities here are the risk of massive consumer frauds and the prospect of another collapse of the financial services industries, dragging down with them the larger "real" economy, just as happened in 2008.

Fourth, and standing as a bridge to the final point, firms that have taken on more legal rights are now more vulnerable to claims about their responsibilities. The legal system in recent years has rapidly evolved to construe business firms not just as juridical persons—capable of concluding contracts in their own name, and so on—but also as quasi-human legal persons. *Citizens United*, for example, rests on the (highly contested) conclusion that the First Amendment's protection of freedom of speech extends beyond natural persons to include business entities acting in their independent capacity as juridical persons, but ones now imbued with an important personal fundamental right.

The *Hobby Lobby* Supreme Court decision further expanded this conflation of the juridical personality of business firms with the constitutional protections made available to natural persons. In that case, the religious views of the owners of a firm were allowed to determine the health care coverage made available to employees of that firm, who did not necessarily share those religious views. The Supreme Court couched matters in terms of the free exercise of religion (by the owners), but this was very strained reasoning. Although one might contort oneself to conclude that firms should enjoy First Amendment rights of free speech, so that those firms can advocate in public forums for policies that reflect their profit-maximizing objectives, firms themselves do not and cannot have religious preferences, and they are incapable of "exercising" them. What is more, and as previously noted, the health care system in America for those under the age of sixty-five years is largely designed around a model in which private employers are the primary health care delivery mechanism. The employees of Hobby Lobby or any other firm, therefore, look to their employer to provide their health care, regardless of any differences in moral principles between employee and owners of the employer. The employer's role, in turn, is directly subsidized by the government (employer-provided health care is not considered taxable income for the employee).

The owners of Hobby Lobby thus took advantage of a secular federal subsidy to impose their religious beliefs on their employees—not simply to exercise their religion—in an area where employees did not have competitive market alternatives. To this author at least, the case's holding seems far afield from any legitimate claim that the Supreme Court was only protecting the owners' rights to the free exercise of their religion. For purposes of this chapter, however, the point is that in *Hobby Lobby*, as in *Citizens United*, the firm essentially was reconceived as possessing rights traditionally thought of as appertaining only to individuals. In turn, the more the lines between the rights of firms and those of individuals are blurred, the less convincing is the distinction of the firm as unencumbered profit maximizer, and owners alone as shouldering any social mortgage.

Fifth, and most interestingly, events have completely overtaken this standard presentation of the very small social mortgage that lies on business assets and activities. Many firms have very recently developed a conscience, it would seem. Starbucks closed for a day to conduct training on racism; Citibank decided not to take on firms in the gun industry as clients. What explains this rapid reversal of the previous consensus that social welfare was advanced by letting firms be profit-maximizers and leaving social obligations to the individual level?

In part, these developments reflect the strong moral compass of some extraordinary self-made men. Howard Schulz, who has just resigned from Starbucks, has a long history of interest in social issues, and Bill Gates left Microsoft largely to devote himself to the deployment of his great wealth to advance important social issues. But the real novelty lies elsewhere.

The new development is social media, which is all-encompassing and all-seeing. Starbucks closed all its stores for a day of racial sensitivity training, not because Howard Schulz randomly thought that this was a good idea, but because a viral video showed the arrest of two men in a Philadelphia Starbucks for the crime of sitting while black. This is a sea change: for the first time, every business finds itself deeply and inescapably enmeshed in every social issue of the day. The issues cannot be avoided by recourse to the old adage that firms are simply amoral, profit-making enterprises, for which social causes are inappropriate distractions from their existential agenda. Every large enterprise today operates in practice in a new world of near-complete transparency, in which every corporate decision or misstep is reflected in uncountable tweets, Instagram posts, and Facebook likes.

The irony here is that through the all-seeing lens of social media, the social values of firms, which traditionally have been not just permitted but encouraged to abstain from any expression of social consciousness, will become explicit, highly articulated, and unavoidable. Firms will scramble to define these values against a backdrop of conflicting constructs of the social good, expressed in the anarchistic, reaction-driven, and sometimes thoughtless way that dominates all Internet interactions. Will we end up with pro-gun banks and anti-gun banks appealing to different customer bases? At the same time, individuals largely will remain unmoored from any larger social consensus of the common good: even basic notions of citizenship seem no longer to be part of the shared social enterprise. It is ironic, to say the least, to think of corporate CEOs agonizing over how to position their firms along the margins of every social issue of the day, while most individuals remain untrained in any moral tradition and therefore rely on rough intuition and tribal identity to express any social values.

If written today, *Sollicitudo rei socialis* would no doubt contain a large section on social media. On one hand, social media has become a quasi-moral force of great power that directly influences the behavior of our largest corporations. On the other hand, social media often has a mob-rule feel to it, and there certainly is no consistent and well-articulated moral philosophy at work. It is an often-helpful but sometimes dangerous interjection of highly salient moral claims into the operations of business.

What, then, can we make of all this? Social media as applied to businesses is too powerful to ignore but too volatile and underdeveloped in its consensus moral framework to carry much of the weight of the social mortgage. Concerning more formal policy instruments, the most useful are still the traditional measures of identifying negative externalities and market failures attributable to systematic asymmetries in power or information. It is important—and entirely consistent with *Sollicitudo rei socialis*—not to treat business as inherently suspect. Economic development has lifted literally billions out of extreme poverty over the last two generations, and by doing so has broadened the opportunities of these individuals to fulfill their own authentic development narrative. The most powerful policy instrument available to instantiate the social mortgage—taxation—can reduce the engine of growth if applied too vigorously; as a general matter, economists do not like taxation much at all, but when given the choice they prefer to tax savers over firms. The wealth generated by great business success does not vanish into thin air, but rather is captured by individuals and available for taxation at that level. This is the direction in which the terms of the social mortgage should be outlined.

Still, the reasons cited for questioning the two-step in this section do make a difference. Kenneth Goodpaster and Michael Naughton argue in chapter 6 of this volume that an "institutional insight," analogous to the social mortgage, identifies broader obligations that firms should endorse. In chapter 4 Gregory Beabout outlines the understanding of agency and autonomy most appropriate for the businessperson concerned with promoting positive social impact. But even if firms do not recognize any version of this obligation, the profits of those firms that pass to owners bear with them the social mortgage of the firm. The wealth of the wealthy bears a social mortgage not only because all wealth does but also because, for reasons of economic efficiency, our society does not require a firm to pay its social mortgage directly.

PUBLIC POLICY AS INSURANCE

The social mortgage, supported by both religious insight and a secular recognition of the force of luck in life, leads to the question of what we should do about it. The answer is that society ought to take action to assist those left behind in life, through communal, governmental effort funded by tax revenues. The most useful way to think of this action is with the metaphor of insurance.

Private insurance—say, for your car or house—pools risk, and the essence of insurance is mutuality. We each pay a manageable monthly premium and then, when one of us has fire damage at home, the insurance provider pays the victim for his or her financial loss—often much more than that individual ever paid in premiums. This all works because most of us never have that fire, but we enjoy the certainty of mutual assistance if we do. Insurance enhances the welfare of all members of the group. This theme of mutuality is also the essence of our government—"the things we decide to do together."

The insights arising from the social mortgage and the power of luck lead us to address misfortune that market mechanisms cannot address. Private market insurance is powerless against unfortunate circumstances of birth or unemployment due to technological change. Public insurance, conversely, can reach these cases because public policy instruments can look backward as well as forward in applying the intuitions' underlying insurance to situations that do not strictly constitute insurance in the commercial sense.

Social insurance is not a code word for gratuitous "transfers" or "entitlements." Instead, it acknowledges that the spending and taxing sides of government can be designed to work together to assist those in need by sharing the costs across society. The "benefits" paid by insurance in this metaphorical sense take the form of income support programs and investments in human capital: health care and education for the poor, retraining and relocation payments for unemployed workers, and the like. As we have seen above, these feed directly into the virtuous circle of inclusive growth strategies. The insurance metaphor resonates in public policy discourse and helps to focus government interventions where they will be most productive.

Private insurance does not make bad random events disappear; houses still burn down, and cars still crash. Insurance has value because it mitigates the financial consequences for an individual of an adverse fortuity, by spreading the cost to the group. And private insurance does not mend broken hearts, though it does mitigate the financial consequences of adverse events. The same is true for social insurance. This is all we can do as a social matter; the rest points in the direction of inner development of the individual, which is not the proper province of social initiatives.

The difference between insurance as product and insurance as metaphor is only whether the insurance we describe is one that fits the technical definition of insurance as it is ordinarily understood in commercial markets. In either case, by adopting insurance as the frame from which to respond to the problems of the unfortunate, it is possible to refine our intuitions about when government intervention might be feasible and desirable.

The philosopher John Rawls suggested a famous "behind the veil" thought experiment, where we all are sentient and rational disembodied beings about to pass through the veil and be born. We know that there are many circumstances into which we may be born, and many paths our futures might take regardless of those circumstances. Some futures are materially abundant, and others foretell lives of desperation, but we do not know which future will be ours. We are enthusiastic about embarking on the adventure of life, but anxious about the worst possible outcomes.[16]

Because we are rational, we wish to buy insurance before we launch ourselves into life—but being disembodied, we have no money with which to do so. The dilemma is resolved by the progressive income tax, in which we all agree to pay into the common pool disproportionately more of our future winnings, in order to support those who suffer the worst run of brute luck. The progressive income tax thus complements the insurance metaphor, with premiums necessarily paid in arrears rather than up front, where the resources thus collected are applied to the common pool to fund legitimate claims made against the pool.[17]

Because insurance here serves as a metaphor as well as an actual program, government can "pay claims" through investments as well as through direct transfers. Investing in the human capital of poor children through better funding for public education is the way we address the existential fortuity that poor families by definition do not have the resources to match rich ones in their investments in the human capital of their children.

In other words, public investment in human capital is one mechanism for implementing comprehensive insurance in response to the social mortgage, whether founded on religious insight or the power of brute luck. A universal basic income or means-tested programs can address issues like nutrition security, and universal health insurance can offer better health outcomes. These are the base conditions required to prosper in the modern world. But it is public investment that offers an economic path forward for an individual, and in doing so a more equal and productive overall economy.

The principal burden of the social mortgage will fall on wealth and the highest individual incomes. Importantly, however, the social mortgage does not need to take the form of steeply progressive income taxes. Indeed, the United States today has a more progressive overall tax system than most other countries—for example, Germany, whose government policies mitigate marketplace inequality far more than does the United States. How can these two thoughts be reconciled? The secret is on the other side of the ledger: government spending is almost by definition highly progressive, and in practice dominates any feasible progressive tax structure. What is needed is more revenue to fund more programs; within reason, the progressivity of the tax instruments employed to collect that revenue is much less important than is getting the revenue in the door, whence it can fund highly progressive social programs.

This is why European value-added taxes (VATs)—which are routinely derided in the United States as cruelly regressive—actually advance the agenda of the social mortgage. These VATs bring in enormous revenue with less economic deadweight loss than do steeply progressive income taxes, and the progressive application of VAT revenues to sensible public programs makes the overall fiscal system—the net of taxing and spending—more progressive than the US fiscal system, where a small but progressive tax system starves public income support, insurance, and investment programs of the funds they need to satisfy any fair reading of the obligations that the social mortgage should impose.

My book *We Are Better Than This* argues that the United States needs to increase public spending by about 2 percent of GDP to satisfy the moral and economic obligations staring at us.[18] This is a large sum of money—about $400 billion annually. Yet a typical reader's shock at the audacity of this suggestion also indicates how little we do today to acknowledge the social mortgage. Fortunately, we have ample fiscal space to make this measure of the social mortgage concrete.

To begin, the United States today is the lowest-taxed large economy in the world. We combine low taxes and high inequality; but the two, in fact, are connected. This is the point of the social mortgage and the inclusive growth literature. Considering all federal, state, and local taxes as a proportion of GDP, in 2016 the average national total tax collection in the industrialized nations (the OECD) was 34.3 percent; the United States, by contrast, collected only 26 percent of GDP. Moving the US to the average for advanced nations would generate an additional $1.5 trillion ($1,500 billion) per year.

If we accept just how contingent our lives really are, and therefore the importance of the metaphor of insurance as an ordering principle in our political and social systems, we instantiate what I call an empathetic economy. As we reflect on how government should spend and tax, we open a window into our national fiscal soul. We see at once that today our fiscal soul is sick. Yet, if we can inculcate in ourselves humility and concern for others that are the hallmarks of maturity, we can do better than this.

CONCLUSION

This chapter began with the notion of the social mortgage in Catholic social thought and added a secular reason—the force of luck in achieving prosperity—for endorsing this sort of obligation facing all who hold wealth. For both religious and secular reasons, those of us who are prosperous have an obligation to assist the unfortunate.

Recent economic research by international organizations—both the International Monetary Fund and the Organization for Economic Cooperation and Development—has made clear that certain fundamental efforts to assist the poor and further the common good lead to "inclusive" growth. Most important here are investments in the human capital of the poor and society's infrastructure, funded by taxes on capital.

The traditional argument in favor of economic efficiency—that moves the social mortgage from firms to the owners of firms—are overstated but contain a fundamental insight. Firms should be limited in cases of negative externalities and other market failures due to systematic asymmetries of power or information. But a reasonable concern for efficiency does call for the social mortgage on firms to be conveyed with the profits on those firms that move to owners.

A recognition of this mortgage should lead the owners of businesses to endorse what are in essence societal insurance programs that use tax revenues to fund inclusive growth. The fiscal policies necessary to breathe life into the social mortgage are not destructive of economic growth, but rather (and surprisingly) are accretive to it. The social mortgage, therefore, is not a rearrangement of wealth in a zero-sum game; instead, it is a call to action to fund those income-support, insurance, and investment programs that can put the country on a higher growth path. Public institutions and instruments are required to take advantage of these opportunities, but the social mortgage is not a vehicle for takers to dominate makers. Instead, it is a vehicle by which we can both honor our moral obligations to others and point the country in the direction of greater growth, more broadly shared.

NOTES

1. John Paul II, *Sollicitudo rei socialis*, 42.
2. John Paul II, 46.
3. This finds echoes in the work of John Rawls.
4. John Paul II, *Sollicitudo rei socialis*, 43.
5. John Paul II.
6. John Paul II, 32.
7. John Paul II, 41.
8. John Paul II, 35.
9. "The Church does not propose economic and political systems or programs, nor does she show preference for one or the other, provided that human dignity is properly respected and promoted, and provided she herself is allowed the room she needs to exercise her ministry in the world." John Paul II, *Sollicitudo rei socialis*, 41.
10. International Monetary Fund, *Fiscal Policy*.
11. Ostry, Berg, and Tsangarides, "Redistribution."
12. Organization for Economic Cooperation and Development, "In It Together."
13. Many years ago, when I was the chief nonpartisan tax resource to Congress, I had the opportunity to talk with the secretary-general of the OECD. I confessed that I was struggling with an issue that constantly popped up in Congress, which was whether tax policy ideally should advance environmental goals by taxing polluters more or instead by subsidizing emerging technologies like solar and wind. His advice was succinct but profound: "Tax the bads, and let the goods take care of themselves." It was a little simplistic, in that in some cases subsidies are needed to enable a new technology to achieve critical mass, but the fundamental point was that competitive markets, through the discipline of prices, reach allocative efficiency without the interposition of congressional (or other) judgments. The trick, in the secretary-general's aphorism, is to ensure that market prices incorporate all relevant social costs, and then stand back and let the market do its thing.
14. One can easily imagine counterarguments that such a policy would penalize first-time job holders, whose work experience might be mind-numbing but who gain valuable discipline, experience, and money from being part of the labor market. At one time, McDonald's claimed to be the first job of 20 percent of all working Americans: should we penalize or congratulate them for that?
15. The two themes intersect in optimal tax theory. There the idea is that a society has an independent preference for a certain degree of equality of economic outcomes, which it sets out to achieve by taxing income or wealth and "redistributing" the tax revenues to those further down the economic scale. But all practical taxes engender some quantum

of "deadweight loss"—of lower pretax wealth creation, because behavior is changed due to the imposition of the tax, whether on income, wealth, or consumption. In particular, taxpayers always have available a tax-free good: leisure—just chucking it in and going to the beach. At the margin, some individuals who would have chosen to work (i.e., to be productive wealth creators) in a world without taxes will choose instead to quit their job (or withdraw their savings), pack the sunscreen and beach towels, and head for the sand. Optimal tax theory sets out to propose tax structures that minimize deadweight loss in light of the productive capacity of the economy and society's independent preference for some assumed level of economic equality.

16. To put it in terms employed by Rawls, if we all were disembodied beings behind the veil who were offered the opportunity to trade away the potential economic upsides in life for no risk of downsides (i.e., a guaranteed equality of all incomes), we would refuse. This is the fundamental weakness in Rawls's policy prescriptions—the "behind the veil" model is a very useful thought experiment, but the rational actors whom he posits striking bargains behind the veil lack a robust appetite for the adventure of life. Phrased differently, his disembodied beings overinsure.

17. Ronald Dworkin has explored the insurance metaphor as a moral principle in some detail. This metaphor supplies an independent reason for preferring progressive rate structures beyond the standard explanation of the declining marginal utility of money.

18. Kleinbard, *We Are Better.*

CHAPTER 10

When Are Market Decisions Morally Legitimate?

K. J. Martijn Cremers

This volume focuses on the moral legitimacy of business in Catholic social thought, with most authors focusing on a careful examination of the internal workings of businesses. Still, any inquiry into the morality of business also requires a consideration of the morality of markets, specifically whether market decisions (by individuals or businesses) are morally legitimate. The answer to this question depends both on one's economic assumptions about the market and on one's perspective on morality. In this chapter, we discuss a variety of economic assumptions about markets. For morality, we use the basic standard of justice as the minimum requirement for morally legitimate behavior toward others, justice both as one's obligation toward others and as a virtue through which one pursues human goods with excellence.

We argue that market decisions—that is, particular market transactions—are morally legitimate only (benefiting rather than disadvantaging others) if they meet three requirements. First, they need to satisfy transactional justice (also called commutative justice or justice-in-exchange), which requires that both sides of any market transaction benefit from the transaction and receive approximately equal value. Second, the individual market transaction should not diminish, but rather contribute to three interrelated "shared goods" of market competition. These are information sharing, risk sharing, and discipline sharing, processes through which individual transactions can indirectly benefit those not directly participating in those transactions.

The third requirement concerns market activities that affect business firms: these actions must be either sufficiently committed to the long-term strategy of the firm—and thus to fruitful cooperation with the firm's other stakeholders—or have sufficiently limited market power so the activities do not have an adverse impact on the other stakeholders. The danger is that in some circumstances strong market competition renders it more difficult for other stakeholders (e.g., the employees, customers, and suppliers) to cooperate, thereby limiting the extent to which these other stakeholders can participate, limiting the firm's contributions to human flourishing.

To prepare for this argument, the chapter begins with three critical assumptions that also serve to narrow our discussion: that the private interests sought through the market transaction are good in themselves, that many human goods cannot be achieved through market transactions, and that the focus of the chapter is on transactions in a competitive market (rather than decisions regarding longer-term economic cooperation).

The chapter next explores the widespread notion from economics that competitive market transactions serve the public interest as long as markets are efficient. We highlight the main economic assumptions needed for this notion to hold as well as the limitations of these assumptions. In particular, three characteristics that are widespread in actual markets undermine the efficiency of markets: asymmetric information, incomplete markets (or incomplete contracting), and limited substitutability (or market control). Due to these limitations, the private interests of one party may conflict with the private interests of other parties, harm the shared goods of market competition more generally, and limit the ability of all the other stakeholders to cooperate with the firm to the detriment of the firm's ability to contribute to human flourishing.

THREE CRITICAL ASSUMPTIONS
REGARDING MARKET TRANSACTIONS

This chapter cannot address all the issues related to the moral legitimacy of market actions. Thus, we make three key assumptions to focus our analysis.

The Interests Pursued Individually Are Moral

The first assumption of the analysis of this chapter is that the interests pursued by decision-makers in market transactions are in themselves morally legitimate. Put differently, we assume that the private interests pursued through market transactions are actually good and contribute to human flourishing, such that we can also refer to these morally legitimate private interests as private "goods" that are good. Under this assumption, the central question to be answered can be rephrased: is the way in which these private goods are pursued through market transactions morally legitimate?

Many Private Goods Cannot Be Satisfied by the Market

The second assumption is that our discussion is only relevant to those human wants and needs that can actually be addressed or satisfied by market transactions. In his encyclical letter *Centesimus annus*, Pope Saint John Paul II addresses the question of whether "the free market is the most efficient instrument for utilizing resources and effectively responding to needs." He answers that the question can be answered affirmatively only "for those needs which are 'solvent,' insofar as they are endowed with purchasing power, for those resources which are 'marketable,' [and] insofar as they are capable of obtaining a satisfactory price."[1]

In other words, markets are inherently limited in the kinds of goods that they allow to be pursued, or the needs that they can satisfy, namely, needs that involve tradable goods and services. However, "many human needs find no place on the market,"[2] such as the need for meaningful relationships with God and other persons, which ultimately cannot be satisfied through market transactions (even if participation in markets can contribute to human relationships).

Further, markets only "work" for people who have the skills, access, and wealth to participate in the market. Pope Saint John Paul II explains that this is a major limitation, as he argues that

> perhaps the majority [of persons in the world] today do not have the means to take their place in an effective and humanly dignified way within a productive system in which work is truly central. They have no possibility of acquiring the basic knowledge which would enable them to express their creativity and develop their potential. They have no way of entering the network of knowledge and intercommunication which would enable them to see their qualities appreciated and utilized. Thus, if not actually exploited, they are to a great extent marginalized.[3]

In other words, if people are effectively barred from participating in the productive economy (i.e., excluded from the market), then social institutions other than the market are required to overcome the exclusion, to "help people to acquire expertise, to enter the circle of exchange, and to develop their skills in order to make the best use of their capacities and resources."[4]

This is the responsibility of everyone who is participating productively in the market economy, as we are exhorted by Pope Francis in his letter *Evangelii gaudium*, where he challenges us that "today we also have to say 'thou shalt not' to an economy of exclusion and inequality."[5]

The Focus Is on Market Decisions

The third and final major assumption of this analysis is that it only pertains to "market decisions," defined as transacting in markets through competitive exchanges without compulsion, as distinguished from decisions in nonmarket, social environments that are not operating through the market mechanism. The market mechanism involves three closely connected components: a process of "adversarial" bargaining regarding private benefits (i.e., competition), independent transactions, and substitutability.

First, exchanges in markets are "adversarial," in the sense that goods and services are exchanged between two or more transacting parties where the more one party receives, the less the other party gets (at least in an objective sense, even if, based on their own preferences and circumstances, all parties subjectively prefer what they are getting to what they are giving up). For example, if I sell 100 shares of IBM stock to you, the more you pay me for those shares, the better it is for me and the worse for you.

Second, exchanges in competitive markets are assumed to be independent individual transactions, rather than one instance of an ongoing association involving repeated interactions over a longer period of time. For example, I sell 100 shares of IBM to you at a certain price at a particular point in time, without any further expectations of future transactions. Selling a product with an extended warranty would go beyond an individual and independent transaction, unless the warranty itself would be separately exchangeable through the market mechanism.

Third, the market mechanism is assumed to be competitive in the sense that each of the transacting parties could make an essentially identical exchange with another party. In other words, both the exchanging parties and the item exchanged are substitutable. For example, if I want to sell 100 shares of IBM stock and you do not offer me the price I am looking for, there are many other parties to whom I could offer to sell these shares. Similarly, if you are looking to buy a certain product in a competitive market, you can choose from a variety of sellers offering comparable products.

These three basic ingredients further help to distinguish the competitive mechanism in markets from the cooperative mechanism that characterizes many interactions in business (including many interactions that also take place in markets). In contrast to the competitive mechanism as narrowly defined above, cooperative associations involve the pursuit of social or shared benefits, interdependence in longer-term relationships beyond a given trans-action, and/or a certain complementarity between the cooperating parties.

ECONOMIC ARGUMENTS FOR THE MORAL SUPERIORITY OF MARKETS

Economic theory indicates that under the specific conditions of competitive market equilibrium, the pursuit of private economic interests in markets can serve the public (or shared) interest. In the first subsection below, we will briefly discuss this theory. The second subsection considers how the public interests are advanced by the pursuit of private economic interests in compet-itive markets, namely, through their contribution of what we call the "shared goods of market competition." In the third subsection, we discuss the three central assumptions—and their limitations—necessary for attaining a com-petitive market environment and for the pursuit of private interests in mar-kets to have such public or shared benefits.

The Economic Theory of Competitive Market Equilibrium

As Jennifer Herdt explains in chapter 2, a moral endorsement of markets has a long history. In economic theory, the idea that pursuing private eco-nomic interest in markets serves the public interest is expressed in the two fundamental theorems of welfare economics.[6] The first fundamental theo-rem asserts that under competitive market equilibrium, no individual can be made economically better off unless another individual is made worse off (which is called a Pareto-optimal allocation of economic goods and services). This is consistent with the famous argument made by Adam Smith in *The Wealth of Nations*:

> As every individual, therefore, endeavors as much as he can both to employ his capital in the support of domestic industry, and so to direct that industry that its produce may be of the greatest value; every indi-vidual necessarily labors to render the annual revenue of the society as great as he can. He generally, indeed, neither intends to promote the public interest, nor knows how much he is promoting it. By preferring the support of domestic to that of foreign industry, he intends only his own security; and by directing that industry in such a manner as

its produce may be of the greatest value, he intends only his own gain, and he is in this, as in many other cases, led by an invisible hand to promote an end which was no part of his intention. Nor is it always the worse for the society that it was no part of it. By pursuing his own interest, he frequently promotes that of the society more effectually than when he really intends to promote it.[7]

The second theorem says that, in a competitive market equilibrium, redistributing wealth among individuals can produce any desired (Pareto-optimal) allocation of goods and services. In other words, if one does not like the allocation resulting from the competitive market, then any desired optimal allocation can be achieved through redistribution of wealth among the individuals competing in the market.

Together, the first and second fundamental theorems of welfare economics suggest that the main task of government is twofold. On one hand, government should promote those rules, regulations, and institutions that facilitate the functioning of the market, such that a competitive market equilibrium can best be approximated in practice.[8] On the other hand, it means that when there is a competitive market, any governmental action other than redistribution of wealth would distort the Pareto-optimal allocation of goods and services and lead to economically inefficient outcomes. Therefore, from this theoretical economic perspective, governments should strictly limit their interference in competitive markets involving morally legitimate products and services, as the main coordination needed for the optimal functioning of markets is provided by the "invisible hand" of market prices that guide demand and supply of these products and services.

Therefore, the question posed in the title of this chapter has an easy initial answer: market transactions are morally legitimate whenever markets are in competitive equilibrium. In this case, the pursuit of private interests in a competitive market gives rise to three different shared goods that benefit even those who are not involved in the market transaction themselves, including a Pareto-optimal distribution of goods and services based on the initial distribution of wealth among everyone participating in the market. However, this initial answer hinges on whether markets actually are in, or close to, a competitive equilibrium, which is discussed below.

The Shared Goods of Market Competition

In well-functioning markets, individual market transactions give rise to benefits that are shared beyond the parties directly involved in any particular transaction. Such benefits associated with market transactions we call "shared goods" (or "common goods") of market competition. In particular, we can distinguish three different, though related, shared goods of competition: information sharing, risk sharing, and discipline sharing.

Information Sharing

First, each market transaction involves a good (i.e., product, service, contract, security) that is sold at some price, which is a piece of information in a competitive market equilibrium that is easily observable or cheaply obtainable. The knowledge of other transactions in which they themselves are not involved allows all market participants to learn about demand and supply. At the most basic level and in normal circumstances, if the price of a certain good increases, the (actual or anticipated) supply of the good has declined or its (actual or anticipated) demand has increased. Therefore, every time a market participant is indicating a willingness to transact in the market, that person is providing some information about demand and supply to the market that is then shared across all participants in the market.

The shared information (1) helps individual market participants to make better decisions (as prices inform them about relative needs or preferences of others); (2) serves as the primary coordination device—or the invisible hand—in the market (e.g., a decrease in the price will lead to different reactions for low-cost and high-cost producers of a certain good); and (3) facilitates participation in the market, even for parties that do not have relevant information beyond the price.

The sharing of information through prices facilitates participation because it reduces the risk that a party will misunderstand the actual benefit of that product. If a product comes with very desirable benefits, it will have a high market price, which will inform people about its benefits. In this case, a deep ex-ante understanding of what those benefits are is not necessary. If information is widely shared in markets and thus prices reflect such shared information, then this helps consumers to buy products before they fully understand them. For example, when some new technological device comes out that is more expensive, if the higher price reflects the shared information from others that the device comes with superior benefits, then this would allow one to buy the new device before fully understanding all its benefits (which may require sustained use of the device). Further, because well-functioning markets offer many similar, competing products with different attributes, people have an incentive to become better informed. If there were only one product to buy, why spend significant time exploring the details or learning about how it works? If many products are available, it is worth spending some time to do research for one's own direct benefit, from which others can also benefit through the market mechanism.

Risk Sharing

Second, competitive markets allow participants to share risks, which again generates shared benefits for others. For example, if an entrepreneur sells equity in her firm to outside investors, then the upside and downside potentials of the firm are shared among a wide group of people. The entrepreneur can use the proceeds of the sale for consumption and investment in the firm, but also to invest in other firms, and thus have a better-diversified exposure to various business risks instead of a concentrated risk arising only from her own firm. Such diversification would lower the overall risk for the entrepreneur, allowing her to take additional risks that she would have been more reluctant to undertake in the absence of such diversification. This, in turn, allows the firm to pursue additional opportunities that can benefit everyone involved in the business. In other words, by sharing risks in the market (or through "co-insurance"), the entrepreneur can contribute more to the benefit of others.

Discipline Sharing

Third, market competition facilitates "outside options" and thereby provides a mechanism to share a drive for greater effort and excellence (i.e., "market discipline"), leading to more efficient allocation of resources and greater participation. A competitive market for resources and jobs facilitates a more effective allocation of the available resources (including land, investment capital, technology, and machinery), as well as to better job opportunities for workers. For example, if a firm owns land that can be more productively used by another firm and if there is a competitive market for land, then the firm can easily sell the land to another firm at a price that reflects (at least partly) this higher productivity. This creates an incentive to sell their land to the firm that can more productively use it, which can also be thought of as competitive pressure to sell. After all, if other firms are using the opportunity provided by the market to sell underutilized land at such a price that they benefit from this, then these other firms will be able to better compete and thus create more competitive pressure. The incentives and competitive pressure created by markets are shared benefits that accrue to all firms that have access to the market.

Another way to express the same idea is that by participating in the market, one creates outside opportunities for others, which effectively allows one to "share discipline"—or encourage the drive for others to also improve—through the market mechanism. For example, if the business practice at one firm has become a bit lax or inefficient, and some resources are underutilized, this would lead to inferior or relatively expensive products and insufficient opportunity to advance for the people working at those firms. A competitive market incentivizes the manager of the firm to better utilize the available resources and offer the people working there better opportunities. After all, if the manager would not improve the utilization of the resources and not offer better work opportunities, the firm may suffer a decline in sales of its products and may lose its employees to better outside opportunities, with adverse consequences for the manager and the business. In other words, the outside opportunities afforded by the competitive market produce shared benefits—even if no one at a firm actually leaves for another firm.

ASSESSING THE ECONOMIC ARGUMENT

Despite its popularity—the economic argument for trusting markets to generate the public good—there are numerous reasons to doubt it.

A Competitive Market Equilibrium Rarely Occurs

The private and the shared benefits of markets only arise if certain conditions hold. There are three conditions that are required for a competitive market equilibrium to be possible (i.e., for the first and second fundamental theorems of welfare economics to apply), namely, the lack of significantly unequal information, power, and control in the market among its participants.

Information

First, significantly unequal distribution of information means that some market participants have a much better understanding of the products and services sold and are unable to easily or cheaply share such information with others. The classic example of such asymmetric information is used cars, where the seller (typically the previous owner or the car dealer) has a much better understanding of the quality of the car than the buyer. If a customer is unable to ascertain such quality independently—for example, because this would be too expensive, or because the quality of the car may only become clear after a certain amount of use—the market mechanism becomes less effective. In particular, willingness to buy the product depends not just on the price and whatever information about the product can be shared but also on the reputation of and legal remedies available against the seller. If buyers rarely buy products subject to asymmetric information, or if it is difficult to reliably gauge the seller's reputation or learn of the experiences of other buyers, the problem of asymmetric information becomes more severe.

This problem is not easy to solve. One significant problem is what economists call "adverse selection," a problem that makes the goal of the "good goods" presented by David Cloutier in chapter 7 even more challenging. If it is difficult for buyers of a product to distinguish between high and low quality, sellers whose products actually have high quality are "selected out" of the market because they find it difficult to persuade customers that the higher quality is worth the higher price. As a result, sellers of lower-quality products can drive sellers of higher quality out of the market.

A particularly interesting example of the problems of asymmetric information and adverse selection is given by mortgage-backed securities (i.e., securities that distribute cash flows paid by a pool of mortgages) in the recent global financial crisis. Many such mortgage-backed securities were not subject to asymmetric information when first sold to investors, as the value of their collateral (i.e., the houses) was high relative to the cash flows that these securities promised to pay. In that case, investors did not have any incentive or need to investigate the value of the collateral or the ability of the homeowners to afford their mortgages, as more precise information would hardly change the estimate of the security and thus was not worth collecting. However, these securities suddenly became very difficult to value after the unexpected (and unprecedented) large decline in house prices, at which point more precise information about house values and homeowners' ability to pay the mortgage became very relevant. But this information was not readily available or (for most investors) easily understood. As it abruptly became costly to gauge their value, the private market in mortgage-backed securities broke down because trading securities requires some sense of what the security is worth.

Power

The second limitation is that some market participants may have more power than other market participants. Here we define power as the ability to change the circumstances of others without these others having the ability to reciprocate. A simple example is given by a market externality such as pollution, where the polluters have power over those whose environment they pollute, if the polluters do not have to compensate those who suffer the damaging effects of the pollution. In this case, the pollution is not fully incorporated in the market price of the polluter's products. The social cost of pollution is external to the market.

Differential power generally arises from markets or contracts that are "incomplete": when market participants cannot fully insure themselves against all risks to which they are exposed. For example, if a firm buys a product that requires a long-term service contract provided by another firm, the first firm is subject to the risk that the latter firm will go out of business. Other examples occur when products require significant switching or learning costs, or when the product (e.g., certain highly specific equipment or technology) is valuable to the firm buying it but not to anyone else. The buyer of such equipment is subject to the business risk that their customers may stop buying their supplies, in which case the equipment cannot be resold. In addition, it may be difficult to insure against this risk, in which case their customers will have a certain degree of power over them, especially if there is a limited number of such customers, which is captured by the next limitation: unequal control.

Control

Third, markets may be subject to unequal control if some market participants can more easily find another party to transact with than can others, or some can transact at much lower cost. Whenever a seller is selling a product that has no close substitute, the seller has some power over the buyers, as happens when a new product is still under patent protection. Or a seller may have superior power if the seller is relatively large compared with the other sellers, particularly in a context of many small buyers. Other instances of unequal control arise due to sudden changes in circumstances, as when people need to quickly buy or sell. In this case, one may not have enough time to bargain with multiple parties, giving others significant power over them.

Finally, unequal information, power, and control tend to go together. For example, market participants with less information tend to have less power and control, and market participants with superior information tend to have superior power and control.

Implications for the Economic Argument

The point here is not to argue that inequalities in information, power, and control are necessarily inefficient or morally suspect. Rather, the point is that such inequalities are widespread. This has a definitive impact on the general moral endorsement of self-interested economic activity promised by the two fundamental theorems of welfare economics. Although they are theoretically elegant, they are simply not generally valid in practice. Uncoordinated market transactions do not give rise to a competitive market equilibrium with a Pareto-optimal distribution of all goods and services. One cannot assume that the pursuit of one's private interests in markets will be morally legitimate.

OTHER PROBLEMS

Market transactions may also adversely affect the shared goods of markets. Making the market more competitive may make it more difficult for other stakeholders to cooperate.

Benefiting at the Expense of Others

If information, power, and control are unequally distributed, it could very well be the case that in pursuing one's private interests in market transactions, those with superior information (every used car salesman, TV salesman, financial planner, et al.), power, or control may benefit directly at the expense of others participating in these transactions who have less information, power, or control. This would violate commutative justice, which is the minimum requirement of moral behavior pertaining to exchanges of products, services, or securities.

For example, a seller with better information than the buyer may be able to sell a product at a higher price than the buyer would have paid if the buyer had fully understood the quality of the product. Or a seller may sell a product or service that requires significant subsequent servicing, giving the seller some power over any buyer. Although the buyer's contract may specify such subsequent service, it is hard for contracts to deal with all eventualities, and thus the seller might legally provide less service to the buyer than the buyer may have reasonably expected. The product might break down after the warranty has expired, and the seller may be the only party with the necessary expertise to fix the product, giving the seller power over the buyer.

Three interrelated solutions may help prevent market participants from directly benefiting at the expense of others, namely, increased transparency, accountability, and social responsibility. First, increased transparency can shed light on the advantages of some market participants and help those who are vulnerable to better protect themselves (e.g., by getting more background information, references, or feedback from others).[9] Second, increased transparency in markets can lead to greater accountability (e.g., by allowing consumers to better understand firms' social and environmental policies).

Third, whether market participants care about whether other market participants also benefit depends on their social responsibility. Similarly, the extent to which consumers consider the social and environmental policies of the firms whose products they buy will depend on their general willingness to consider how their actions affect others—that is, it depends on their social responsibility. In turn, it is important that firms recognize the limits of market competition and the extent to which they have superior information, power, and control.[10] The recognition of their ability to benefit at the expense of others is only the first step. The second is their willingness to refrain from doing so, which depends on their social responsibility—that is, whether they judge their social duties toward others as important, whether they are determined to pursue excellence (i.e., virtue, as Andrew Yuengert explains in chapter 3) through their participation in markets. In chapter 6, Kenneth Goodpaster and Michael Naughton focus on a similar issue in their insistence on "the institutional insight."

Harming the Shared Goods of Market Competition

Pursuing one's private interests in economic life can harm the shared goods of market competition, even if the particular transactions are not directly harming the parties with whom one is transacting. As we saw earlier in the chapter, the shared goods of market competition are the shared benefits arising through information sharing, risk sharing, and discipline sharing. These shared goods also benefit people not directly involved in the particular market transactions. As these shared goods naturally arise out of social interactions within the market, and can be thought of as the shared goal or "telos" of the market, the harming of shared goods is inconsistent with the pursuit of excellence (and particularly the virtue of justice) by the participants in the market.

Consider the example of a firm whose shares are being traded in a setting with asymmetric information, incomplete contracting, and limited competition. Let us assume the firm produces highly specialized equipment and technology that requires substantial investments over the long term. In such a setting, corporate insiders have a better understanding than outside shareholders. It is difficult for outside shareholders to fully appreciate the growth opportunities and associated risks involved, especially if it takes considerable time before the growth opportunities are realized and the value of these investments becomes apparent to outsiders. Due to their limited information, investors may be buying and selling shares in this firm based on speculative rumors. Such speculative trading can move the share price further away from fundamental value or cause more volatility in the price, decreasing information sharing in the market and rendering the share price less informative. Speculation has a greater ability to affect the price of the shares if there is more asymmetric information about the firm's investments, rendering it harder for investors to interpret any new information about the firm and distinguish between accurate and unfounded news.

There is a limit on how much speculative trading can matter. At some point, if the market price moves too much from the fundamental price, traders will have an incentive to collect the specialized information needed to understand the discrepancy from the fundamental price and take advantage of it, and by their corrective trading move the market price toward the fundamental price. The cycle of speculative trading followed by corrective trading creates additional volatility in the share price, which decreases the shared good of risk sharing. Finally, if the actual performance of the company and the share price are less closely related, this lowers the disciplinary effect that market prices have on the people running the firm.

Harming Stakeholder Cooperation

The pursuit of one's private interests in markets may also harm the extent to which the firm and its stakeholders can cooperate, a goal clearly endorsed by the CEOs interviewed by Regina Wolfe, as presented in chapter 1. Good cooperation in turn requires a joint commitment to the long-term strategy of the firm shared by all stakeholders. Too much competitive pressure may render cooperation between stakeholders more difficult, particularly if there is limited commitment of shareholders to the long-term strategy. Shareholders of publicly traded firms in general have a limited commitment to the long term because such shareholders always have the option to sell their shares (the "Wall Street Walk"), vote for different directors at the annual meeting, agree to a takeover bid, or support an activist shareholder (e.g., a hedge fund) pressuring the board of directors to change the strategy. If market transactions can make it more difficult for the firm's stakeholders to cooperate, this may harm the ability of the firm to contribute to society. This is another way the "institutional insight" recommended for business firms in chapter 6, by Kenneth Goodpaster and Michael Naughton, is so important.

Specifically, if the firm's shareholders can threaten to change the corporate strategy in the short term, the firm cannot credibly commit to a long-term strategy vis-à-vis its stakeholders. For firms whose investments are subject to significant asymmetric information and incomplete markets, such a limited commitment renders implementing any long-term strategy difficult. The asymmetric information causes uncertainty for investors about whether the long-term strategy is performing well and may cause investors to (rationally) misinterpret poor performance in the short term as indicating poor long-term prospects. In incomplete markets, the firm and its stakeholders (including employees, customers, and suppliers) have to make specific long-term investments, which will generally be significantly less valuable if the firm's strategy changes. As a result, short-term shareholder market pressure can render long-term commitments by any other stakeholders more difficult or costly. For example, employees will be more reluctant to learn the specific innovative technology that the firm is developing if there is too much uncertainty about whether the firm's shareholders have the necessary patience.

A further complication arises if the outside shareholders (or customers and suppliers) cannot be sure that the owner-entrepreneurs are making the right investment decisions, or perhaps are wasting money. Due to asymmetric information, this can be hard for outside shareholders to assess in the short-term period if the firm has made long-term investment decisions that lower current earnings and whose future payoffs are uncertain. As a result, the longer it takes before any growth opportunities are realized, the more likely it is that the outside shareholders will infer that the entrepreneurs-managers are wasting money, and the lower the firm's share price will be, and the more likely it is that outside investors will try to change the long-term strategy of the firm.

The solution is to create stronger shareholder commitments to the firm's longer-term strategy—especially for those shareholders who have the most influence on the firm's longer-term strategy, have the longest investment horizons, and/or find it easiest to exit, such as large institutional shareholders. Their temptation to focus on the short term—itself rising out of their being intermediaries with clients of their own that are often evaluating their performance over relatively short-term horizons—may harm the ability of the other stakeholders to cooperate with the firm, to the detriment of the firm's ability to make long-term investments and contribute to human flourishing. Because this would also harm the long-term performance of the firm, it is very much in the interests of these shareholders to commit to the long term, especially for firms that are more subject to asymmetric information and incomplete markets or are doing more long-term investments.

One solution is to implement "commitment devices," allowing such shareholders to commit to the long-term strategy of the firm—that is, legal agreements limiting their ability to make drastic changes to the firm's strategy in the short term. The first is longer terms for directors by adopting a staggered board, where directors might serve three-year terms and where in each annual election only one-third of directors is up for (re-)election, as opposed to a unitary board, where all directors serve one-year terms. The second is a supermajority requirement to change the firm's charter (i.e., the corporate "constitution") or bylaws (i.e., main procedures) or agree to any merger, which require a strong consensus among all shareholders before any such decisions are made.[11]

CONCLUSION

In the elegant economic theory of competitive market equilibrium, the pursuit of private interests in market transactions is always associated with shared benefits that accrue to all market participants and all corporate stakeholders. However, the three central economic assumptions for this theory to hold are widely violated in actual markets, which are generally subject to asymmetric information, incomplete contracting, and limited competition (or limited substitutability, with some market parties having some control over market prices). As a result, the pursuit of private interests in market transactions may involve benefiting at the expense of others, harming the shared goods of market competition, and limiting cooperation within the firm. In justice, market transactions are only morally legitimate if they do not do these things.

NOTES

1. John Paul II, *Centesimus annus*, 34
2. John Paul II.
3. John Paul II, 33.
4. John Paul II, 34.
5. Francis, *Evangelii gaudium*, 53.
6. For a formal treatment of both theorems, see Mas-Colell, Whinston, and Green, *Microeconomic Theory*. The discussion in the text benefited significantly from my joint work with Simone Sepe—including Cremers and Sepe, "Shareholder Value"; Cremers, Masconale, and Sepe, "Commitment"; and from other papers written by Sepe, e.g., Bratton and Sepe, "Shareholder Power." For a closely related discussion on corporate governance, see Cremers, "What Corporate Governance Can Learn."
7. Smith, *Wealth of Nations*, 363–64.
8. E.g., this means both that those rules should require a certain amount of transparency and provide a system to hold people accountable for violating market rules and that regulations should allow for relatively easy and free contracting between individuals and have

few restrictions on how people can associate (or that market institutions should as far as possible be self-regulated).

9. Challenges to greater transparency are the questions of who decides what information needs to be disclosed, who can verify such information, and who will bear the costs of disclosure or help people to understand the additional information. For example, as more people are investing in mutual funds for retirement or to help pay for their children's education, the market for financial advice has become more important to help people understand and navigate the plethora of financial products. Financial advisers and other financial intermediaries help investors through their advice, but they can also be costly to investors. Increased financial intermediation has resulted in a few very large financial institutions—like Vanguard and BlackRock—managing a large fraction of investor wealth, which concentration itself may give these large financial institutions considerable market power. The role of regulations falls outside the scope of this chapter.

10. Market participants would normally (and in justice) receive some compensation for acquiring information that is useful for others.

11. For more discussion on staggered boards, see Cremers, Litov, and Sepe, "Staggered Boards"; and Cremers and Sepe, "Shareholder Value." For more discussion on the importance of supermajority requirements as commitment devices, see Cremers, Masonale, and Sepe, "Commitment."

Afterword

James L. Heft

The research project and conference that generated this volume set out to ask some of the most fundamental questions about the moral legitimacy of business in Catholic social thought. The authors, including many of the most able in the field, dug deep into both the internal purpose of the business firm and every firm's obligations to society at large. The insights available here will be of significant service to many. At the same time, however, it is helpful to recall how this particular effort forms a part of a longer-term project aimed at better understanding the relation of faith and economic life, sponsored by the Institute for Advanced Catholic Studies.

In the summer of 2007, a group of scholars met in Chicago to discuss the possibility of a long-term research project that would not only harness Catholic social thought more effectively to interdisciplinary and empirically grounded studies in economics but also find ways for that project to influence Catholic social thought nationally and internationally. Led by the economist and theologian Daniel Finn—and collaborators Paul Caron of France, Clifford Longley of England, and James Heft, SM—the group explored ways to foster a body of international research that addressed the critical questions, nearly all now global, that would build upon, critique, and advance Catholic social thought on economics. In Chicago, they decided to organize an international conference to be held at the University of Southern California the following year. At the time, they had no idea that a year later the world's economies would plunge into frightening free fall. As I write these words, we are now in the midst of another major global financial crisis, the one precipitated by COVID-19. The need for intelligent, humane, generous, realistic, and morally grounded economic research could not be more timely and urgent.

The 2008 conference resulted in *The True Wealth of Nations: Catholic Social Thought and Economic Life* (Oxford University Press, 2010), the first of now five volumes in this distinguished series.[1] The sixth research project, on the character of justice in democratic and pluralistic societies, is already being planned. Twice in the past decade, the Institute for Advanced Catholic Studies has been invited to hold its research conferences at the Vatican, the first hosted by the Pontifical Council for Justice and Peace and the second by the Pontifical Academy of Social Science. The participants in all six of these projects believe that Catholic social thought can make a major contribution to creating a more just society, even as it learns from scholars of different religions and disciplines.

CLOSING GAPS FOR A BETTER WORLD

In typical Catholic fashion, the Institute for Advanced Catholic Studies recognizes that faith and reason are compatible. They can enrich each other and even purify each other. To create an ecology in which faith and reason can interact fruitfully, two gaps in our modern culture need to be closed.

First, there is the gap between theory and what is happening on the ground. For example, in the earlier True Wealth of Nations study on the common good, scholars from the social sciences, who by profession study what is occurring, and theologians, who are specialists in Catholic social thought, explored what they could learn from each other.

In writing this current volume, scholars had the benefit of studying interviews with business leaders who face decisions that are often not black and white and who have to make practical judgments that involve inescapable trade-offs, situations where hard decisions have to be made. The True Wealth project aims to overcome the gap between theory and concrete experience.

Second, there is the gap that exists between secular reasoning and religious thinking. The Catholic philosopher Charles Taylor has noted the remarkable fact that the academy in the Western world is more secular than the culture in which it exists. The Lutheran sociologist Peter Berger put it humorously, but pointedly, when he suggested that if India is the most religious country in the world and Sweden the least, then the United States is a nation of Indians ruled by Swedes.[2] In other words, the power elites in the United States, and especially the cultural elites, including most of the faculty members in our leading universities, are secular in their thinking, whereas the majority of ordinary people remain quite religious. Using Berger's typology, Taylor adds that "unbelieving sociologists of religion often remark how their colleagues in other parts of the discipline express surprise at the attention devoted to such a marginal phenomenon."[3] What Taylor says certainly applies to the field of economics.

The crucial importance of overcoming these gaps between a theologically grounded body of Catholic social thought and the work of secular thinkers in multiple academic disciplines was addressed at Westminster Hall in London in September 2010, where Pope Benedict XVI expressed what has been from the very beginning the goal of the entire True Wealth research program:

> The central question at issue, then, is this: where is the ethical foundation for political choices to be found? The Catholic tradition maintains that the objective norms governing right action are accessible to reason, prescinding from the content of revelation. According to this understanding, the role of religion in political debate is not so much to supply these norms, as if they could not be known by nonbelievers—still less to propose concrete political solutions, which would lie altogether outside the competence of religion—but rather to help purify and shed light upon the application of reason to the discovery of objective moral principles. This "corrective" role of religion vis-à-vis reason is not always welcomed, though, partly because distorted forms of religion, such as sectarianism and fundamentalism, can be seen to create serious social problems themselves. And in their turn, these distortions of religion arise when insufficient attention is given to the purifying and structuring role of reason within religion. It is a two-way process. Without the corrective supplied by religion, though, reason too can fall prey to distortions, as when it is manipulated by ideology, or applied in a partial way that fails to take full account of the dignity of the human person. Such misuse of reason, after all, was what gave rise to the slave trade in the first place and to many other social evils, not least the totalitarian ideologies of the twentieth century. This is why I would suggest that the world of reason and the world of faith—the world of secular rationality and the world of religious belief—need one another and should not be afraid to enter into a profound and ongoing dialogue, for the good of our civilization.[4]

Catholic social thought represents the Church's effort to bridge the gap between the world of reason and the world of faith. The True Wealth research project is committed to build this bridge between Catholic social thinking and economic thinking, not just in the United States but also globally.

The first sentence of Daniel Finn's introduction to this volume asks this poignant question: "Can a religion whose founder taught love of neighbor as the most fundamental moral principle give moral approval to profit-seeking business firms in a global economy?" Or, to put the question in terms similar to Pope Benedict's address, can Catholic social thought help purify and shed light on the moral principles derived from the careful use of reason, as well as learn from secular reasoning in order to develop clearer ways to express the moral teachings of Jesus?

THE SCOPE OF INSTITUTE RESEARCH:
THE "BENEDICT PROJECT"

Since coming to the University of Southern California in 2006, the Institute for Advanced Catholic Studies has also supported original and often interdisciplinary research in other fields of inquiry, including interreligious dialogue, Catholicism and modernity, engineering and Catholic social thought, religious freedom, the Catholic literary imagination, the Catholic vision of education, four Generations in Dialogue programs, religiously unaffiliated youth, and the sociology of the American parish. In all, the institute has published twenty books of original research. Soon it will acquire its own campus near the University of Southern California, where scholars from different disciplines and different religions can spend sabbaticals together for extended periods of research and conversation focused on the Catholic intellectual tradition.

It has been an extraordinary privilege to be a part of so many of these research projects, to find ways to support them, and to witness the commitment and dedication of the many scholars who are not afraid to enter and sustain the dialogue between faith and reason. As Martin Schlag puts it in this volume, these scholars have chosen not the Benedict Option, but the Benedict Project. They do not wish to isolate themselves from the modern world, but to enter into it and build bridges of understanding and collaboration. For this, we should all be thankful.

James L. Heft, SM
Alton Brooks Professor of Religion
University of Southern California
President Emeritus, Institute for Advanced Catholic Studies

NOTES

1. *The Moral Dynamics of Economic Life: An Extension and Critique of Caritas in veritate* (Oxford University Press, 2012); *Distant Markets, Distant Harms: Economic Complicity and Christian Ethics* (Oxford University Press, 2014); *The Empirical Foundations of the Common Good* (Oxford University Press, 2017); and this volume.
2. Berger, Davie, and Fokas, *Religious America, Secular Europe?* 12.
3. Taylor, "Secularization," 4.
4. Benedict XVI, "Meeting."

BIBLIOGRAPHY

Acemoglu, Daron, and James Robinson. *Why Nations Fail: The Origins of Power, Prosperity and Poverty*. New York: Crown, 2012.

Akrivou, Kleio, and Jose Victor Oron. "Two Kinds of Human Integrity: Towards an Ethics of the Inter-Processual Self." In *The Challenges of Capitalism for Virtue Ethics and the Common Good*, edited by Kleio Akrivou and Alejo Jose G. Sison, 221–53. Cheltenham, UK: Edward Elgar, 2016.

Alford, Helen. "The Influence of Thomistic Thought in Contemporary Business Ethics." In *The Handbook of the Philosophical Foundations of Business Ethics* 1, edited by Christopher Luetge. Dordrecht: Springer, 2013.

Alford, Helen, and Michael Naughton. *Managing As If Faith Mattered: Christian Social Principles in the Modern Organization*. Notre Dame, IN: University of Notre Dame Press, 2001.

Allmark, P. J. "An Aristotelian Account of Autonomy," *Journal of Value Inquiry* 42, no. 1 (2008): 41–53.

Alzola, Miguel. "Virtuous Persons and Virtuous Actions in Business Ethics and Organizational Research." *Business Ethics Quarterly* 25, no. 3 (2015): 287–318.

Annas, Julia. *Intelligent Virtue*. Oxford: Oxford University Press, 2011.

Appleby, Joyce. *Economic Thought and Ideology in Seventeenth-Century England*. Princeton, NJ: Princeton University Press, 1978.

Aquinas, Thomas. *Libros Politicorum Aristotelis Expositio*, Book 4, Lectio 4, edited by Raimondo Spiazzi. Rome: Marietti, 1966.

———. *Summa Theologica*. Translated by the Fathers of the English Dominican Province. New York: Benziger Brothers, 1948.

Aristotle. "Nicomachean Ethics." In *The Basic Works of Aristotle*, edited by Richard McKeon and translated by David Ross, 935–1126. New York: Random House, 1941.

———. *Nicomachean Ethics*. Trans. C. Rowe. Oxford: Oxford University Press, 2002.

———. "Politics." In *The Basic Works of Aristotle*, edited by Richard McKeon and translated by Benjamin Jowett, 1127–1324. New York: Random House, 1941.

Arrow, Kenneth J. "An Extension of the Basic Theorems of Classical Welfare Economics." *Proceedings of the Second Berkeley Symposium on Mathematical Statistics and Probability*, edited by J. Neyman. Berkeley: University of California Press, 1951.

Aufderheide, J., and R. Bader, eds. *The Highest Good in Aristotle and Kant*. Oxford: Oxford University Press, 2015.

Austin, N. *Aquinas on Virtue*. Washington, DC: Georgetown University Press, 2017.

Bakan, Joel. *The Corporation*. New York: Free Press, 2004.

Baker, Bruce. "Free Markets with Caritas: A Transformational Concept of Efficiency." In *Free Markets with Solidarity and Sustainability*, edited by Martin Schlag and Juan A. Mercado. Washington, DC: Catholic University of America Press, 2016.

Bannock, Graham, R. E. Baxter, and Ray Rees. "Rent-Seeking Behaviour." In *The Penguin Dictionary of Economics*, 7th ed, by Graham Bannock, R. E. Baxter, and Ray Rees. London: Penguin Books, 2003.

Barbalet, Jack. *Weber, Passion, and Profits*. Cambridge: Cambridge University Press, 2008.

Bartlett, Christopher, and Sumantra Ghoshal. "Changing the Role of Top Management: Beyond Strategy to Purpose." *Harvard Business Review* 72, no. 6 (1994): 79–88.

Beabout, Gregory R. *The Character of the Manager: From Office Executive to Wise Steward*. London: Palgrave Macmillan, 2013.

———. "Management as a Domain-Relative Practice That Requires and Develops Practical Wisdom." *Business Ethics Quarterly* 22, no. 2 (2012): 405–32.

———. "Practical Wisdom, Practices, and Institutions." In *Handbook of Virtue Ethics in Business and Management*, vol. 1, edited by Alejo Jose G. Sison, Gregory R. Beabout, and Ignacio Ferrero. Berlin: Springer, 2017.

———. "What Counts as Respect?" In *Medicine, Health Care, and Ethics: Catholic Voices*, edited by J. Morris. Washington, DC: Catholic University of America Press, 2007.

Beadle, Ron. "MacIntyre's Influence on Business Ethics." In *The Handbook of Virtue Ethics in Business and Management*, vol. 1, edited by Alejo G. Sison, Gregory R. Beabout, and Ignacio Ferrero, 59–67. Dordrecht: Springer, 2017.

Becker, Gary. *The Economic Approach to Human Behavior*. Chicago: University of Chicago Press, 1976.

Bellah, Robert N., Richard Madsen, William M. Sullivan, Ann Swidler, and Steven M. Tipton. *Habits of the Heart: Individualism and Commitment in American Life*. Berkeley: University of California Press, 1985.

Benedict XVI. *Caritas in veritate*. 2009. http://w2.vatican.va/content/benedict-xvi/en/encyclicals/documents/hf_ben-xvi_enc_20090629_caritas-in-veritate.html. June 29, 2009.

———. "Inaugural Address at the Fifth General Assembly of CELAM." Aparecida, May 13, 2007. http://w2.vatican.va/content/benedict-xvi/en/speeches/2007/may/documents/hf_ben-xvi_spe_20070513_conference-aparecida.html.

———. "Meeting with Representatives of British Society, Including the Diplomatic Corps, Politicians, Academics, and Business Leaders." September 17, 2010. http://www.vatican.va/content/benedict-xvi/en/speeches/2010/september/documents/hf_ben-xvi_spe_20100917_societa-civile.html.

———. *Spe salvi*. 2007. http://www.vatican.va/content/benedict-xvi/en/encyclicals/documents/hf_ben-xvi_enc_20071130_spe-salvi.html.

Benestad, J. Brian. *Church, State, and Society*. Washington, DC: Catholic University of America Press, 2011.

Bennis, Warren G., and James O'Toole. "How Business Schools Lost Their Way." *Harvard Business Review*, May 2005, 96–104.

Benson, Robert L., and Giles Constable, eds., with Carol D. Lanham. *Renaissance and Renewal in the Twelfth Century*. Cambridge, MA: Harvard University Press, 1982; repr. Toronto: University of Toronto Press, 1991.

Berger, Peter, Grace Davie, and Effie Fokas. *Religious America, Secular Europe? A Theme and Variation*. Burlington, VT: Ashgate, 2008.

Biéler, André. *Calvin's Social and Economic Thought*. Geneva: World Council of Churches, 2005.

Bloch, Marc. *Feudal Society*, 2 vols. London: Routledge, 1989.

Boatright, J. "From Hired Hands to Co-Owners: Compensation, Team Production, and the Role of the CEO," *Business Ethics Quarterly* 19, no. 4 (2009): 471–96.

Bonaventure. *Apologia pauperum contra calumniatorem*. Vol. VIII. Opera Omnia. 11 vols. Quaracchi, 1882–1902.

Bowles, Samuel. *The Moral Economy: Why Good Incentives Are No Substitute for Good Citizens*. New Haven, CT: Yale University Press, 2016.

Brandon, John. "Why I Started a Business: 5 Unusual Founder Stories." *Inc.*, n.d. www.inc.com /john-brandon/5-real-founder-stories-what-really-motivated-you.html.

Bratton, William, and Simone Sepe. "Shareholder Power in Incomplete Markets." Unpublished manuscript.

Brinker, Jennifer. "SLU Catholic Studies Centre Serves as Nexus for Faith, Academics," *St. Louis Review*. Febuary 15, 2018. http://stlouisreview.com/article/2018-02-15/slu -catholic-studies.

Brinkman, Bill, and Dan O'Brien. "Transforming Healthcare: A Study in Practical Wisdom." *Journal of Management Development* 29, nos. 7–8 (2010): 652–59.

Brooks, David. *The Road to Character*. New York: Random House, 2015.

Brown, Peter. *Through the Eye of a Needle: Wealth, the Fall of Rome, and the Making of Christianity in the West, 350–550 AD*. Princeton, NJ: Princeton University Press, 2012.

Bullarium Franciscanum. Vols. I–VIII. Edited by J. Sbaralea and C. Eubel. Rome, 1759–1908.

Calvin, John. *Commentary on the Acts of the Apostles*. Translated by Henry Beveridge, vol. 1. Orig. pub. Calvin Translation Society. Grand Rapids: Baker Book House, 1979.

———. *Commentary on a Harmony of the Evangelists*. Translated by William Pringle, vol. 1. Orig. pub. Calvin Translation Society. Grand Rapids: Baker Book House, 1979.

———. *Institutes of the Christian Religion*. Translated by Henry Beveridge. Grand Rapids: Wm. B. Eerdmans, 1990.

Cambridge English Dictionary. "Management Science." https://dictionary.cambridge.org/us /dictionary/english/management-science.

Campbell, Colin. "Consuming Goods and the Good of Consuming." In *Consumer Society in American History: A Reader*, edited by Lawrence B. Glickman. Ithaca, NY: Cornell University Press, 2000.

Campbell, R. H., and A. S. Skinner. *Introduction to Adam Smith, An Inquiry into the Nature and Causes of the Wealth of Nations*. Oxford: Clarendon Press, 1976.

Carey, Phillip. *Augustine's Invention of the Inner Self*. Oxford: Oxford University Press, 2003.

Catechism of the Catholic Church. Vatican City: Liberia Editrice Vaticana, 1993. http://www .vatican.va/archive/ccc_css/archive/catechism/p3s1c3a2.htm.

Cavanaugh, William. *Being Consumed: Economics and Christian Desire*. Grand Rapids: Wm. B. Eerdmans, 2008.

Chaput, Charles J. *Strangers in a Strange Land: Living the Catholic Faith in a Post-Christian World*. New York: Henry Holt, 2017.

Chakrabarty, Dipesh. *Provincializing Europe: Postcolonial Thought and Historical Difference*. Princeton, NJ: Princeton University Press, 2008.

Clement of Alexandria. "Who Is the Rich Man That Shall Be Saved?" In *The Ante-Nicene Fathers*, vol. 2. Grand Rapids: Wm. B. Eerdmans, 1951.

Cloutier, David. *The Vice of Luxury*. Washington, DC: Georgetown University Press, 2015.

———. "What Can Social Science Teach Catholic Social Thought about the Common Good." In *Empirical Foundations of the Common Good*, edited by Daniel Finn. New York: Oxford University Press, 2017

Cohen, J. "Rational Capitalism in Renaissance Italy." *American Journal of Sociology* 85 (1980): 1342–50.

Congregation for the Doctrine of Faith and the Dicastery for Promoting Integral Human Development. *Oeconomicae et pecuniariae quaestiones: Considerations for an Ethical Discernment Regarding Some Aspects of the Present Economic-Financial System.* 2018. http://www.vatican.va/roman_curia/congregations/cfaith/documents/rc_con_cfaith_doc_20180106_oeconomicae-et-pecuniariae_en.html.

Cooper, John. "Stoic Autonomy." *Social Philosophy and Policy* 20, no. 2 (2003): 1–29.

Cremers, K., and J. Martijn. "What Corporate Governance Can Learn from Catholic Social Teaching." *Journal of Business Ethics*, 2016.

Cremers, K., J. Martijn, Lubomir Litov, and Simone Sepe. "Staggered Boards and Long-Term Firm Value, Revisited." *Journal of Financial Economics* 126 (2017).

Cremers, K., J. Martijn, Saura Masconale, and Simone M. Sepe. "Commitment and Entrenchment in Corporate Governance." *Northwestern Law Review* 110, no. 4 (2016).

Cremers, K., J. Martijn, and Simone Sepe. "The Shareholder Value of Empowered Boards." *Stanford Law Review* 68 (2016).

Curran, Charles. *Catholic Social Teaching, 1891–Present.* Washington, DC: Georgetown University Press, 2002.

Davis, John B. *The Theory of the Individual in Economics.* London: Routledge, 2003.

Debreu, Gerard. "The Coefficient of Resource Utilization." *Econometrica* 19 (July 1951), 273–92.

De Koninck, Charles. "The Primacy of the Common Good Against the Personalists." http://ldataworks.com/aqr/V4_BC_text.html.

De Vries, Jan. "The Industrial Revolution and the Industrious Revolution." *Journal of Economic History* 54 (1994): 249–70.

Dobson, John. "Against MacIntyre: The Corrupting Power of Practices." *The Handbook of Virtue Ethics in Business and Management*, vol. 1, edited by Alejo G. Sison, Gregory R. Beabout, and Ignacio Ferrero, 89–98. Dordrecht: Springer, 2017.

Donaldson, T., and J.P. Walsh. "Toward a Theory of Business." *Research in Organizational Behavior* 29, no. 35 (2015):181–207.

Eisenhardt, K. M. "Agency Theory: An Assessment and Review." *Academy of Management Review* 14, no. 1 (1989): 57–74. https://www.jstor.org/stable/258191.

Ferguson, Adam. *An Essay on the History of Civil Society.* Edinburgh, 1767.

Finn, Daniel. *Moral Ecology of Markets: Assessing Claims about Markets and Justice.* Cambridge: Cambridge University Press, 2006.

Flynn, Patrice. "Global Capitalism and Values-Based Businesses: The Case of Cooperatives and Benefit Corporations." In *Free Markets with Solidarity and Sustainability*, edited by Martin Schlag and Juan A. Mercado. Washington: Catholic University of America Press, 2016.

Francis. *Evangelii gaudium.* 2013. http://w2.vatican.va/content/francesco/en/apost_exhortations/documents/papa-francesco_esortazione-ap_20131124_evangelii-gaudium.html.

———. *Laudato si.* 2015. http://w2.vatican.va/content/francesco/en/encyclicals/documents/papa-francesco_20150524_enciclica-laudato-si.html.

Francis of Assisi. *Regula Bullata, Die Opuscula des Hl. Franziskus von Assisi*, edited by K. Esser. Rome: Grottaferrata, 1989.

Frank, Robert H. *Luxury Fever.* New York: Free Press, 1999.

Frankena, William. *Ethics*, 2nd Edition. Englewood Cliffs, NJ: Prentice Hall, 1973.

Frankfurt, Harry. "Freedom of the Will and the Concept of a Person." *Journal of Philosophy* 68, no. 1 (1971).

Freeman, R. Edward. "A Stakeholder Theory of the Modern Corporation." In *The Corporation and Its Stakeholders*. Edited by Thomas Beauchamp. Upper Saddle River, NJ: Prentice Hall, 1998.

Friedman, Milton. *Capitalism and Freedom*, 40th anniversary ed. Chicago: University of Chicago Press, 2002.

———. "The Social Responsibility of Business Is to Increase Its Profits." *New York Times Magazine*, September 13, 1970.

Gay, Craig. "Sensualists without Heart." In *The Consuming Passion: Christianity and the Consumer Culture*, edited by Rodney Clapp. Downers Grove, IL: IVF Press, 1998.

Ghosh, Peter, ed. *Max Weber and the Protestant Ethic: Twin Histories*. Oxford: Oxford University Press, 2014.

Ghoshal, Sumantra. "Bad Management Theories Are Destroying Good Management Practices." *Academy of Management Learning & Education* 4, no. 1 (2005): 75–91.

Goodpaster, Kenneth. "Business Ethics and Stakeholder Analysis." *Business Ethics Quarterly* 1, no. 1 (1991).

———. *Conscience and Corporate Culture*. Chichester: Wiley, 2007.

———. "Corporate Responsibility and Its Constituents." In *Oxford Handbook of Business Ethics*, 126–57. Oxford: Oxford University Press, 2009.

———. "Goods That Are Truly Good and Services That Truly Serve: Reflections on *Caritas in veritate*." *Journal of Business Ethics* 100 (2011): 9–16.

———. "Human Dignity and the Common Good: The Institutional Insight." *Business and Society Review* 122 (2017): 1–24.

Gorski, Philip S. "The Little Divergence: The Protestant Reformation and Economic Hegemony in Early Modern Europe." In *The Protestant Ethic Turns 100: Essays on the Centenary of the Weber Thesis*, edited by William H. Swatos Jr. and Lutz Kaelber, 165–90. Boulder, CO: Paradigm, 2005.

Gratian. *Decretum*. Corpus iuris canonici. Graz: Akademische Druck-u. Verlaganstalt, 1959.

Grisez, Germain. *Living a Christian Life*. Quincy, IL: Franciscan Herald Press, 1993.

Guardini, Romano. *The End of the Modern World*. Translated by Joseph Theman and Herbert Burke. Wilmington, DE: ISI Books, 1998.

———. *Letters from Lake Como: Explorations on Technology and the Human Race*. Translated by Geoffrey W. Bromiley. Grand Rapids: Wm. B. Eerdmans, 1994; Kindle edition.

Haakonssen, Knud. *Natural Law and Moral Philosophy: From Grotius to the Scottish Enlightenment*. Cambridge: Cambridge University Press, 1996.

Habiger Institute for Catholic Leadership. *True Leadership*. Montclair, NJ: Sophia Consulting, 2015.

Haidt, Jonathan, and Anthony Randazzo. "The Moral Narratives of Economists." *Econ Journal Watch*, 12, no. 1 (2015): 49–57.

Handy, Charles. "What's a Business For?" *Harvard Business Review*, December 2002. https://hbr.org/2002/12/whats-a-business-for.

Hanley, Ryan. *Adam Smith and the Character of Virtue*. Cambridge: Cambridge University Press, 2009.

Harkless, Gresham, Jr. "20+ Entrepreneurs Explain Why They Started Their Businesses." CBNation, 2014. https://hear.ceoblognation.com/2014/04/18/20-entrepreneurs-explain-started-businesses/.

Hawthorne, Fran. *Ethical Chic: The Inside Story of the Companies We Think We Love*. Boston: Beacon Press, 2012.

Heath, Joseph. "Business Ethics Without Stakeholders." *Business Ethics Quarterly*, 2006.

Heclo, Hugh. *On Thinking Institutionally*. Boulder, CO: Paradigm, 2008.

Herdt, Jennifer A. "Eudaimonism and Dispossession: Augustine on Almsgiving." In *Augustine and Social Justice*, edited by Teresa Delgado, John Doody, and Kim Paffenroth, 97–112. Lanham, MD: Lexington Books, 2015.

———. *Religion and Faction in Hume's Moral Philosophy*. Cambridge: Cambridge University Press, 1997.

Hill, Thomas. "Happiness and Human Flourishing in Kant's Ethics." *Social Philosophy and Policy* 16, no. 1 (1999): 143–75.

Himes, Kenneth, ed. *Modern Catholic Social Teaching*. Washington, DC: Georgetown University Press, 2005.

Hirsch, Fred. *The Social Limits to Growth*. Cambridge, MA: Harvard University Press, 1976.

Hirschfeld, Mary L. *Aquinas and the Market: Toward a Humane Economy*. Cambridge, MA: Harvard University Press, 2018.

———. "What Theology Should and Should Not Learn from the Social Sciences about the Common Good." In *Empirical Foundations of the Common Good: What Theology Can Learn from Social Science*, edited by Daniel K. Finn. Oxford: Oxford University Press, 2017.

Hirschman, Albert. *The Passions and the Interests: Political Arguments for Capitalism Before Its Triumph*. Princeton, NJ: Princeton University Press, 1977.

Hollenbach, David, SJ. *The Common Good and Christian Ethics*. Cambridge: Cambridge University Press, 2002.

Hont, Istvan, and Michael Ignatieff, eds. *Wealth and Virtue: The Shaping of Political Economy in the Scottish Enlightenment*. Cambridge: Cambridge University Press, 1983.

International Monetary Fund. *Fiscal Policy and Long-Term Growth*. IMF Policy Paper. Washington, DC: International Monetary Fund, 2015. https://www.imf.org/external/np/pp/eng/2015/042015.pdf.

Jakab, Eva. "Property Rights in Ancient Rome." In *Ownership and Exploitation of Land and Natural Resources in Ancient Rome*, edited by Paul Erdkamp, Koenraad Verboven, and Arjan Zuiderhoek, 106–31. Oxford: Oxford University Press, 2015.

Jensen, M. C., and W. H. Meckling, "Theory of the Firm: Managerial Behavior, Agency Costs and Ownership." *Journal of Financial Economics* 3, no. 4 (1976).

John Paul II. *Centesimus annus*. 1991. http://w2.vatican.va/content/john-paul-ii/en/encyclicals/documents/hf_jp-ii_enc_01051991_centesimus-annus.html.

———. *Evangelium vitae*. 1995. www.vatican.va/content/john-paul-ii/en/encyclicals/documents/hf_jp-ii_enc_25031995_evangelium-vitae.html.

———. *Laborem exercens*. 1981. http://w2.vatican.va/content/john-paul-ii/en/encyclicals/documents/hf_jp-ii_enc_14091981_laborem-exercens.html.

———. *Sollicitudo rei socialis*. 1987. www.vatican.va/content/john-paul-ii/en/encyclicals/documents/hf_jp-ii_enc_30121987_sollicitudo-rei-socialis.html.

John XXIII. *Mater et Magistra*. www.vatican.va/content/john-xxiii/en/encyclicals/documents/hf_j-xxiii_enc_15051961_mater.html.

Jones, Daniel Stedman. *Masters of the Universe: Hayek, Friedman, and the Birth of Neoliberal Politics*. Princeton, NJ: Princeton University Press, 2012.

Kant, Immanuel. *Grounding of the Metaphysics of Morals*. Indianapolis: Hackett, 1993.

Kennedy, Brian. "Most Americans Trust the Military and Scientists to Act in the Public's Interest." Pew Research Center, 2016. www.pewresearch.org/fact-tank/2016/10/18/most-americans-trust-the-military-and-scientists-to-act-in-the-publics-interest/.

Kennedy, Robert. *The Good That Business Does*. Grand Rapids: Acton Institute, 2006.

Keynes, John Maynard. *The General Theory of Employment, Interest, and Money*. New York: Harcourt, 1964.

Kimmel, Allan J. *People and Products: Consumer Behavior and Product Design*. London: Routledge, 2015.

Kirzner, Israel. *Competition and Entrepreneurship*. Chicago: University of Chicago Press, 1978.

Kleinbard, Edward. *We Are Better Than This: How Government Should Spend Our Money*. Oxford: Oxford University Press, 2015.

Knight, Kelvin. "MacIntyre's Critique of Management." In *Handbook of Virtue Ethics in Business and Management 1*, edited by Alejo Jose G. Sison, Gregory R. Beabout, and Ignacio Ferrero. Berlin: Springer, 2017.

Kolster, Thomas. *Goodvertising: Creative Advertising that Cares*. London: Thames & Hudson, 2012.

Korsgaard, Christine. "Aristotle and Kant on the Source of Value." *Ethics* 96, no. 3 (1986).

Kühler, M., and N. Jelinek, eds. *Autonomy and the Self*. London: Springer, 2013.

Kuyper, Abraham. *Lectures on Calvinism* (1898). Grand Rapids: Wm. B. Eerdmans, 1931.

Laczniak, Gene, Nicholas J. C. Santos, and Thomas A. Klein. "On the Nature of Good Goods and the Ethical Role of Marketing." *Journal of Catholic Social Thought* 13, no. 1 (2016): 63–81.

Langholm, Odd. *Economics in the Medieval Schools. Wealth, Exchange, Value, Money & Usury according to the Paris Theological Tradition, 1200–1350*. New York: E. J. Brill, 1992.

———. *The Legacy of Scholasticism in Economic Thought: Antecedents of Choice and Power*. Cambridge: Cambridge University Press, 1998.

Lehmann, Hartmut, and Guenther Roth, eds. *Weber's Protestant Ethic: Origins, Evidence, Contexts*. Cambridge: Cambridge University Press, 1993.

Leo XIII. *Rerum novarum*. 1891. http://w2.vatican.va/content/leo-xiii/en/encyclicals/documents/hf_l-xiii_enc_15051891_rerum-novarum.html.

Lewis, Bradley. "Is the Common Good an Ensemble of Conditions?" *Archivio di Filosofia* 534, nos. 1–2 (2016).

Little, Lester K. *Religious Poverty and the Profit Economy in Medieval Europe*. Ithaca, NY: Cornell University Press, 1978.

Luther, Martin. "Trade and Usury" (1524). In *Luther's Works*, edited by W. I. Brandt and H. T. Lehmann, vol. 45. Philadelphia: Muhlenberg Press, 1962.

Kimmel, Allan J. *People and Products: Consumer Behavior and Product Design*. London: Routledge, 2015.

Koch, Charles G. *Good Profit*. New York: Crown Business, 2015.

Marcoux, Alexei. "A Fiduciary Argument against Stakeholder Theory." *Business Ethics Quarterly* 13 (2003): 1–24.

MacIntyre, Alasdair. *After Virtue: A Study in Moral Theory*, 2nd ed. Notre Dame, IN: University of Notre Dame Press, 1984.

———. *After Virtue: A Study in Moral Theory*, 3rd edition. Notre Dame, IN: University of Notre Dame Press, 2007.

———. *Ethics in the Conflicts of Modernity: An Essay on Desire, Practical Reasoning, and Narrative*. Cambridge: Cambridge University Press, 2016.

———. "The Irrelevance of Ethics," *Virtue and Economy: Essays on Morality and Markets*, edited by Andrius Bielski and Kevin Knight, 7–22. London: Routledge, 2016.

———. *Whose Justice? Which Rationality?* Notre Dame, IN: University of Notre Dame Press, 1988.

Maines, T. Dean, and Michael Naughton. "Middle Level Thinking: The Cultural Mission of Business Schools." *Journal of Management Development* 29, nos. 7–8 (2010): 669–77.

Mäkinen, Virpi. *Property Rights in the Late Medieval Discussion on Franciscan Poverty*. Leuven: Peeters, 2001.

Mandeville, Bernard. *Fable of the Bees; or, Private Vices, Publick Benefits*, edited by F. B. Kaye. Oxford: Oxford University Press, 1924.

Mankiw, N. Gregory. *Principles of Economics*, 4th edition. Mason, OH: South-Western, 2007.

Maritain, Jacques. "The Person and the Common Good." https://maritain.nd.edu/jmc/etext /cg.htm.

Mas-Colell, Andreu, Michael Whinston, and Jerry Green. *Microeconomic Theory*. Oxford University Press, 1995.

McCall, Brian M. "Corporations, Politics, and the Common Good." In *The Challenges of Capitalism for Virtue Ethics and the Common Good*, edited by Kleio Akrivou and Alejo Jose G. Sison, 185–220. Cheltenham, UK: Edward Elgar, 2016.

McCloskey, Dierdre N. *The Bourgeois Virtues*. Chicago: University of Chicago Press, 2006.

Meeropol, Michael. "Another Distortion of Adam Smith: The Case of the 'Invisible Hand.'" Working Paper 79. Amherst: Political Economy Research Institute at University of Massachusetts–Amhers, 2004.

Mele, Domenec. "Virtues, Values, and Principles in Catholic Social Teaching." In *The Handbook of Virtue Ethics in Business and Management* 1, edited by Alejo G. Sison, Gregory R. Beabout, and Ignacio Ferrero, 153–64. Dordrecht: Springer, 2017.

Millgram, Elijah. "Incommensurability and Practical Reasoning." In *Incommensurability, Incomparability, and Practical Reason*, edited by Ruth Chang, 151–69. Cambridge, MA: Harvard University Press, 1997.

Moore, G. E. *Principia Ethica*. Cambridge: Cambridge University Press, 1903.

Moore, Geoff. "On the Implications of the Practice/Institution Distinction: MacIntyre and the Application of Modern Virtue Ethics to Business." *Business Ethics Quarterly* 12, no. 1 (2002): 19–32.

———. *Virtue At Work: Ethics for Individuals, Managers, and Organizations*. Oxford: Oxford University Press, 2017.

———. "The Virtue of Governance, the Governance of Virtue." *Business Ethics Quarterly* 22, no. 2 (2012): 293–318.

Moore, Geoff, and Ron Beadle. "In Search of Organizational Virtue in Business: Agents, Goods, Practices, Institutions, and Environments." *Organizational Studies* 27, no. 3 (2006): 369–89.

Morgaine, Briana. "8 Reasons Why Entrepreneurs Started Their Own Businesses." Bplans, n.d. https://articles.bplans.com/8-reasons-why-entrepreneurs-started-their-own-businesses/.

Moss Kanter, Rosabeth. "Managing Yourself: Zoom In, Zoom Out." *Harvard Business Review*, March 2011. https://hbr.org/2011/03/managing-yourself-zoom-in-zoom-out.

Murdoch, Iris. *Metaphysics as a Guide to Morals*. New York: Penguin Books, 1992.

Nagel, Thomas. *What Does It All Mean?* New York: Oxford University Press, 1987.

Naughton, Michael. *The Logic of Gift: Rethinking Business as a Community of Persons*. Milwaukee: Marquette University Press, 2012.

Naughton, Michael, and David Specht. *Leading Wisely in Difficult Times: Three Cases of Faith and Business*. New York: Paulist Press, 2010.

Noonan, John T. *The Scholastic Analysis of Usury*. Cambridge: Harvard University Press, 1957.

Novak, Michael. *The Spirit of Democratic Capitalism*. New York: Simon & Schuster, 1982.

O'Brien, William J. *Character at Work: Building Prosperity through the Practice of Virtue*. New York: Paulist Press, 2008.

Olivi, Peter. *Tractatus de emptionibus et venditionibus, de usuris, de restitutionibus*, edited by Giacomo Todeschini. Un trattato di economia politica francescana, 51–108. Rome: Istituto storico italiano per il Medio Evo, 1980.

O'Neill, Onora. *Autonomy and Trust in Bioethics*. Cambridge: Cambridge University Press, 2001.

Organization for Economic Cooperation and Development. *In It Together: Why Less Inequality Benefits All*. Paris: OECD Publishing, 2015. http://dx.doi.org/10.1787/9789264235120-en.

Oslington, Paul. *Political Economy as Natural Theology: Smith, Malthus and Their Followers*. New York: Routledge, 2018.

Ostry, Jonathan D., Andrew Berg, and Charalambos G. Tsangarides. "Redistribution, Inequality, and Growth." International Monetary Fund, Staff Discussion Note 14, 2014. https://www.imf.org/external/pubs/ft/sdn/2014/sdn1402.pdf.

Paul VI. *Octogesima adveniens*. 1971. http://www.vatican.va/content/paul-vi/en/apost_letters/documents/hf_p-vi_apl_19710514_octogesima-adveniens.html.

———. *Populorum progressio*. 1967. http://w2.vatican.va/content/paul-vi/en/encyclicals/documents/hf_p-vi_enc_26031967_populorum.html.

Pearce, Colin D. "Aristotle and Business: An Inescapable Tension." In *The Handbook of the Philosophical Foundations of Business Ethics*, vol. 1, edited by Christopher Luetge, 23–43. Dordrecht: Springer, 2013.

Phillipson, Nicholas. "Culture and Society in the 18th-Century Province: The Case of Edinburgh and the Scottish Enlightenment." In *The University in Society, Volume 2: Europe, Scotland, and the United States from the 16th to the 20th Century*, edited by Lawrence Stone, 407–48. Princeton, NJ: Princeton University Press, 1974.

Pinkaers, Servais. *The Sources of Christian Ethics*. Washington, DC: Catholic University of America Press, 1995.

Pius XI. *Quadragesimo anno*. 1931. http://w2.vatican.va/content/pius-xi/en/encyclicals/documents/hf_p-xi_enc_19310515_quadragesimo-anno.html.

Pomeranz, Kenneth. *The Great Divergence: China, Europe, and the Making of the Modern World Economy*. Princeton, NJ: Princeton University Press, 2000.

Pontifical Council for Justice and Peace. *Compendium of the Social Doctrine of the Church*. Vatican City: Liberia Editrice Vaticana, 2005. www.vatican.va/roman_curia/pontifical_councils/justpeace/documents/rc_pc_justpeace_doc_20060526_compendio-dott-soc_en.html.

———. *The Vocation of the Business Leader*. Rome: Pontifical Council for Justice and Peace, 2012.

Preston, R. H. "Christian Socialism." In *The Blackwell Encyclopedia of Modern Christian Thought*, edited by A. McGrath. Oxford: Blackwell, 1993.

Ratzinger, Joseph. "Christliche Orientierung in der pluralistischen Gesellschaft? Über die Unverzichtbarkeit des Christentums in der modernen Gesellschaft." In *Vom Wiederauffinden der Mitte. Grundorientierungen: Texte aus vier Jahrzehnten*, edited by Schülerkreis. Vienna: Herder, 1997.

———. "Europe in the Crisis of Cultures." Trans. Adrian J. Walker. https://www.theway.org.uk/endeanweb/ratzinger32-2.pdf.

Reno, R. R. *Resurrecting the Idea of a Christian Society*. Washington, DC: Regnery Faith, 2016.

Rodgers, S., and S. Gago. "A Model Capturing Ethics and Executive Compensation." *Journal of Business Ethics* 48 (2003): 189.

Royce, Josiah. *The Religious Aspect of Philosophy*. New York: Harper & Row, 1965.

Rule of St. Benedict, edited and translated by Bruce L. Venarde. Cambridge, MA: Harvard University Press, 2011.

Rushkoff, Douglas. *Throwing Rocks at the Google Bus*. New York: Penguin, 2016.

Sandel, Michael J. *What Money Can't Buy: The Moral Limits of Markets*. Reprint edition. New York: Farrar, Straus & Giroux, 2013.

Sayous, André-E. "Calvinisme et capitalism à Genève de la Réforme à la fin du 18e siècle," *Annales d'histoure économique et sociale*, Paris, 1935, 227.

Scheler, Max, and Werner Stark. "The Thomist Ethic and the Spirit of Capitalism." *Sociological Analysis* 25, no. 1 (1964): 4–19.

Schlag, Martin. *The Business Francis Means: Understanding the Pope's Message on the Economy*. Washington, DC: Catholic University of America Press, 2017.

———. "Economic and Business Ethics in Select Italian Scholastics (ca. 1200–1450)." In *Handbook of the Philosophical Foundations of Business Ethics*, edited by Christoph Luetge, 179–204. Dordrecht: Springer, 2013.

———. *Handbook of Catholic Social Teaching: A Guide for Christians in the World Today*. Washington, DC: Catholic University of America Press, 2017.

Schlag, Martin, and Juan A. Mercado. "Freedom as the Call to Being." In *Free Markets with Solidarity and Sustainability*, edited by Martin Schlag and Juan A. Mercado. Washington, DC: Catholic University of America Press, 2016.

Schwartz, Barry, and Kenneth Sharpe. *Practical Wisdom: The Right Way to Do the Right Thing*. New York: Riverhead Books, 2011.

Seetubtim, Mo. "10 Reasons Why You Should Start Your Own Business." *Huffington Post*, December 6, 2017. www.huffingtonpost.com/mo-seetubtim/10-reasons-why-you-should -start-your-own-business_b_8046036.html.

Selznick, Philip. *Leadership in Administration*. New York: Harper & Row, 1957.

———. *Leadership in Administration: A Sociological Interpretation*. Berkeley: University of California Press, 1957.

Sensen, O., ed. *Kant on Moral Autonomy*. Cambridge: Cambridge University Press, 2013.

Sison, Alejo Jose G., and Joan Fontrodona. "The Common Good of the Firm in the Aristotelian-Thomistic Tradition." *Business Ethics Quarterly* 22, no. 2 (2012): 211–46.

Smith, Adam. *An Inquiry into the Nature and Causes of the Wealth of Nations*, edited by R. H. Campbell and A. S. Skinner. Oxford: Clarendon Press, 1976.

———. *The Wealth of Nations*. London: Methuen, 1904.

Smith, Vernon. *Rationality in Economics: Constructivist and Ecological Forms*. Cambridge: Cambridge University Press, 2008.

Solomon, Michael. *Consumer Behavior: Buying, Having and Being*, 6th ed. Upper Saddle River, NJ: Pearson / Prentice Hall, 2004.

Stackhouse, Max. "Weber, Theology, and Economics." In *The Oxford Handbook of Christianity and Economics*, edited bty Paul Oslington, 307–36. Oxford: Oxford University Press, 2014.

Stigler, George J. *The Economist as Preacher and Other Essays*. Chicago: University of Chicago Press, 1982.

Stiglitz, Joseph, *The Price of Inequality*. New York: W. W. Norton, 2012. https://www.theatlantic .com/business/archive/2015/11/stiglitz-heres-how-to-fix-inequality/413761/.

Stohr, Karen. "Virtue Ethics and Kant's Cold-Hearted Benefactor." *Journal of Value Inquiry* 36, nos. 2–3 (2002): 187–204.

Stone, Brad. *The Upstarts: How Uber, Airbnb, and the Killer Companies of the New Silicon Valley Are Changing the World.* New York: Little, Brown, 2017.

Sullivan, Bob. *Gotcha Capitalism.* New York: Ballantine Books, 2007.

Sunstein, Cass R. *Why Nudge? The Politics of Libertarian Paternalism.* New Haven, CT: Yale University Press, 2014.

Sweetland Edwards, Haley. "The Masters of Mind Control." *Time,* April 23, 2018, 30–37.

Tanner, Kathryn. *Capitalism and the New Spirit of Capitalism.* New Haven, CT: Yale University Press, 2019.

Tawney, R. H. *Religion and the Rise of Capitalism.* New York: New American Library, 1926.

Taylor, Charles. "Leading a Life." In *Incommensurability, Incomparability, and Practical Reason,* edited by Ruth E. Chang, 170–83. Cambridge, MA: Harvard University Press, 1997.

———. "Secularization." Unpublished manuscript.

———. *Sources of the Self.* Cambridge, MA: Harvard University Press, 1989.

———. "What Is Human Agency?" In *Philosophical Papers,* 15–44. Cambridge: Cambridge University Press, 1985.

Time. "Invest in Technology." April 2, 2018.

Tirole, Jean. *Economics for the Common Good.* Princeton, NJ: Princeton University Press, 2017.

Todeschini, Giacomo. *Franciscan Wealth: From Voluntary Poverty to Market Society.* Trans. Donatella Melucci. Saint Bonaventure, NY: Franciscan Institute, 2009.

Tornielli, Andrea, and Giacomo Galeazzi. *This Economy Kills: Pope Francis on Capitalism and Social Justice.* Trans. Demetrio S. Yocum. Collegeville, MN: Liturgical Press, 2015.

Troeltsch, Ernst. *The Social Teachings of the Christian Churches.* Trans. Olive Wyon. Chicago: University of Chicago Press, 1976.

Twenge, Jean. *iGen.* New York: Simon & Schuster, 2017.

US Department of Defense. *Inspector General Report DODIG-2013-041.* Washington, DC: US Government Publishing Office, 2013.

Werhane, Patricia. "The Role of Self-Interest in Adam Smith's *Wealth of Nations*." *Journal of Philosophy* 86 (1989): 669–80.

Valeri, Mark. "Religion, Discipline, and the Economy in Calvin's Geneva." *Sixteenth Century Journal* 28 (1997): 123–42.

Vatican Council II. *Gaudium et spes.* 1973. www.vatican.va/archive/hist_councils/ii_vatican _council/documents/vat-ii_const_19651207_gaudium-et-spes_en.html.

———. *Lumen gentium.* 1965. https://www.vatican.va/archive/hist_councils/ii_vatican _council/documents/vat-ii_const_19641121_lumen-gentium_en.html.

Veblen, Thorstein. *The Theory of the Leisure Class.* New York: Macmillan, 1899.

Vimeo. "Upload, Livestream, and Create Your Own Videos, All in HD." https://vimeo.com /42713491.

Visser 't Hooft, W.-A. *The Background to the Social Gospel in America.* Haarlem: Bethany Press, 1928.

von Nell-Breuning, Oswald. *Reorganization of Social Economy.* Milwaukee: Bruce, 1936,

Walsh, Jim, and Thomas Donaldson. "Toward a Theory of Business." *Research in Organizational Behavior* 29, no. 35 (2015): 181–207.

Waterman, Anthony Michael C. *Political Economy and Christian Theology Since the Enlightenment: Essays in Intellectual History.* New York: Palgrave Macmillan, 2004.

————. *Revolution, Economics, and Religion: Christian Political Economy, 1798–1833*. Cambridge: Cambridge University Press, 1991.

Weber, Max. "Asceticism, Mysticism and Salvation." In *Economy and Society: An Outline of Interpretive Sociology*. New York: Bedminster Press, 1968.

————. *The Protestant Ethic and the Spirit of Capitalism*, trans. Talcott Parsons. New York: Charles Scribner's Sons, 1958.

White, Gillian B. "Stiglitz: Here's How to Fix Inequality." *The Atlantic*, November 2015. www.theatlantic.com/business/archive/2015/11/stiglitz-heres-how-to-fix-inequality /413761/.

Wilber, Charles K. "Contributions of Economic Theory to an Understanding of the Common Good in Catholic Social Thought." In *Empirical Foundations of the Common Good: What Theology Can Learn from Social Science*, edited by Daniel K. Finn, 114–41. Oxford: Oxford University Press, 2017.

William of St. Amour. "*De quantitate eleemosynae*, edited by A. Traver; 'William of Saint-Amour's Two Disputed Questions De quantitate eleemosynae and De valido mendicante.'" *Archives d'histoire doctrinale et littéraire du Moyen Age* 62 (1995): 295–342.

Withy, Katherine. "Authenticity and Heidegger's Antigone," *Journal of the British Society for Phenomenology* 45, no. 3 (2015): 239–53.

Wood, Diana. *Medieval Economic Thought*. Cambridge: Cambridge University Press, 2002.

Wright, Thomas. *The Passions of the Minde in Generalle*. London, 1601.

Wu, Tim. *The Attention Merchants: The Epic Scramble to Get Inside Our Heads*. New York: Alfred A. Knopf, 2016.

Yuengert, Andrew M. *The Boundaries of Technique: Ordering Positive and Normative Concerns in Economic Research*. Lanham, MD: Lexington Press, 2004.

Zingales, Luigi. *A Capitalism for the People: Recapturing the lost genius of American prosperity*. New York: Basic Books, 2012.

CONTRIBUTORS

GREGORY R. BEABOUT is professor of philosophy at Saint Louis University. His research and teaching are in ethics, the history of philosophy, and Catholic social thought. Much of his work applies personalism and the tradition of the virtues to business and the professions. His books include *Ethics: The Art of Character; Virtue Ethics in Business and Management; The Character of the Manager; Beyond Self-Interest: A Personalist Approach to Human Action*; and *Applied Professional Ethics*.

DAVID CLOUTIER is associate professor of moral theology at the Catholic University of America in Washington. A graduate of Carleton College and Duke University, he is the author of *The Vice of Luxury: Economic Excess in a Consumer Age* and *Walking God's Earth: The Environment and Catholic Theology*, and he co-edited *Naming Our Sins: How Recognizing the Seven Deadly Vices Can Renew the Sacrament of Reconciliation*.

K. J. MARTIJN CREMERS is the Martin J. Gillen Dean and the Bernard J. Hank Professor of Finance at the University of Notre Dame's Mendoza College of Business. Before joining Notre Dame in 2012, he was a faculty member at Yale University's School of Management from 2002 to 2012. His research and teaching areas are investment management, corporate finance, corporate governance, corporate law, business ethics, and Catholic social thought.

DANIEL K. FINN is Clemens Professor of Economics and Professor of Theology at Saint John's University and the College of Saint Benedict. He is a former president of the Catholic Theological Society of America, the Association for Social Economics, and the Society of Christian Ethics. His books include *Consumer Ethics in a Global Economy* and *Christian Economic Ethics*. He is the director of the True Wealth of Nations research project at the Institute for Advanced Catholic Studies.

KENNETH E. GOODPASTER, who received an AB in mathematics from Notre Dame and a PhD in philosophy from the University of Michigan, is professor emeritus at the University of Saint Thomas in Minnesota. He taught moral philosophy at Notre Dame during the 1970s before joining the Harvard Business School faculty in 1980. In 1990, he accepted the David and Barbara Koch Chair in Business Ethics at Saint Thomas. In 2014, he was honored by the Society for Business Ethics for a "Career of Outstanding Scholarly Achievement in the Field of Business Ethics."

THE REVEREND JAMES L. HEFT, SM (Marianist), is the Alton Brooks Professor of Religion at the University of Southern California and founder and president emeritus of the Institute for Advanced Catholic Studies. His areas of interest include Catholic education, the history of Catholicism, interreligious dialogue, and interdisciplinary studies. He is the author and editor of twelve books—most recently, *Empty Churches: Disaffiliation in America*, co-edited with Jan Stets; and *The Future of Catholic Higher Education: The Open Circle*.

JENNIFER A. HERDT is the Gilbert L. Stark Professor of Christian Ethics at the Yale University Divinity School. She has published widely on virtue ethics and early modern and modern moral thought. Her most recent book is *Forming Humanity: Redeeming the German Bildung Tradition* (2019). Her book *Putting on Virtue: The Legacy of the Splendid Vices* was selected as a Choice Outstanding Academic Title in 2008. She was the president of the Society of Christian Ethics in 2020.

MARY HIRSCHFELD is associate professor of economics and theology in the Humanities Department at Villanova University. She received a PhD in economics from Harvard and a PhD in moral theology from Notre Dame. She is a member of the College of Fellows at the Dominican School of Philosophy and Theology and of the Institute for Human Ecology at the Catholic University of America. Her book, *Aquinas and the Market: Toward a Humane Economy*, is the recipient of the Economy and Society International Award bestowed by the Fondazione Centesimus Annus Pro Pontifice and the Aldersgate Prize bestowed by Indiana Wesleyan University.

EDWARD D. KLEINBARD was the Robert C. Packard Chair in Law at the University of Southern California's Gould School of Law. Previously, he served as chief of staff at the Joint Committee on Taxation, the nonpartisan tax resource for Congress. His work focused on government taxation and fiscal policy, including *We Are Better Than This: How Government Should Spend Our Money* and his last book, *What's Luck Got To Do With It?*

MICHAEL J. NAUGHTON is the director of the Center for Catholic Studies at the University of Saint Thomas in Minnesota, where he holds the Koch Chair in Catholic Studies and is a full professor in the Department of Catholic Studies. He is author, co-author, and/or co-editor of twelve books and monographs and over sixty articles. He serves on multiple boards, including as board chair for Reell Precision Manufacturing, which has plants and offices in the United States, Europe, and Asia. He also serves as a trustee at the University of Mary.

MONSIGNOR MARTIN SCHLAG, JD, STD, is professor for Catholic social thought and holds the Alan W. Moss Chair for Catholic Social Thought at the Center for Catholic Studies at the University of Saint Thomas in Minnesota. His is also director of Saint Thomas's John A. Ryan Institute for Catholic Social Thought.

REGINA WENTZEL WOLFE is professor emerita at the Catholic Theological Union and Senior Wicklander Fellow at DePaul University's Institute for Business and Professional Ethics. She was Christopher Chair in Business Ethics at the Brennan School of Business at Dominican University and served on the theology faculty at Saint John's University in Minnesota. She is co-author of the second edition of *Alleviating Poverty Through Profitable Partnerships* and *Global Women Leaders: Breaking Boundaries* and co-editor (with David J. Bevan and Patricia H. Werhane) of *Systems Thinking and Moral Imagination*.

ANDREW M. YUENGERT is the Seaver Professor of Social Science at Pepperdine University. He is a former president of the Association of Christian Economists, and he edited its journal, *Faith & Economics*. His most recent book is *Approximating Prudence*. His next book project, *Prophecy and Praxis: Practical Wisdom and Catholic Social Teaching*, is currently under review. He has been a Madison Fellow at Princeton University and a visiting professor at the Catholic University of America.

INDEX

Lightning Source UK Ltd.
Milton Keynes UK
UKHW011827060322
399651UK00002B/40